The Quiet People of India

Norval Mitchell in mess uniform with OBE and Frontier Service medal, 1943

The Quiet People of India

by

Norval Mitchell

The Memoir Club

© Norval Mitchell 2006

First published in 2006 by
The Memoir Club
Stanhope Old Hall
Stanhope
Weardale
County Durham

All rights reserved.
Unauthorised duplication
contravenes existing laws.

British Library Cataloguing in
Publication Data.
A catalogue record for this book
is available from the
British Library

ISBN: 1-84104-146-7

Typeset by TW Typesetting, Plymouth, Devon
Printed by CPI Bath

Contents

List of illustrations

*Photographs by Mary Mitchell.

*Photographs by Mary Mitchell.

Acknowledgements

Mr P N L Nicholson, my contemporary and friend at Oxford who has become a distinguished writer and broadcaster in Canada since those distant days, has given me invaluable advice after reading my first draft. Sir Olaf Caroe has given me information which was not available to me when I first wrote the chapters dealing with the North West Frontier of India, and has saved me from several grievous errors. I hope that I have done justice in the narrative to his distinguished but far too brief period of office as Governor. He received no justice at the time. Finally I acknowledge the part played in this production by my friend Sir Malcolm Knox. I expected and was given the analytical, astringent and constructive criticism which is characteristic of him. To all of them I am very grateful.

Norval Mitchell
Twynholm
Kirkcudbright
3 December 1976

Foreword

These memoirs were written in 1975 by A N Mitchell, known generally in his youth by the name Alf but latterly by his ancient Scots name, Norval. It seems that he wrote them for his own interest rather than in the hope of fame and he did not make any great efforts at publication beyond sending a copy to the India Office. They cover his life up to the day in 1947 when, on sailing away from India for the last time, he symbolically threw his topi into the sea.

The manuscript was typed by his wife, Mary Mitchell. His children inherited copies which lay around until we decided that they merited publication. Apart from filial piety we thought that there were two good reasons why they deserved a wider public. The first is that they are a new and refreshing illumination of the lives of the famously small number of people (small even in the last years of the Raj) who effectively ran the Indian sub-continent. That is the reason for the part of the book starting with his embarkation for India in 1930. The second reason is that the earlier part of the book may show why a young man with no relevant family traditions should develop a burning and uncompromising sense of duty and integrity coupled with an inspirational mission for public service – by which we mean serving others rather than serving the Raj. Those Victorian virtues, shared by many of his colleagues, were personified by Norval Mitchell.

His own title for his memoirs was little more than a working title – *Years That Have Ended*. The title which we have chosen is taken from his text as an early indication of where his deepest interests lay. It was the title which he gave to a speech in 1934 when he was invited to address the Kiwanis Club in Chicago about his life in India: *The Quiet People of India*. Throughout these memoirs what stands out most is his concern to improve the lot of the ordinary people, often in the face of crippling budget constraints after the Depression and of the dead hand of unimaginative bureaucracy. The improvement of education, healthcare and agriculture recur as priorities in almost all the positions which he held. His mastery of several languages, the result of hard work and flair as a linguist, helped him to get close to those who needed help.

The distinguished anthropologist Verrier Elwin, who held Norval Mitchell in high esteem, paid him the compliment of inviting him to make a contribution to his book *The Muria and their Ghotul* (OUP, 1947) in the form of an Appendix on the language of the Muria people of Bastar State. In Bastar he also compiled a grammar of another aboriginal language, Maria Gondi, as an essential aid to education in village schools. Dr Albert Simeons, Chief Medical Officer of Kolhapur State during his time there, subsequently wrote several novels of which the first, set in the community of lepers and entitled *The Mask of a Lion* (Alfred A Knopf, 1952), was dedicated to 'Alfred and Mary' in recognition of their support for his work on behalf of lepers.

His periods of duty in the North West Frontier Province enabled him to make penetrating observations about the frontier tribes. Events on the frontier since the Soviet invasion of Afghanistan, not least the activities of Al Qaeda and the Taliban, show that an understanding of the historical background is crucially important, and his insights and stories are not only entertaining but as useful today as they were then.

In his last years in India he became disillusioned by the changing nature of his tasks: dealing with 'social unrest or outright rebellion', which, after he left India, were followed by 'one of the worst disasters in history' – the millions who died in the inter-communal massacres that followed independence. And yet, unlike the classic caricature of the 'Empire Builder' writing of lands conquered and battles won, Norval Mitchell described as one of his proudest achievements, during World War II and with Japan threatening, the suppression of a dangerous rebellion in Orissa in which only one life was lost on either side – and that an accident. He was awarded the OBE for his success.

His four children are proud to publish his story.

David Mitchell
Editor

Editor's Note

In 1968, when my father wrote his biography of Sir George Cunningham, the publishers encouraged him to write his own memoirs, with an understanding that they would be interested in representing him. Seven years later, circumstances had changed and those publishers were no longer interested. My father was disappointed, but was always modest and had little interest in marketing himself, even to his own family. He sent a copy of the manuscript to the India Office and consigned the project to oblivion.

The India Office copy has been found by several subsequent authors and researchers and is quoted extensively by Charles Chenevix-Trench in *Viceroy's Agent* (Jonathan Cape, 1987).

Fortunately, my mother, Mary Mitchell, made several copies of her original typescript and gave them to her four children. We read it with great interest and filed it away. In 2002, 14 years after my father's death, I decided, after my own retirement, to look for a publisher. With little knowledge of how publishers specialize, I ran into several brick walls before finding The Memoir Club. With their enthusiastic encouragement as a spur, I enrolled my sister, Genevra, my brothers, Bill and Malcolm and my son Julian as helpers and this book is the result.

My mother's contribution includes many of the photographs. I inherited from her an album of negatives, taken between 1938 and 1943, which I was able to scan and print. These help bring to life our family, my father's personality and the environment in which he worked.

As Editor, I am grateful to my family members and The Memoir Club for working together to make a dream come true.

David Mitchell

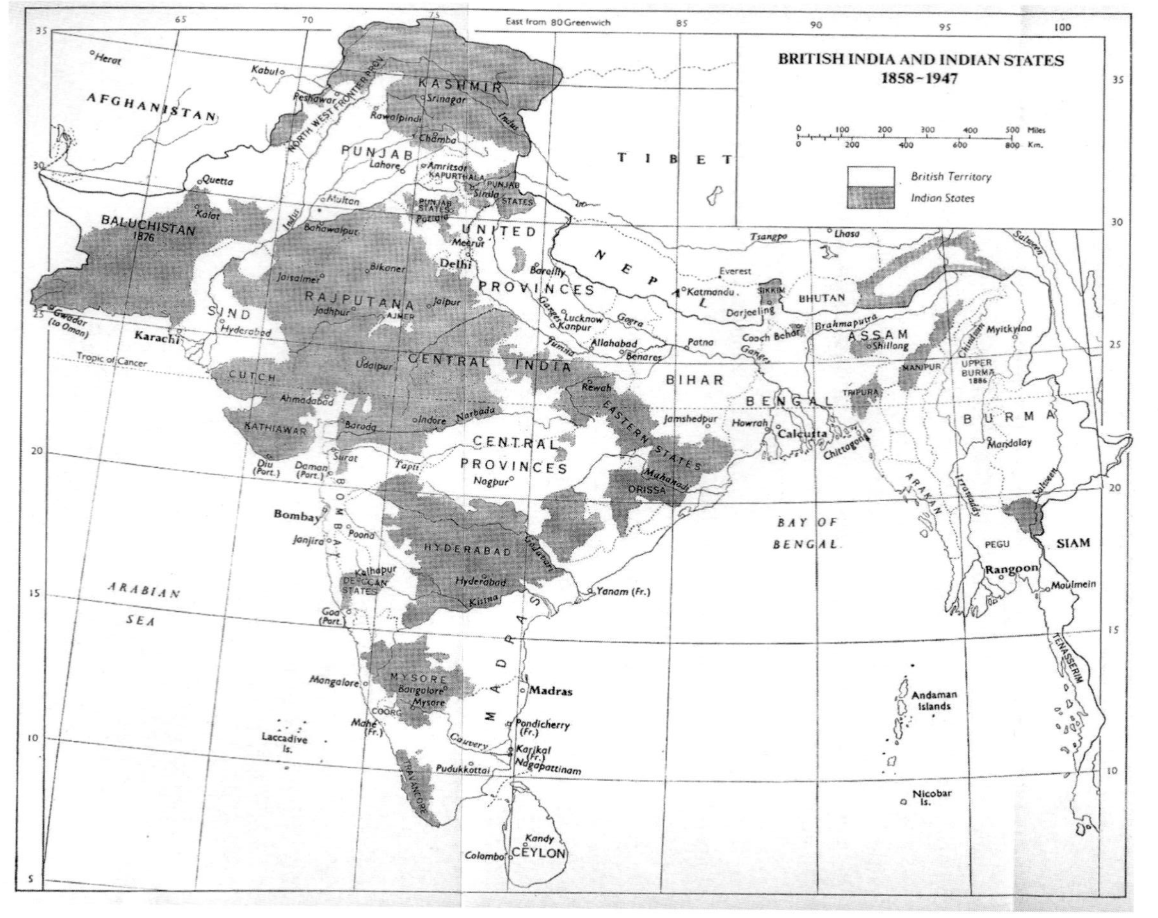
BRITISH INDIA AND INDIAN STATES
1858–1947
Miles
Km.
British Territory
Indian States
East from 80 Greenwich
TIBET
AFGHANISTAN
BALUCHISTAN
1876
KASHMIR
NORTH WEST FRONTIER PROV.
PUNJAB
PUNJAB STATES
KAPURTHALA
SIND
RAJPUTANA
AJMER
UNITED PROVINCES
NEPAL
SIKKIM
BHUTAN
ASSAM
MANIPUR
TRIPURA
UPPER BURMA
1886
BURMA
ARAKAN
PEGU
SIAM
TENASSERIM
BIHAR
BENGAL
CENTRAL INDIA
CENTRAL PROVINCES
EASTERN STATES
ORISSA
CUTCH
KATHIAWAR
BOMBAY
HYDERABAD
DECCAN STATES
MYSORE
COORG
TRAVANCORE
MADRAS
CEYLON
BAY OF BENGAL
ARABIAN SEA
Andaman Islands
Nicobar Is.
Laccadive Is.
Tropic of Cancer
Herat
Kabul
Peshawar
Rawalpindi
Srinagar
Chamba
Lahore
Amritsar
Simla
Patiala
Multan
Quetta
Kalat
Bahawalpur
Bikaner
Jaisalmer
Jodhpur
Jaipur
Meerut
Delhi
Bareilly
Lucknow
Kanpur
Allahabad
Benares
Patna
Katmandu
Everest
Darjeeling
Lhasa
Tsangpo
Cooch Behar
Shillong
Myitkyina
Mandalay
Rangoon
Moulmein
Karachi
Gwadar (to Oman)
Hyderabad
Udaipur
Ahmadabad
Baroda
Indore
Rewah
Jamshedpur
Howrah
Calcutta
Chittagong
Diu (Port.)
Daman (Port.)
Surat
Nagpur
Bombay
Poona
Janjira
Kolhapur
Goa (Port.)
Hyderabad
Yanam (Fr.)
Mangalore
Bangalore
Mysore
Mahe (Fr.)
Madras
Pondicherry (Fr.)
Karikal (Fr.)
Nagapattinam
Pudukkottai
Kandy
Colombo
Indus
Ganges
Jumna
Gogra
Brahmaputra
Chindwin
Irrawaddy
Salween
Narbada
Tapti
Mahanadi
Godavari
Kistna
Cauvery

Map of India

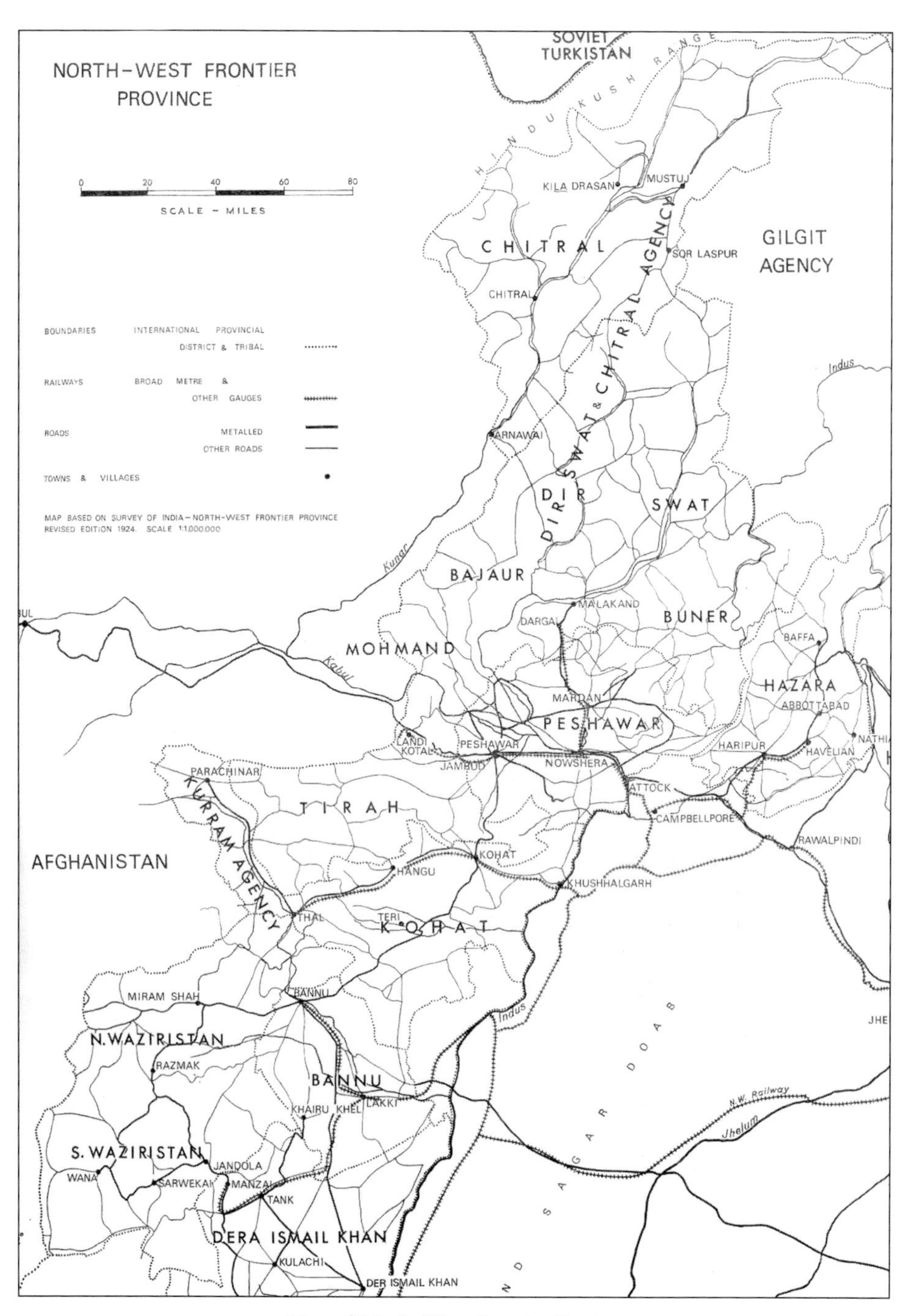

Map of North West Frontier Province

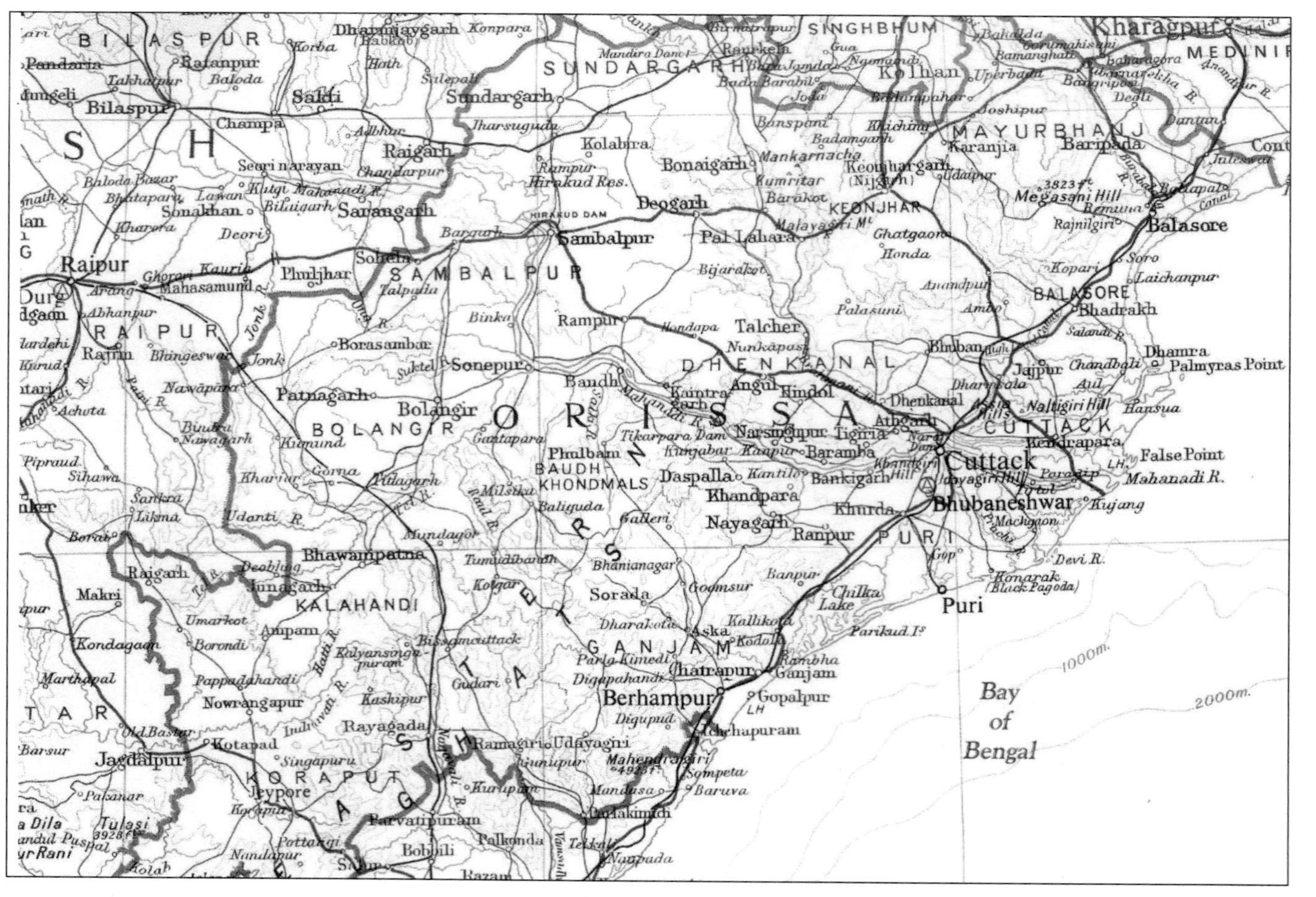

Map of Orissa

Chapter 1

Not on papyrus but in my heart.
Irenaeus

A SECOND CENTURY BISHOP OF LYONS so described the record of his childhood memories. Anything preserved in such an archive is liable to be unreliable. However fortunate or however miserable may be the ambience of the child's first years, he will remember colours, light and shadow, sounds and scents, pain and pleasure, warmth and cold. Affection, if he be born fortunate, he takes for granted; and of hate he is usually incapable. The unfortunate knows and remembers hunger and fear. However subjective and coloured by imagination these memories may be, lacking definition of time and place, they are nonetheless a part of the adult's mature personality. As Irenaeus went on to say,

> The lessons received in childhood; growing with the growth of the soul, become identified with it.

Later, less pleasant matters will enter this record. At this point it is agreeable to recall the things that a fortunate child may remember.

I never knew my father, William Mitchell, who was born and bred in Dundee, Scotland. At the time of my birth on 18 December 1906, he was General Manager of the Lautaro Nitrate Company in Taltal, Chile, and in 1907 he travelled to England with my mother and me. He returned to Chile in the autumn of that year and in May 1908, when I was 18 months old, he died from the delayed effects of the derailment of a freight train on which he was riding. My mother Mary Mitchell had remained in England awaiting the birth of my sister, which took place in February 1908. When she was left a widow, she moved temporarily into 2 Ailsa Place, Twickenham. It is of this house that I have my earliest memories. It was a large semi-detached one which had been rented by my mother's parents, Mr and Mrs Peter Nicholas Scholberg.

Mr Scholberg was a Norwegian mining engineer; in 1908 he was 74. His wife, Sarah Monk, was the daughter of a Cornish mining engineer working in the extreme north of Norway, who died an untimely death. It was said in the family that he fell into a sluice while in a rage and there drowned. Up to that point Sarah Monk and her elder sister, Mary, had been going to London for their education, but this was now cut off by poverty. The whole family returned to Cornwall, whence both their parents had come, and settled in Liskeard, where Sarah played the organ in the Wesleyan chapel.

Peter Scholberg, on the exhaustion of the Norwegian tin mines, had migrated to Chile and staked out a large number of claims (perhaps 200) in the copper and gold producing areas of the barren north. Thence he returned to marry my grandmother in that same Wesleyan Chapel on August 30 1869, appearing in the records only as 'gentleman'. His father is there as 'mining engineer'; he himself is likewise in my mother's baptismal certificate in 1880. At this time he was a wealthy man, a fact from which, owing to his seven surviving children being more generous than thrifty, little benefit accrued to his descendants.

Now vignettes occur in my memory. There was helping the gardener to sweep up leaves in the drive. I rode on the cross-bar of his bicycle when he went shopping. There were walks with Nurse Dicker along the Thames. One of my mother's brothers introduced me to contemporary manners. He would ask me what I would like; and the proper answer was 'a glass of port and a bicky, please'.

It was in the summer of 1909 that we all, including Nurse Dicker, arrived to live in the village of Dollar in Clackmannanshire. The sun was very warm as I scrambled up the steps of the station and out into the open space to the north. This was a single railway line, now long closed, between Alloa and Kinross. It must have been one of the most peaceful and sleepy lines in the British Isles. Twenty-five years later in India I remembered it as I travelled in the Grand Trunk Express from Nagpur to Delhi in the month of March: momentary turmoil at each station and then the resumption of progress through the warm country and the scents of field and forest.

From the station we were transported, probably in an open landau, to our new abode. This was Sobraon Villa, a semi-detached house, screened by a high hedge from the road to its south; an important road now, which will take the motorist to Stirling in a quarter of an hour, but then a dusty, sleepy thing. At the age of two and a half I was entranced. The two Misses Falconer, from whom my mother rented the house, told me the names of all the flowers in the garden. I can now only remember the pansies, and goodness knows why; but it may have been that they described them as Pan's eyes. This produced a *frisson*. Then in the hall the ladies stood by apprehensively as I climbed onto a chair and from that onto a dresser in order to examine a very large and sombre oil painting depicting the sack of Jerusalem by the Emperor Titus in 70 AD.

Of the winter of 1909–10 I recall extreme cold combined with the smell of manure in the fields. Nurse Dicker would take us for walks, my sister in her pram and me on foot. That is why I noticed the cold. But the road south out of Dollar past the bleaching mills to the bridge over the river Devon is indissolubly linked for me with Nurse Dicker's contribution to my education, that was her teaching of the songs of the day such as 'All hands on deck there's a pretty little craft in sight'; 'Has anybody here seen Kelly, Kelly from the Isle of Man?'; 'Ta ra ra boom de-ay': and others.

But cheerful little Nurse Dicker, so trim in her bonnet and uniform, was young and her eyes were lifted to far horizons. She was with us in Scotland. She returned with us to the south in 1911, shortly after my grandfather's death. And she went with us in February 1912 – my grandmother, my mother, my sister and me – to the Riviera for a month in Nice and a month in Menton. She enjoyed the Mardi Gras carnival at least as much as we children did; and she may well have been as puzzled as we were by the colossal wagon depicting a man astride a whale with the Mona Lisa under his arm. At that moment, it seems, no better solution had been offered to the theft from the Louvre. But then she disappears from the scene, and we were told that she had got married and gone to New Zealand.

In the summer of 1911 the memory of the coronation of King George V is of a perfect day in midsummer. In the afternoon all the children of the village, whose total population was only 1800, took their places below the steps of the main entrance to Dollar Academy. Each of us in turn received from the Provost, in robes and chain, a Coronation mug, decorated with the likenesses of King George and Queen Mary. This was to be, I suppose, a possession for ever. But, more important, it contained a bag of sweets, and we very small children (I was 4 years old) sat in small circles on the grass of the Academy's grounds eating our sweets in the declining sunlight and expatiating on our own affairs as if our brief northern summer could never end.

Two of my clearest memories come soon after. In the winter of 1911–12 we travelled to Bournemouth to join my grandmother Scholberg, who was briefly staying there, and thence paid a visit to London. Our time there was spent at a modest hotel in the Cromwell Road. Even – or perhaps especially – in London the pram with my sister, and with me alongside, had to go out regularly. Often this meant the considerable walk to Kensington Gardens and the Round Pond; but not always. One morning the murmur went round the hotel that, owing to the violence of the suffragettes, not a single pane of glass was unbroken in Kensington High Street. It were better not to venture north that morning.

But the occasion which I especially remember was a winter afternoon with the darkness coming on. We had gone up to the point where the Cromwell Road is met from the south by the Gloucester Road. We were heading for a shop by the Underground Station whose 'jujubes' were famous. Unexpectedly I saw an opening on the east side of the street, which led to a mews. And there, drawn up in line, were about a dozen lamp-lighters with their staves. The man in charge gave an order and they trotted out and turned north to the Cromwell Road. I followed. At the junction some went west, some went east, and on either hand the street lights, kindled by the magic staves, shone out until the darkness and the mist were illuminated as by 'silver lamps in a distant shrine'.

One other memory of that winter was not happy or romantic. It was when we arrived in London, at Paddington Station, that a porter loaded our luggage into a cab. Off we went accompanied by the clop of the horse's feet on the wet, wooden paving blocks; and behind us, the whole way, there splashed the running feet of a thinly-clothed man hoping for a small tip for unloading the luggage at the other end.

We were back in Scotland when in the summer of 1912 I was told that I was to go to school in September. This was a new establishment in Dollar, organized by two sisters, the Misses Bremner. Fees were charged. I have been told that these were £5 per year. I went with my mother to be formally entered and we were told by the elder Miss Bremner that mine was the very first name to go down in the book. There I stayed for three years, with one interval in 1914, and for the first time came in contact with the less gentle world outside the family. The first year, when I only attended in the morning, was marked by the regularity with which a girl of my age, Betty Johnstone, was top of the class.

But in the summer of 1913 my thoughts were first directed to India. My sister and I caught chicken-pox, and my mother read to me Kipling's *The Jungle Book* as I lay in bed. Then a few days later it was revealed that I had won a prize – goodness knows for what – which took the form of a book called *When Mother was in India.* Like the spore of bracken an idea had found its way into my mind.

What I remember of Dollar is only minor events in an ambience of peace and quiet. We were on a visit to my grandmother in 1914 when the Great War broke out. She had rented a large house in Llanishen, then a quiet village three miles north of Cardiff. She wished to be near her second son Dr H A Scholberg who had settled there after qualifying in medicine at St Bartholomew's Hospital.

The house belonged to a Professor Mackenzie* of the University College of South Wales, and contained many of his effects including some hundreds of books. These meant nothing much to me at first. It was after 1915 that I was driven to concede that *The Crock of Gold* was more to my taste than Kant's *Critique of Pure Reason*; and ponderous folio editions of *Don Quixote* and *Robinson Crusoe* drew me strongly by the engravings with which they were illustrated. The house had neither gas nor electricity. It was only semi-detached from its neighbour, but its entrance hall with its tessellated floor, its three stories, a wing with kitchen etc at ground level and three servants' bedrooms at second floor level, placed it unequivocally in the wealthier Victorian middle-class category.

It was in the congested drawing-room that I was told on the 4 August 1914 that we were at war with Germany. The sun was brilliant on the lawn beyond the south windows. On the east side of the room a glass door led to a conservatory flooded by the sun. In the room itself the red plush on the furniture, the fringes of beads on the standard lamps and the black varnish of the piano quietly reflected the sun.

I stood and wondered what war meant. At that time there were two aspects. First, I was strongly indoctrinated at the kindergarten school, where I spent that summer, with imperialist ideas. There on the wall was the map of the world with the British Empire coloured red. Good or bad it was very impressive. On another wall was a picture of Lord Kitchener of Khartoum which to a child was awe-inspiring. But I was very sad to hear that, for those of our neighbours who owned horses, all horses were being commandeered (a new word), the price of which I was told was £40 – the equivalent of £400 today. I was sad because I had seen how confused and frightened were the horses which someone had decided should draw gun carriages through Cardiff by way of the very narrow Duke Street, which has since disappeared.

Then, however, we went back to Dollar; and there was enough of the summer left for us to see the Argyll and Sutherland Highlanders marching down the Ochil Hills, through the village and away westward again to Stirling with the pipes playing. It was a *braw sicht*. It was, of course, not long before the same soldiers had to go. From an upper window of a well-known shop in Stirling, Maclachlan and Brown, we watched one of the very early departures. The sicht was braw all right. Look, there is so-and-so and the other lad. And the piper, aged seventeen, Malcolm Sarrel, who only a week before had taken his part in our concert in aid

* Sir Malcolm Knox remembers that 'J S Mackenzie of Cardiff was one of Edward Caird's Glasgow pupils and was, therefore well brought up on Kant and Hegel'.

of the Red Cross. They must have gone very soon into battle. The piper's death was told to us three weeks later and there began the dark flowering of the mourning dresses in our streets.

In the summer of 1915 we finally left Dollar. Again I was sad; but several reasons contributed (one of them financial) to the need for us to join my grandmother's household in Llanishan. Nor was I entirely leaving Scotland. My mother had been directed towards the preparatory school St Ninians in Moffat, Dumfriesshire. There she met Mr A M Simpson, who was solicitor to the school and Town Clerk. My mother, having settled my entry to the school, organized our migration to Llanishen and then returned to Scotland for some two or three months' service as a Voluntary Aid Detachment (VAD) nurse in Arnsbrae Hospital, Alloa. When the time came for me to take the great step of going to a boarding school, it was necessary for my mother's sister, Sara Scholberg, to escort me from Cardiff to Moffat. This meant for her an interruption of her duties as a land girl.

We met my mother in Moffat and stayed for several nights, until the school term began, at a very small unlicensed hotel named the Hopetown. There was no eluding the war. On the first night that we were there the man of the house left his wife and infant son, his leave finished, to go to the war with the KOSBs; and he too was soon killed at Gallipoli.

The opportunity was taken to enjoy Moffat's tourist facilities. Four-horse brakes took us one day to Raehills Glen, where I was almost uncontrollably excited to see a deer cross the road ahead of us. On another day the trip was up the Moffat water and on to St Mary's Loch, a two-hour journey. The lunch at Tibbie Sheils Inn, the worst I have ever eaten, requires no racking of the memory – watery lentil soup, tough mutton, and even tougher prunes with only part-cooked rice pudding. There are still deer at Raehills. No doubt Tibbie Sheils has by now forgotten the difficulties of 1915 as it still caters for tourists. St Ninian's School is also, after grave vicissitudes, still there. It was initially built in 1879 as a school by a Mr Dowding, father of Air Chief Marshall Dowding who conducted, to the salvation of his country, the air defence of England in 1940. The headmastership and ownership descended, as it were, in the female line. Dowding was followed by a son-in-law, Rundle; and Rundle was succeeded in 1906 by his son-in-law, the Rev Frank Wingate Pearse. I hope that I shall cause no offence to any of his descendants if I record my memories and my later opinions of this extraordinary man.

When I first saw him he was something over fifty years old. He was six feet four inches in height, lean and very broad. His face was also broad and his hair, long, grey and windswept, was receding from a noble forehead. I never heard him speak of his parents. But he was clearly Welsh, and he told me that his MA degree was from Trinity College, Dublin. At some time he had lived in Rochester and rowed for the local boat club. It should have been simple later to supplement this scanty information; but I never had the opportunity; and it is how he appeared to a small boy that I wish to record.

He was an expert fisherman, a very good golfer, and probably a good club rugby football player. His severity was, as I see it in retrospect, excessive though no doubt of its period. I was quite a harmless type of child, yet in my thirteen terms at the school (as I totted up when I left) I had been beaten by him thirteen times – an average per term which conveniently required no calculation of decimals. He used a light rattan cane with which he delivered not more than six strokes.

Certain senior boys, captains of dormitories, were also authorized to beat, though I do not remember for what offences. They, however, could only use a shoe (the heel) or a hair brush with a handle. Of this type of corporal punishment also I acquired an average share. I do not think that I suffered any psychic trauma as the result. I may even have been improved, if painful and conspicuous weals on the buttocks are an improving influence on ordinary children. I would not, however, myself adopt this method of instilling discipline when that responsibility fell on me.

Mr Pearse's basic idea was that courage was the most important element in character. I recall with distaste his method of driving on a rugby football team. There was very little encouragement in his cries, rather was there a continuous raving designed to keep these small creatures working to the limit of the endurance of pain and fatigue. And most of us were very small. When I left the school on 18 December 1919, which was my thirteenth birthday, I had on the previous day been recorded as exactly five feet tall and as weighing exactly six stone. In due course our own sons exceeded these attainments. But it is only just to recall that none of us ever seemed to resent our treatment. We accepted the standards with which we were required to comply.

On one occasion I felt acute embarrassment as the result of this acceptance. We played a match against a neighbouring school, Warriston, and they were taking a drop-kick out of their own 'twenty-five'. I charged down the kick (I hope within the rules) and received the man's boot on the inside of my right elbow. Among mature players no one would even notice this. Among small boys it could hardly be regarded as a natural action. And so that evening, during our preparation period, I was called out in front of all. Not by Mr Pearse. Never; but by one of the recurring temporary assistant masters who appeared during those war years. He was a Mr Andrews, plump, affable and probably inefficient. He drew the attention of the other boys to my devotion to duty, hoped that they had taken the point (my arm was temporarily useless), and sent me back to my seat. The other boys were unimpressed. But Mr Andrews was a humane man.

He finally left the staff as the result of a rather pathetic incident. At breakfast (he lived in the main building and took his meals in the main hall) he asked for a second piece of toast. Someone, I do not know who but I suspect Mrs Pearse, refused it with the eternally recurrent reference to the fact that there was a war on. Mr Andrews came into our class in high indignation and, before starting our lesson, wrote large on the blackboard a limerick describing his humiliation. I remember the two lines:

I now understand
Why the Scots leave their land.

Yet I do not think that any of us came near to disliking Mr Pearse. Among the boys he was never known as anything but The Bump. This was one of those sharp-eyed ideas which occur to little boys. The name came from a by no means conspicuous swelling behind one of his ears. Of course, like all little boys, before adolescence tends to emphasize the margin between the genuinely clever and the naturally not so clever, we were all very shrewd. We noticed the almost besotted way in which this behemoth, so severe towards us, always addressed his wife as 'My lady' and rose to his feet when she appeared. He probably lived to some extent in a world of the imagination; perhaps the rather attractive world of Conan Doyle's *The White Company*, which, among other books, he would read aloud to us on winter evenings.

He clearly took great pleasure in reading to us John Buchan's *Prester John*. This presented us with one of those utterly clean characters, whose faith and fitness, the result in each case of the opposition to, and the avoidance of, something which was not defined but clearly meant wickedness, carried him through exceptional physical hardships. It is perhaps permissible to wonder whether John Buchan himself, at that time not very long out of Tweedsmuir Parish, Glasgow University and Brasenose College, would have wished his early works to have been used to indoctrinate the succeeding generation.

Mr Pearse was an Anglican clergyman. The Rector of St John's Episcopalian Church in Moffat, Mr Moloney, gave Mr Pearse every co-operation in conducting services. I remember Mr Moloney as a tall figure with a longish but clipped beard and a monotonous voice. Those of us who attended the Episcopalian Church were sifted in order to ascertain whether we could sing in the choir. I achieved this dubious success. And so for all those years, with my fellow victims, I attended morning and evening services in the school chapel on every weekday, and the morning and evening services on Sundays in St John's Church. In the latter we went through the whole order of morning and evening prayer.

For those not familiar with the Prayer Book I would mention the interminable psalms which are one of its features. It is not surprising that even towards the end of my life not one of the one hundred and fifty is unfamiliar. In this rather drear introduction to the God of our fathers, however, there was still the figure and the voice of Mr Pearse reading – six foot four of low church clergyman kneeling at a lectern below the steps of the chancel – the litany. We chanted the responses. But I feel sure that no one who ever heard him would forget Mr Pearse saying 'By Thine agony and bloody sweat'.

I was more intrigued by 'fornication and all other deadly sin'. I had not the slightest idea what this meant, though I could sing 'Good Lord deliver us' with a good show of pious sincerity. I was certainly not prepared to enquire. Twice I had been in peril in this strange field of human knowledge. The first was when, on one of our frequent scripture (Old Testament) readings, I interrupted to ask what was meant by the words 'went a whoring after', something I am doubtful whether I know today. But Mr Pearse gave me a nasty look which implied that I knew perfectly well and was a subversive influence who should be watched. The time came when he heard me say 'Oh! Help'. I had read it in *The Scout* weekly magazine. He called me up with all guns firing. Did I not know that he knew that I was craftily muffling the (presumably obscene) phrase 'Oh! Hell'? My transparent astonishment impressed even his calvinistic mind. I was not beaten; but I learned what it meant to be crafty.

Mrs Pearse at this time middle-aged, had undoubtedly been extremely pretty in her earlier years. She was obviously devoted to her husband, and, as happens with older people on occasion, still looked very pretty when she looked at him. She could be very kind to those whom she liked and unkind to those whom she did not. I did not come in the former category. She taught me French.

So in this strange place I stayed to the exact age of thirteen. I was drilled in Latin and Greek – Latin by Mr Pearse; Greek more especially by his daughter Molly, a potential graduate of Oxford but not qualified by the Statutes of the time. To her I had to recite my Greek irregular verbs even though, as happened sometimes, the lesson coincided with her dressing for a dance. 'Come in, Mitchell. You must have seen your mother like this often enough.' And so I would downward turn my burning eyes at mysteries so bright, and go through my paradigms. I had been almost a mouse in the wainscot at her wedding. I watched her ride the blow of her husband's death in France, which left her with an infant son. And I knew her and her second husband up to 1930. She always seemed to me both brave and good.

In March 1919 I was awarded a scholarship at Shrewsbury School. My transfer to Shrewsbury was put off till January 1920, because the school would not take boys before their thirteenth birthday. This is, therefore, a suitable point to record that to leave St Ninian's and the country round Moffat was for me very sad. All the Spartan regimen seems, as I look back, to have raised no resentment. One hot bath a week, supplemented by the communal small *balneum* in the changing room – ample hot water and Sunlight soap to remove the mud and sweat of the football or the run round Gallow Hill were ample compensation for the compulsory cold shower at 7.10 am daily throughout the two winter terms (it was a length of the swimming bath in summer). We knew that the junior master in charge of this exercise was content to accept the drops on one's shoulders, sprinkled by a judicious use of the dampened forelock, as evidence of immersion.

In summer there were frequent fishing expeditions. Mr Pearse could be kind, indeed must have been at heart kind. It was just a matter of what you consider to be kindness. Once my mother took me by train from Cardiff to London in order to join the party of St Ninian's boys leaving Euston at the end of the holidays by the 10.00 am train. On the previous day, she had bought me a bicycle at Gamages and this involved, of course, a special ticket and the consignment of the bicycle to the guards van. She sent me up the platform (which seemed endless) to join the party of which Mr Pearse was in charge. As the hands of the clock drew on to 10.00, I was showing signs of anxiety, not (if I were honest with myself) about the bicycle but because I did desperately want the last goodbye. Mr Pearse saw this and said, quite like an ordinary man, 'don't bother, Mitchell. She's a clever little thing.' If he had been mistaken in his confidence, he would probably have gone and loomed over the guard. In fact my mother, a little breathless, arrived with a minute or so to spare and with everything done.

So nostalgic was I that three years later I indented on my poor mother for additional money at the end of the Michaelmas term at Shrewsbury and on 18 December, 1922, travelled north to Moffat. Both Mr and Mrs Pearse received me with great kindness and, now sixteen, I was allowed a glass of claret at supper. I was in no way daunted by having to arrive at 7.45 pm to find snow everywhere; nor can I remember objecting to leaving on 20 December at 7.15 pm and travelling all night to reach Plymouth at 11.00 am (we had moved there from Llanishen in 1920). The point was that I had once more been to Scotland and to a particular part of Scotland; and had been able to see certain people who had been good to me when I was a child.

Mr Pearse I was to see twice again in 1930. Nothing suggested that the school was other than prosperous or he other than contented. In November 1930 my wife and I went to India to start our own life together and I never saw him again nor saw Scotland for fifteen years. News did, however, somehow seep through to us, much of it from an old boyhood friend at St Ninian's, Norman Maclaurin (he was a Captain in Skinner's Horse in Risalpur when I was posted to Nowshera in 1934). Mrs Pearse died during these years and he gave up the school. He seems to have had no financial ability; the school was encumbered with debt; and he received little or nothing for its sale to two very much younger men. He obtained the Rectorship of St John's Church and with it the manse for a roof over his head. A housekeeper looked after him. But he must have been very poor. 'Just a poor old man' said one informant after he died. This was no proper epitaph for a Stoic.

Chapter 2

A time to plant
Ecclesiastes III 2

I STAYED AT SHREWSBURY from January 1920 to July 1925. I moved up the school in the normal way; but since I was only thirteen when I started in the Upper Fifth, I finished by spending three years in the Classical Upper Sixth. My athletic achievements were as disparate as they were mediocre, though I was unlucky to miss my First VIII rowing colours in 1925 through a severe attack of pneumonia which nearly killed me. I gather that prayers were even said for me in chapel. I was awarded a Domus Exhibition at Balliol College, Oxford, in December 1923, shortly before my seventeenth birthday. Like so many precocious achievements this one proved to be something of a flash in the pan. I failed to convert the exhibition into a scholarship when I took the same examination a year later; and even then I felt that the spark of scholarship was dying simply because I was trying (or being asked) to do too much. Some boys did better than I did with as heavy loads. By a paradox, their greater distinction in, say, athletics might give them less academic pressure on their time.

Shrewsbury allowed people like me no more than two periods a week for private study out of school. In my final summer, aged eighteen and with almost my whole school career behind me, I was required, with my Balliol Exhibition in my pocket, to sit the Oxford and Cambridge Higher Certificate examination, which I had already successfully taken three times before. This pressure of the nose to the academic grindstone was increased by the numerous other tasks which fell to be done by the senior boys in general. There were for me the offices of president of two or three societies, the editorship of the school magazine and the submission at least four times a week of compositions in Latin and Greek prose and verse.

Yet the Headmaster took a very serious view of my conduct one night. Lights out was at 10.15 pm. About 10.30 pm I was sitting up in bed with an electric torch preparing a passage from the New Testament in Greek for a lesson at 7.45 am next morning. Another torch flashed on me from the doorway and I said rather sharply 'Who's that?' It was the Headmaster, of whose School House I was a member. At that time I was past caring what was done to me. For four years I had been getting up winter and summer at 6.30 am so as to keep pace with the day by day work for classes which started at 7.45 am. I was, of course, very senior. I was blatantly in breach of the rules. But what choice had I after a day (Sunday) which included attendance at three chapel services, two choir practices, an afternoon lesson in school, and all the tide of work from the previous week leading up to the week to come? The Headmaster could only see that a breach of discipline by a senior boy was a grievous offence.

Nonetheless Shrewsbury in my view was, during the Headmastership of Canon H A P Sawyer, a very good school. It bore his mark everywhere. His predecessor, Dr C A Alington, was a much more conspicuous figure and very much loved by his staff and at least by the senior boys who knew him well. His *Shrewsbury Fables*, originally delivered as addresses in chapel, were the sort of product of which Canon Sawyer would have been quite incapable. Alington's subsequent active life as Headmaster of Eton and Dean of Durham, like his literary output, is public knowledge.

When he was appointed Headmaster of Eton, he was replaced in January 1917 by a very different man. Sawyer was an enthusiastic alumnus of Queen's College, Oxford, where he narrowly missed a Blue for Rugby football. He became successively a master at Highgate School and Headmaster of St Bees School in Cumbria. He was of short stature but strongly built. In middle life he grew stout, a fact which was all too manifest in his ordinary clerical clothes. But his face was strongly, even nobly, cast. When I travelled down from Moffat in the Lent Term of 1919 to sit the scholarship examination, I stayed in the School House as the guest of him and Mrs Sawyer. My impression of that occasion is dim apart from the night-long chiming of church clocks in the town beyond the river. It was, however, a moment at which my mother, very rightly, decided to take a hand in what Mr Pearse was planning for me. This was that the Shrewsbury examination should be taken for the sake of experience with a view to an attempt at Winchester later in the year.

My mother arranged, therefore, an appointment with Canon Sawyer and travelled from Cardiff for the purpose. He actually called me out of the examination room to see her. Years later she admitted that she felt very maternal as I came blinking out into the light of day. The main result of the visit however, was her instant and unmoving decision that I must go to Shrewsbury. Odd arguments were adduced against poor Winchester. The main one was that it was low-lying and damp. There was also a suggestion that the soup was served in wooden plates. The truth was that she conceived an absolute faith in Sawyer from which she never saw reason to retreat.

Sawyer did have much difficulty when he first arrived at Shrewsbury. He was outwardly so much the antithesis of Alington that he was actually unpopular with, and mocked by, some. His scholarship was not of a high order. He was absent-minded; and in administrative matters he was sometimes regarded as almost an imbecile. This, of course, could not possibly be true, otherwise his fifteen years of office could not have been as successful as they were. At Shrewsbury, as at other schools, some remote, but of necessity divine, power is often urged in Latin song to agree that the school may flourish. The 'Carmen' was composed by Alington and is in a very neat, up-to-date type of Latin which might have puzzled a Roman. *Floreat Salopia* does not mean 'May Shropshire flourish' but 'May Shrewsbury (*sc.* school) flourish'. In Sawyer's time it did. Scholarships in unlikely numbers were year after year won to Oxford and Cambridge. All athletic clubs maintained surprising records of success, the Boat Club most conspicuously so because it competed not only against other schools but also against the strongest colleges in the Ladies Plate at Henley. It was not coincidence that all this happened at this time.

Although I have made above certain adverse criticisms of the Shrewsbury of those days, I would, however, point out that one aspect of these matters illustrated Sawyer's prime quality. This was integrity. Discipline was in his view indivisible, a field in which no compromise could be admitted. He was quietly jovial, unobtrusively kind. How kind he was, and for how little return, others besides me must sometimes feel – with John Masefield:

> O grave, keep shut lest I be shamed.

As regards the alleged incompetence, someone possessed of a mischievous sense of humour once applied to a Masters' Meeting certain lines from Milton's *Paradise Lost*:

> Chaos umpire sits,
> And by decision more embroils the fray
> By which he reigns: next him high arbiter
> Chance governs all.

The reference was to the senior master, A F Chance. He was a house-master of an age approaching retirement. He was a very fine scholar, having been a Porson Prize winner during his time at Trinity College, Cambridge. In his time he had been a fine cricketer. But he was, when I knew him, of another time altogether. There was something of Lord Kitchener or of Mr Harold Macmillan in the moustache which just escaped dominating the face; something Olympian in his stature and his

Student at Balliol

gait. But he was not one to assert himself at meetings. I never saw him treat Sawyer other than with a courtesy which was sincere. My affection for Artie Chance was based on a certainty of his integrity. This must however, be coupled with the warm smell of cigar smoke and claret which always infused his criticism of my Greek iambics when I brought them to him of an evening.

After I went up to Oxford in 1925 I often visited Shrewsbury; and one example of Sawyer's kindness was his employment of my services to correct the Classical Upper Sixth examination papers in Plato's *Republic.* It may have been true that he could not spare the time to do it himself; but he certainly knew that the fee was important to me. He and Mrs Sawyer were always clearly pleased to see people like myself who were still not much more than the adolescents whom they had known. In the course of time I went to India and connection with Shrewsbury was cut. Here again however, my remote postings received some news. More especially there was news of the celebrations in 1932 of the jubilee of the school's move from the town to Kingsland. These coincided with the second time that the First VIII won the Ladies Plate at Henley; and likewise reproduced the *annus mirabilis*, 1923–24, in scholastic and athletic successes. Canon Harold Athelstane Parry Sawyer retired in a cloud of glory.

I saw him once more. On his retirement he was appointed Chaplain of Corpus Christi College, Oxford. During 1934 1 was on leave from India and was in England during September and October. I was very fortunate to be able to get in contact with my old friend and Shrewsbury contemporary, D S Colman, at that time Dean of Queen's College. He took me round to Corpus and we took a glass of sherry with Sawyer. He was very cheerful, but he was shrunken and rather vague. The news of his death reached me in 1939 in a remote spot in the Himalayas long after I would have wished to know, and with no means of expressing my condolences to anyone concerned. His ashes were buried under the chapel sanctuary.

Life at Shrewsbury fifty to fifty-five years ago was on the whole very happy, though with some strange survivals from the past. In the summer term of 1920 I found myself, together with an equally small boy from Ireland called Figgis, the most junior scum* in the School House. The feeding system was still rather poor, since the war was not long over and rationing of many foodstuffs was still in force. But all boys by force of convention, joined with one or two others to share such additional food as their parents or their pocket money might provide.

For Figgis and me there was only one choice. We must (to use the local language) 'firm' together. We were also the only two boys in the house who, since we had joined one term later than most boys did, had not been through a curious ordeal which still survived from the barbarian past. It was called 'Study Singing'. New boys were required to present themselves outside a certain study on a certain evening. Inside were the four senior boys of the house below the status of house monitor. They were called Hall Firm and were headed by a person called the Hall Constable.

This person was elected by an open vote of the house at the beginning of each term; and by convention was appointed a house monitor in the following term. Even Sawyer never broke this convention. On the Hall Constable's elevation, Hall Firm would co-opt a fourth member. In this devious way the house monitors always included one or two who had *de facto* been elected by the boys themselves. In that study was a table. The members of Hall Firm sat against it with sticks in their hands. One at a

* This disagreeable word was synonymous with 'fag' in other schools, or with the slightly more elegant Shrewsbury word 'dowl' from the Greek word for 'slave'.

time the little boys were admitted and told to stand on the table. Thus exposed, they were then put through an interrogation on a very wide range of things that a Shrewsbury boy was expected to know. Some were simply related to the colours of the houses or the school teams. Some were geographical. Some brought in the nicknames of masters or ceremonies. If a boy did not know enough of the answers, he had to appear again later.

But in any case the ordeal ended by the examinee being ordered to sing a song and dance the while on the table. The sticks of the committee were cracked about the examinee's feet to ensure that he really leaped in the dance. Then, released from the inquisitors, he must run the gauntlet down the corridor of other members of the house bearing pillow-cases loaded with such heavy objects as shoes. With these they belaboured the graduands. It was a lot of nonsense, and in a way it sounds much worse than it was. No one was really beaten. But everyone was in a sense humiliated by superior force in much the same way that a dog is trained. I can sometimes see a glint of merit in this, but no one today would think so. Even then it was dying out. So also, at Sawyer's insistence, was the use of a piece of wood called a 'swiper' – for the beating by house monitors of wrong-doers. This looked much like a rounded chair leg and, as I can testify, was a brutal thing. It was substituted by a light cane, which was quite enough.

In any case barbarism was not a feature of the school, and nearly every boy soon came to love it and the country in which it lay. Summer had a Tennysonian quality. Winter was not severe. Even then there was pleasure in games or running. A friend of mine and I, neither of us being runners of any class, once set ourselves a point-to-point course of nine miles which we completed in rather less than an hour and which involved twice swimming a canal. I am sure we were only typical of a sort of absorption in our environment. Like Charles Sorley's 'Ungirt Runners' we would

> Run because we like it
> Through the broad bright land.

Many of us were enchanted by the reading of English literature and Latin and Greek literature and history. These, with prose and verse composition in those languages, formed the bulk of our work. We gave no thought to the rights and wrongs of abandoning scientific or mathematical studies after passing the School Certificate. After all, our scientific and mathematical friends seemed to think and feel much the same as those studying History or the Classics when extra-curricular activities were involved. Of the latter there were many; but after so many years I remember especially the School Orchestra, the Chapel Choir and the much bigger Concert Choir.

Perhaps the loveliest experience of any for me was in the summer of 1922. On 29 June I was one of a party which went to Bradfield College to see their Greek play. My diary records a swim in the Thames in the morning and an excellent lunch at the Elephant, presumably in Pangbourne. 'The play starts at 3.15 pm and we return by 5.35 pm. This is by no means all.' The two available square inches record details long forgotten. But still green is the memory of the Thames on a perfect summer day; of the exquisite beauty of the open air theatre set among trees, so that the green of the trees and the grey of the stone-work merged with no sharp division; and of the play itself, moving like a dream. It is true to say that the light southern wind in the trees made hearing very difficult. But that did not matter. The play was Sophocles' *Antigone*. We knew it very well. What we had previously lacked, but would not lack again, was the mystery and beauty of the words and their sadness in the soft air and gentle light of summer.

I must make one final point. The summer, the winter, the libraries with their exquisite woodwork and their silence, and a multitude of details which went to make up a civilized society, must necessarily have been dependent for their affectionate recollection on the quality of the staff. It was in this field that Sawyer seemed to have an uncanny insight. An old member of the staff told some of us in 1972 how Sawyer had recruited him fifty years before. It was simply an accidental meeting in a railway compartment leading in a matter of minutes to the offer of a post. Sawyer's intuition in these matters seems to have been infallible. Certainly, in the case that I have quoted, the rather dazed recruit stayed with much distinction for the rest of his life. It did seem in 1920 that there were one or two less good masters, especially the occasional one whom the boys, with that unerring cruelty of the young towards weakness, would 'rag' and torment to the threshold of tears. By the time I left however, in 1925, the staff must have been consistently good throughout. Some of them, all now of course in retirement or dead, were my life-long friends, so perhaps I should declare an interest.

After leaving Shrewsbury at the end of July 1925 I spent a long vacation in Wiltshire. My aunt Sara and her husband, Jacob Seaward lived near Winterslow, originally in a Palladian house called Roche Court which they rented with its park, woodland and downland from Lord Nelson. The sundial on the lawn commemorated the peace of Amiens in 1814. When the estate came onto the market, they could only afford to buy the woodland and downland with a cottage at the south-west corner called Owls Castle. In this summer they vacated the cottage so that my grandmother might stay there for a few months. But there was no room for me in the cottage and I slept in another cottage at the top of the steep road which led uphill westwards. Each night as I left Owls Castle to walk up the hill I would see the ripe barley on either side of the road, the clear stars and the phases of the moon; and I would sing vigorously a ballad which was then popular:

> Oh this is the crown of the year,
> The glory and crown of the year.
> Fields all a-shine with sheaves in a line
> And never a harvester there.

I would reach the cottage which was owned by an old couple named Mr and Mrs Ind. He was happy to explain that his name appeared on the coinage of the realm – which was true, since the monarch's name in those days was on any coin followed not only by the abbreviation for *Fidei Defensor* but also by Ind Imp, *Indiae Imperator*. There I would sleep like a child on a feather mattress, wake early and be greeted at 6.30 am by Mrs Ind with a cup of strong, sweet tea. I was for the first of several times in my life mentally rather than physically exhausted. But this time was a hiatus between what had gone before and what was to come. I had no calls on my time, no demands for work. Indeed, having no responsibilities, and being too young to be in love with anyone in particular, my conscience left me free.

Jacob Seaward lent me a gun and an elderly Labrador bitch called Jess. Every single day, week after week, Jess and I threaded our way through the hazel copses which covered the space between second-growth beech, oak and ash. We shot vermin to start with – stoats, weasels, jays, and rabbits if one could be sure before firing that they were not pregnant does. Walking very slowly and silently along the rides and deer paths one in a sense became integrated with the sounds, the colours, the variegated light and shade, and the smells of that type of woodland. The solitude from human beings, and the curious paradox of the silence of nature which is full of sounds, had then, as later in my life, a very quickly healing effect.

I am sure that many people would say that this simply means that a rest was needed which could equally well be acquired by a golf holiday in Ireland or Scotland. I am equally sure that those people would be right. Indeed I did have a short golf holiday in Cornwall at this time with a friend and his family. But the two things are not comparable. A game such as golf with friends is a great enjoyment. It has no resemblance to walking the woods with a dog.

I have been told that the academic staff at Oxford sometimes criticized Shrewsbury School for the unnecessarily strict control which was kept over senior boys in the academic field. I have suggested above that such control was mistaken. Almost all control vanished at Oxford. A man's tutor would recommend certain lectures to be attended, but there was no compulsion. Looking back fifty years I cannot but feel that this was right. I eagerly fell in with the new freedom. I bought a bicycle (a substantial commitment for a poor student) and miraculously escaped having it stolen. On this I might leave the college at 8.55 am for a lecture on Demosthenes at Queen's College at 9.00 am. For much of the year the weather would be wet and the streets muddy. I would arrive, therefore, at Queen's wearing a gown, of course, wet and muddy. The lecturer was dull and dealt with what I am convinced was a dull subject. It required a genius or a film star to breathe life into the legal orations of that Athenian. This man was neither.

When the lecture ended, one made a dash for the bicycle, emerged on the High Street and dauntlessly pedalled through rain, mud and the fumes of motor buses to the Ashmolean to hear H M Last of St John's College lecturing on the pre-history of Herodotus. The lectures were both learned and infused with imagination. But how do you give the attention which is due to such quality of teaching if your bicycle is insecurely padlocked somewhere outside the Ashmolean, your head looks like a haystack, you are in something of a sweat, and your only pair of flannels, with your second best shoes, are splattered with mud?

It was at this time that my intention to go to India became fixed. I have already mentioned how the seed was sown when I was six years old. Five years later, during a half-term holiday at St Ninian's School, my contemporary and friend H H J Cadell invited me out to lunch with his parents. After lunch we walked in the rain until it was time to return to the school, and my friend's father, a retired colonel of the Indian army, asked me what I intended to do in life. I did not know. Had I considered service in India? No. He then spoke of his own days there, but especially of the Indian Civil Service (ICS); and of 'the Political', whose full title was then the Foreign and Political Department of the Government of India (it became the Indian Political Service in April 1937).

I can still see the rain running down the lane about my feet as what he told me brought other pictures to my mind. For some reason I particularly saw myself sitting under a tree in the darkness by a large camp fire with shadowy figures beyond the fire. What they were doing goodness knows. Neither my knowledge nor my imagination was adequate to explain. When I went home at the end of that term, however, my mother was delighted to hear that I was going into the ICS and would in due course transfer to the Political. If it should happen, it would justify to her the general line which she had taken about my upbringing.

At Shrewsbury there was one Speech Day when the main speaker took India as his subject. He was Sir Arthur Lawley, former Governor of Bombay. He was urging us to serve India. To me he was preaching to the converted and did not seem to be inspired. Long afterwards I was told that recruitment to the Secretary of State's services in India had fallen off to a dangerous degree after the passage of the Government of India Act, 1919. Further, it was said that the India Office had set in motion a campaign of propaganda to stimulate recruitment. The idea of indoctrination was not a new one even then; and this seemed a harmless example.

On Saturday 1 May 1926 my ideas about service in India were nearly ended. My friend Stacy Colman and I were rowing at bow and two respectively in the Balliol VIII, which was given a holiday on that day. We decided to borrow his brother's two-stroke motor bicycle and go to see Gloucester Cathedral, he driving, I on the carrier – it was not a comfortable, well-sprung pillion. On our way home in the late afternoon we were hit broadside on by another motor bicycle at a cross-roads on Birdlip Hill outside a public house called the Air Balloon. Our opponent broke his front wheel which in its turn inflicted on me a comminuted fracture of the left femur. The others were unhurt, though Stacy was concussed and behaved very amusingly. I finished up in the Cheltenham General Hospital. Nine weeks later I emerged from the hospital with shortening of the left leg, which ultimately reached two and a half inches, and acute angulation.

In September I was invited to stay with my uncle in Cardiff, and one day I went with him, his wife and their son Philip, to a spot near Abergavenny to fish. Not that fishing was for me at the moment. But my uncle's companion in the renting of a beat on the Usk was Mr Cornelius Griffith and he and his wife were there. He was a brilliant surgeon and a much-loved man, a colleague of my uncle in the King Edward Infirmary. Much later I learned that he and his wife had lost their only son in the war. Mrs Griffith saw me hirpling about like a crab on the bank of the river.

After tea she asked him what he would have done if that fellow over there had been their son. He told her. Before we started the drive home he asked me if I would care to come to the hospital next morning and have my leg X-rayed. I said yes. And next morning I was looking at a photograph which even to me seemed to indicate a mess. He asked me what I intended to do in life. I told him about the ICS. He told me that they probably would not take me with a leg like that; but if I would agree that he should operate he would be very happy to take me in when there was a bed available.

After several false alarms a bed did become available on 10 November. In the meantime I had gone up to Balliol two or three weeks before the term began in order to do as much reading for Mods as possible before the operation. My exercise was, somewhat improbably, beagling. After another nine weeks on my back I returned to Oxford for the Lent term and in due course failed, though not by very much, to get a First Class in my examinations.

Once again in the spring of 1927 there was a resurgence of the feeling of freedom. It was not until October that I got back the full use of my leg. But, while I put in a reasonable number of hours of work, the examination for Greats was two years ahead and could hardly be said to loom. There was a yachting trip with four friends to the Norfolk Broads in April. Owing to my relative immobility I was elected ship's cook. This invariably meant that we had our meals at an inn if there was one near our moorings. My touch was especially unreliable with cauliflower. But I could swim long before I could walk properly; and this I could do during the summer at the spot called Parson's Pleasure on the Cherwell. In the long vacation we took our family holiday in Brittany, where tennis was added to swimming; and by mid-September there was no more than a very slight limp as the residue of so many difficult months.

In October of that year I was so far recovered as to be able to start rowing again, and continued uninterrupted till July 1930, with a Trial Cap in December 1928 as the main reward. This was a silly thing to do in view of the fact that I had to sit for Greats in June 1929 and to take the Civil Service examination in London over a period of three weeks in July and August. I was very tired when it was all over, and I very nearly failed in my life's ambition. In Greats I took a very pedestrian Second Class. I had always thought that this would be my goal, since it represented an academic standard high enough for the requirements of the Civil Service examination, and should mean also that I would have enough spare time to do other things, such as rowing (but also to a less extent golf or shooting) which might persuade the Board of Examiners at the interview that I had emerged from my educational years as a balanced person.

'Balanced' is not a word which in retrospect I would apply to myself at that time. My education was highly specialized. This was a good thing provided that specialized knowledge in one field implied a trained mind, and if it could be counter-balanced by other skills. There I fell short. As I emerged from the chrysalis of education at the age of twenty-two, I was still very immature. Two things accelerated the process of growing up.

One was my two sojourns in public hospitals. These were my first introduction to the world of service and suffering. I saw people die

Student at Balliol

quickly, sometimes before they came round from the drunkenness which had led to their injuries. Others had to wait for death. Nurses in those days were abominably treated. Had they not been as probationers very hardy and very devoted, they could not physically have survived. The experience radically changed my attitude to public service. Hitherto, handing down the tablets of the law round a camp fire had been a pleasing idea. But there had now occurred a revelation of what the life of human beings could be in conditions of disease and pain. I still had to learn about hunger and fear as normal elements in the life of so many people. A window had been opened in my mind however, from which I could view the antithesis of the romantic imaginings of youth.

The second event which helped the process of development was my meeting with Miss Mary Elizabeth Couch of Chicago, Illinois. We met at dinner at the Café de Paris in Bray on the evening of a day in 1928 when, as Captain of the Balliol College Boat Club, I had been beaten in two events in one day at Henley Regatta. I asked her to excuse me if I was not very talkative, since I was rather tired. Her instant sympathy, if an out-of-date cliché is permissible, won my heart. She has retained it since. We met several times during that summer – outside Magdalen College, in Brittany and in Paris. After three days we considered ourselves engaged to be married.

She went back to the United States and successfully passed her final examinations at Smith College in the summer of 1929. In September came the news that I had passed my own examination for the ICS, although only just. In the first combined list of the services covered by the examination (which was competitive) I appeared as equal 50th out of 52. This placing improved as the fifty-two men concerned were allotted to the various services of their choice; and my place was somewhere about 35th of the fifty odd available places in the ICS. Nonetheless it was a close shave.

When the full marks of the Civil Service examination were published, it became clear how much chance seemed to influence the result. In the optional subjects, for which one thousand marks were available, and which were always subjects in which the candidate had taken his degree, I did very much the same as I had done at Oxford. But these were in the field of Latin and Greek literature, Ancient History and both ancient and subsequent philosophy. From Thales to Descartes is a long journey. In all this field there is infinite room for difference of opinion on the part of examiners. How then can the candidate be assessed in relation to another candidate offering subjects in which the answers must be either right or wrong? In 1929 the first name on the list was that of a mathematician, far ahead of the rest.

From an experience of mine I incline to think that mistakes could also arise in the attribution of marks to individual candidates. There were five compulsory subjects in the examination, each with a maximum of one hundred marks. This, added to the one thousand marks available for subjects chosen by the individual candidate, gave a maximum total of fifteen hundred. A further three hundred were allocated to the interview. Finally, a candidate might also choose to take an unseen translation paper in a modern language other than French, the latter being one of the five compulsory subjects. In this category I accumulated useful marks. Even Elementary Science was helpful as the result of my purchase, at one penny each, of six paper-bound leaflets on various subjects, treated at beginner's level, such as botany and astronomy.

But the French paper went wrong. It consisted of two quite short passages for translation. At that time I had added to my School Certificate pass with credit in French (1921) a substantial number of months spent in

France over the previous three years. The paper was easy. It took me twenty minutes to transcribe it into English, with some doubt about one word. It would not have looked well to hand in my paper indecently soon, so I carefully re-wrote it, still with the doubt about the single word, but reasonably hoping for 95%. The published list of marks did not confirm my hopes. The figure was 50%.

This could, in an extremely close competition, have meant complete failure for me. My situation was saved by my decision to take an unseen translation examination in Spanish as a modern language other than French. My mother, who was bilingual in English and Spanish, most kindly came to stay in the Hampstead boarding house where I stayed after the end of Henley Regatta until the examination finished in the fourth week of August. There I obtained a copy from the public library of Blasco Ibañez *Blood and Sand* in Spanish; and I bought a Hugo's booklet on the language. For three weeks I gave some time each day to Hugo and

TO WED, LIVE IN INDIA

MISS MARY ELIZABETH COUCH.

[Drake Studio Photo.]

Mr. and Mrs. Ira Johnson Couch of 232 East Walton place announce the engagement of their daughter, Mary Elizabeth, to Alfred N. Mitchell of London, England. Miss Couch graduated from Smith college in 1929 and has spent the last winter studying at Oxford. Mr. Mitchell was in Chicago a year ago as the guest of Mr. and Mrs. Couch for the holidays. He has since graduated from Oxford. The marriage will take place in September, after which Mr. Mitchell and his bride will go to India to make their home, as Mr. Mitchell is in the Indian civil service of the British government. Sept 2 - 1930 - Chicago Tribune

Mary Couch wedding announcement

some time to reading the novel with my mother and trying to acquire a vocabulary. In the end I obtained some 35% for a language which I did not know as compared with the 50% for French, which I knew quite well.

With the competitive examination finished I went to Winterslow to stay with a retired schoolmaster, Mr Witt, and his wife as I had done several times before when I had much studying to do. This time there was no studying to do. I was too tired to bother about the results of Greats or the Civil Service examinations. The morrow could take thought for itself. I read two novels a day, usually sitting in the sun. As in earlier days Jacob Seaward and my aunt Sara were kind to me. Every afternoon I threaded the deer-paths and walked the rides with a dog. The expanses of Salisbury plain to the north and the thickly wooded country connecting us to the New Forest to the south were like a veil of mental peace, a cool breeze about one's temples.

Several weeks later the cure was completed by three pieces of news which reached me in a hotel in Earl's Court. My Second Class in Greats was awarded. My pass into the ICS was spotted by my sister in *The Times* before breakfast one morning. (I can still hear her feet on the stairs as she ran up, calling out the news.) And several weeks later Miss Couch's parents agreed that she and I might be formally engaged to be married.

Chapter 3

Candidates who had obtained places in the ICS were required to spend a year on probation at one of four universities, Oxford, Cambridge, London or Trinity College, Dublin. I elected to go back to Balliol. Indeed, I had already been elected Captain of Boats for a second year on some sort of contingency basis. I rowed in the IV in November, but decided thereafter that I must stop rowing and restrict myself to coaching and administration. So far as university rowing was concerned, there was not a murmur of objection when I informed the authorities that I did not wish to be considered for the Trial Eights. To anticipate, I did coach through the winter and spring, but found myself rowing in the First VIII in the summer of 1930, someone having become a casualty. Then, in what was now a familiar pattern, I rowed in two events at Henley. By that time I did not even have the responsibility of being captain: I simply had a strange conscience and a love of rowing; and there would not be any more after that first week in July 1930.

Now came a gradual transition from being an undergraduate to being admitted to a profession. My fiancée persuaded her kind and generous parents that she required some post-graduate study, such as only Oxford could supply. By means of which I have not even now been clearly informed, she arrived at Christchurch early in November as a paying guest of Canon Cook, Regius Professor of Hebrew. The buildings of Tom Quad are in the highest degree impressive. The rooms that I had up to that time seen were not such as to arouse enthusiasm; but those of Canon Cook's house were exquisite. Equally exquisite was the general cold in winter. This, combined with bathing in her bedroom in a hip-bath charged with two or three gallons of hot water, soon brought on pneumonia. She continued until May studying English with the young Neville Coghill. We were both very warmly pleased when he came to St Andrews University more than forty years later to receive an honorary doctorate, and we were able to meet him before and after the formal dinner.

I must also record that, without telling me, Mary Couch signed up with Mr Dewhurst, my tutor for Hindi. He had been a member of the ICS, but had not progressed very far in the service. He reached the age of retirement as, I believe, a sessions judge roughly equivalent to a county court judge in England. But he was a miraculous linguist.

One by-product of this was that early in 1930 I received an affectionately worded message from Mary in the Devanagri script. In case further evidence of Mr Dewhurst's polymathy is needed, I can at first hand quote Iftikhar-ud-Din, Nawab of Pataudi, the England cricketer and one of my contemporaries at Balliol. He, unlike his equally distinguished son, had not been to school in England. He was an alumnus of the Chiefs' College, Lahore. Yet he told me in full seriousness that Dewhurst knew very much more Persian than he did.

The year was a busy one as I embarked on studies new to me. Ultimately there was a nasty alarm before I could find myself confirmed as a 'covenanted' member of the ICS. The word referred to a document which one had to sign on emerging from probation. It conferred security of tenure. I have always been sceptical. The original was kept by the Secretary of State and his successors in office; and I neither was given, nor did I ask for, a copy. The security of tenure was exemplified in 1931 by a reduction in salary 'by Act of Parliament' of 10% for all members of the so-called Secretary of State's services in India. This was one result of the world-wide financial collapse of that period, beginning in the United States in 1929. Be that as it may, before this one-sided document could be executed, the probationer had to pass a medical test. When I underwent mine, the two doctors involved pulled very long faces, conferred *sotto voce* in a corner and asked me a number of questions about what I had been doing lately. I explained that I had been working and rowing quite a lot. This seemed to meet their requirements, and they said that they would, rather dubiously, pass me.

I left the sooty portals of the India Office in a state of great perturbation. What could be wrong with me? Whom could I consult? Then I remembered that one of my best friends, Kenneth Irvine, was at that moment a house-man in St Thomas's Hospital. In a rather enfeebled manner I set my face across Westminster Bridge and in due course entered another set of sooty portals. Kenneth was fortunately available. He put me through some rather drastic exercises such as stepping onto a chair and down again forty times using only one leg. The stethoscope at rest on his chest, after assessing the thunderous noise from my chest, pronounced me to be suffering from a haemic murmur. Seeing my anxious reaction (he might just as well have been expounding the Eleusinian mysteries), he was quick to explain that this was a trivial and transient phenomenon. My gratitude was as profound then as is my regret today that he was too busy to have lunch with me.

There was one other alarm before this crucial period was passed. A Chief Commissioner of the North West Frontier Province in India, Sir Norman Bolton, told a friend of mine that he suffered from a recurrent nightmare. This was that he was required to pass an examination before he could retire from the ICS in the same way as he had been required to do for admittance. I similarly have a recurrent nightmare after forty-six years. During my probation year 1929–30 I attended lectures in Indian History without appreciating that I would be examined in the subject later. The fact dawned on me after Henley Regatta in early July 1930. It was one of those blows to the plexus. I bought a copy of Vincent Smith's *Oxford History of India* and read it eight times from cover to cover in four weeks; quite long extracts were impressed on my memory; and the end product was adequate.

The year 1929-30 was good in many ways. There was Christmas festivity centred on the house in Stevenage where the Keysell family lived. Mrs Keysell was a first cousin of my mother-in-law to be. Mr Keysell was a product of Shrewsbury, where he obtained his First XI cricket colours, and a prosperous London business man. It was at this time that he was Master of the Carpenters' Company, and as his guest I struggled through (for the first time in my life) a ten-course dinner. Their two daughters and son looked after us very kindly if in different ways. I had a day with the local beagles, inspired by the fact (since even then I was an amateur of etymology) that one of my fellow runners was a Miss Grosvenor.

And so at the end of August 1930 I took ship to America to be married. As a measure of economy I travelled steerage in the *Mauretania*, booking my passage with a firm of travel agents in the High Street, Oxford.

The single fare was seventeen pounds ten shillings, which seemed very reasonable, especially as the chart of the vessel showed that my berth was in a two-berth cabin with a porthole. Only when I boarded the ship did I discover my mistake. The accommodation was below the waterline, from which I inferred that it would be imprudent to open the porthole. The two-berth cabin was in fact simply two berths, one above the other, in a large space holding some thirty-six such berths. In effect one slept on racks such as became the normal form of accommodation in troop-ships during the war. I never noticed if there was any ventilation.

My companion in the lower berth must, I think, have come from Eastern Europe. Certainly we had no language in common. He wore blue trousers and a sleeveless cotton singlet night and day for the whole voyage. He must however, have been secretly addicted to ablutions (not to shaving), since I noticed nothing wrong. And he had a kind heart. He came aboard at Cherbourg. He was probably about the same age as I was and much more little-boy-lost. But when I woke up the next morning, feeling very sea-sick as the ship pitched in an oily swell, he looked hard at me, spoke in his own language and groped under his pillow. Out came a large brown bottle. His sign language was unmistakable.

Never have I felt less inclined to ingest alcohol, but courtesy demanded it. With a feeble salute I took the neck of the bottle in my mouth and gulped. I was galvanized. Years afterwards I realised that this must have been rather inferior Calvados. Then I only knew that I needed air. Returning the bottle to him rather abruptly, with what is conventionally called a muttered word of thanks, I rushed up on deck and stood gulping air. Some minutes later I realized two things. I was no longer sea-sick; and he had made a friend. I can only hope he understood.

A historic and rather sad event marked this voyage. The new German liner, *Bremen*, left Cherbourg twenty minutes after the *Mauretania*, which was launched a few months before I was in 1906. The *Mauretania* in those twenty-four years had never been overtaken on the high seas. She was not to be overtaken then if she could help it. From about 6.00 pm to 2.00 am she tore through the swell, vibrating in every plate and rivet in a struggle which took no account of fuel consumption.

At 2.00 am I woke to realize that all was quiet. She had been doing something like thirty-five knots, but it was not enough. And yet, with the weight of her years on her, she had conceded only twenty minutes in eight hours. Now she had lost the race. The members of the crew were unanimous that it could not have happened in rough weather. I was sure they were right, for I was a passenger from New York to Plymouth in her in January 1929 when, on a normal voyage and losing an hour a day on the clock, she travelled some 650 miles in twenty-three hours against an easterly gale.

The five days of the voyage were fine and hot, with hardly a ripple on the Atlantic swell. I was told that there were 499 of us in the steerage. It was quite credible. Very few spoke English. Those who did seemed to me rather daft. One was a stout Methodist minister from Paterson, New Jersey, who lectured me from day to day, whenever he could get a firm grip on my elbow, about the activities of the vice squad in that place. He was overjoyed to learn that a first cousin of mine was that same Rev John Mitchell who worked alongside him in the Paterson area. Another companion was a rather diffident American student who actually asked me, with an anxious expression on his face, what, in my view, Rodin's statue 'The Thinker' was thinking about.

One fellow traveller I never noticed until we disembarked; probably I was too concentrated on adhering to the strict routine of the ship like my non-Anglophone companions. They were collectively one of the sad memories in my life, sitting endlessly on deck (not on chairs as a rule) talking and occasionally singing to some elementary stringed instrument. Breakfast at 6.00 am, dinner at noon, supper at 6.00 pm – these were the daily milestones. Those who were interested (of whom I was one) might join a queue, jug in hand, at 5.45 pm and have it filled with a very decent red wine. Likewise the food was good.

But I never saw Dr Madariaga until I happened to be standing behind him in the long queue of immigrants on arrival in New York, in a saloon on one of the upper decks. We picked up the pilot about 5.00 pm on a very hot and humid day. We immigrants took five hours to get through the procedure for getting ashore, on our feet with most if not all of our luggage. Then we had to pass through the customs. But a certain Dr Madariaga was more resourceful than I. I saw him fumbling with some papers. He held up one above the level of his eyes, and I was able to see the printed words 'Albanian Embassy' in the top right-hand corner. With the document adjusted to his satisfaction he snapped his fingers towards a very large, lethargic man in khaki uniform and field boots. He showed this man the paper. The man seemed in a sleepy sort of way to be impressed. He beckoned Dr Madariaga to follow him to the head of the queue, whence in a very short time he vanished into the booth where the responsible official was passing us into his country. Dr Madariaga was out in no time and scuttled ashore. From the booth an even larger man, also in khaki uniform and field boots, emerged and rebuked the lesser man: 'Joe, don't ya know the difference between a school-teacher and a diplomat?'

When I reached the Commodore Hotel in New York there was still an hour and a half in which to bathe and eat before catching a midnight train for Chicago. We were married on 9 September 1930, after some ten days of festivities, with my wife's parents displaying astounding generosity and hospitality. I was never then, nor am I now, able to find the appropriate words of appreciation. I could only hope that I showed it in other ways. Moreover, although one of my English friends was there, more American friends appeared than I knew I possessed. It is an unfortunate world in which it has happened that I never again met my best man and good friend of Balliol days, Matthew Baird III of Ardmore, Pennsylvania. He pursued his career in Arizona, I in India.

A few days later we were on our way back to Europe under very different conditions from those in which I had travelled west. Economy was still necessary, but on the all-tourist class *Belgenland* of the Red Star Line the single fare was still only £21. Another $5 secured a cabin on the top deck. But since this was a Belgian ship, the food was admirable and

Mary Couch wedding photo

the crew very attentive. As was natural in mid-September however, the weather in the North Atlantic was very bad, and the 15,000 ton *Belgenland* behaved differently from the giants of the Cunard or White Star lines. She was nonetheless in no way diverted from her nine-day schedule. We had suffered no sea-sickness amongst the crash of crockery in the saloon.

And so one Sunday morning we were delivered at Plymouth – early and in dirty weather – by tender. A few hours later we alighted at Paddington, where my real trouble began. I had forgotten that my mother's Kensington flat, whither we were bound, could not possibly house what our friends by way of wedding presents and my wife's parents by way of trousseau had given us. It all finished up in the left luggage office. The cockney clerk never gave any sign of emotion.

The few weeks left to us in the British Isles were mainly spent in travelling to see friends and relations and to bid them goodbye. We acquired a very old AC car on a buy- and sell-back arrangement from a motor dealer in Great Portland Street. The last thing that the salesman said one Saturday morning was, 'She'll never let you down'. We picked up one suitcase for my wife and one for myself at my mother's flat and started out westwards aiming for Brockenhurst for the week-end. The car quite simply let us down on the outskirts of Blackwater, Hants. The near-side back wheel came off. One way and another we got into Blackwater and into a good hotel. A new axle was promised for Monday morning.

The manager of the hotel fixed up golf for us at his club, the East Berkshire, next day. We seemed to have fallen on our feet until after tea, when I went up to our room to bathe and change. It was then that I detected a small error. In place of my own suitcase I had brought from my mother's flat a spare suitcase of my wife's containing some twelve or fourteen diaphanous evening dresses, but nothing, so far as I could see, of much use to me. There was just time to run out into the town to buy essentials such as a razor and a toothbrush. The ill-starred outing ended on Monday. With a new axle and some golf conflated with a good measure of anxiety and expense we were glad to get back.

This curious period of limbo moved on to its end. The car took us to Shrewsbury, to Moffat and, through a very stormy evening, to Lochearn-head. I wished to see Scotland in farewell, and my wife was in agreement. Then via Ballachulish and Glencoe we reached Dundee to see my father's sisters. And in due course we said goodbye to my mother and sister and joined the *Viceroy of India* at Tilbury.

Chapter 4

Arise, therefore, and be doing, and the Lord be with thee.

I Chronicles, xxii, 16

THE *VICEROY OF INDIA* was the crack ship (if that is a correct term) of the P&O Line, and the mid-November sailing was a special one. From Marseilles to Bombay was normally a voyage of two weeks, to which would be added a week for the Tilbury to Marseilles section. But we took only four days to Marseilles; and after two nights and a day there, the remainder of the voyage took only eleven days. To say that we were embarking on a new life was obvious enough. It may not be easy, however, for some people to appreciate today how great a severance the transition to India was in 1930. Our voyage was the quickest thing so far devised for achieving the transition, and that only happened very occasionally. The airmail was still some five years in the future. For the moment we had no care.

For the first stage the ship was more than half empty. She was not very different from the Atlantic ships in the matter of comfort and luxury. But the Atlantic run was unbroken by any landfall, whereas here we had several. So we had a most interesting period of several hours in Gibraltar. In Marseilles we spent a day such as very seldom falls to the lot of anyone: it was a day suspended between past and future in which little thought was given to either. We went ashore, found a tram which was heading north and rode it to its terminus. From there we continued walking north in the autumn sunshine of Provence (which sounds so much nicer than Bouches-du-Rhône) along a country road. There came a café or auberge, I do not remember which, where we sat at a table shaded by a vine. We drank some wine. We ate omelette and bread and cheese. And so back to the splendours of the *Viceroy*.

From Marseilles the voyage proceeded in no way different from others. At Port Said and Aden we began to see how less pleasant, against our own background, the East was than the West. The Red Sea was tolerable, though hot. Aden was rather repulsive. And so to Bombay. The wharf was utter chaos. All the coolies seemed to be in the terminal stages of pulmonary tuberculosis – haemoptysis (spitting up blood) very frequent – until it occurred to us that they were chewing something which we knew as betel nut and so, up to a point, we were right. No haemo but lots of ptysis!

After a convulsive experience which ended with all our luggage retrieved and entrusted to an agent of Grindlay and Co, we spent one night in Bombay with a view to taking the Bombay–Calcutta mail train next day in the afternoon. In this way we were able to see, in close juxtaposition, the beggars sleeping on the pavements and the retiring Commander-in-Chief, Lord Birdwood, driving in state between the same pavements towards the Gateway of India and the voyage home by the same ship which had brought his successor. Here was poverty of an unimagined degree; and thus for the first time I met the fundamental problem of India, that of over-population. The undivided sub-continent was approximately the same size as Europe excluding Russia. The population in 1931 was over 560,000,000. The agricultural population pressure in the vast Ganges basin was 750 per square mile.

The problem of how such an area can feed that number of human beings is clearly dreadful, before the feeding of urban populations is considered at all. It is fortunate that the Indian cultivator is on the whole competent. Where his health and his diet permit he is hard-working. Much of the country is barren, even desert, but in many areas the quality of the soil makes possible the growing of two crops every year; and in a few areas, such as Orissa, three crops can be grown. Again the so-called black cotton soil of the Deccan produces cotton and sugar-cane, given an adequate monsoon for the former or irrigation for the latter.

Nonetheless the problem was already acute. For India, and even more for Bangladesh, it has continued to grow worse. It was not simply an academic problem for the administrative services in India, it was the origin of all problems and militated against the health and happiness of the people in every field of life. One of many reasons for the all too common antagonism between Indian nationalists and the British administration as a whole was the failure, as many British officers saw the situation, of the Nationalists and the Indian politicians in general to put first things first. The British saw the need for applying every endeavour to the welfare of the people. These words encompassed a vast and varied field including law and order, education, medical and public health services, the production of food crops and cash crops, freedom from fear, whether it be of starvation, of disease or of the oppressor. The Nationalist would say that freedom, by which he meant a withdrawal of all British control, must come before all else. Thereafter all those other things would be added unto the Indian people.

Here lay the dilemma of the man who might be responsible for ordering affairs in India. Edwin Montagu could write, 'The placid pathetic contentment of the masses is not the soil on which Indian nationhood will grow'. There could hardly be much contentment in a country which for three thousand years had been ravaged by war, pestilence and famine. The arrival of British rule brought internal peace, the establishment of law and order and organized measures against disease and want. This might bring acceptance by the people of British government in preference to indigenous autocracy; it could not automatically bring contentment. Kipling wrote of the Indian peasant:

> Whose life is a long-drawn question
> Between a crop and a crop.

This was and is the basic truth.

We arrived at Nagpur, capital of the Central Provinces and Berar, about 9.00 am on a day in November 1930, the middle of the cold weather. I had since dawn been seeing for the first time from the window of our compartment the Indian countryside, the districts being Akola, Amraoti, Wardha and Nagpur itself. Even with the winter sun lighting on them as it drew up the dew, they looked very flat and dull. The Marathi speaking districts of the CP and Berar were for the most part extremely depressing, extremely hot and, so far as the villages were concerned, extremely dirty. This is not to say that the people were by nature dirty. It was simply a case of dense population in the first instance. Then such things as roads, apart from the use of the word to mean ground excluded from cultivation for purposes of travel and transport, barely existed. Such areas, with the villages which they served, were deep in dust in dry weather, deep in mud during the rains.

Since sanitary services did not exist, a village with a population of about two thousand had to make use of the land adjacent to the houses for natural calls. Since there was no public water supply, a communal well must provide water for drinking and for personal ablutions. The washing of clothes was usually done in the village *talao*, called by the British a 'tank'. This was an area of water created by the building of a dam and the collection of water during the rainy season. Sometimes these tanks were picturesque. Stone-built staircases or *ghats* might here and there go down to the water's edge. Trees of great height and beauty might shade the dam and the banks. In a few places there might be temples each with its own staircase down to the water, but this could only be so where the tank was very large. They were usually small, shallow and muddy. The larger could be used to irrigate substantial acreages of rice fields, where (after the crop was taken) snipe were to be taken in abundance.

Large or small however, the tanks were very suitable breeding grounds for hook-worm. Dysentery was universal, whether amoebic or bacillary, usually water-borne. Malaria was endemic, since the anopheles mosquito enjoyed both ideal breeding conditions and complete immunity from human counter-measures. It would have been very easy to acquire an attitude of disgust towards people who lived in this way. To do so would have been very wrong. I realised this when I first went into one of their houses: thick mud walls, thatched roof (of rice straw) and a floor of plastered cow-dung, which was devoid of any offensive smell, made the interior cool and clean.

Nagpur was the most unpleasant place in which I had ever sojourned. The city, whose population then was about 120,000, was congested and filthy. The so-called civil station, where the government officials lived, was spaciously laid out with compounds of several acres for each bungalow. It shared with the city however, the complete lack of water-borne sanitation and the extreme heat. As regards the latter, the day maximum temperature varied from about 80°F at Christmas time to over 120°F in May and June. As regards the former, it was no consolation to recall that in 18th century France the *chaise percée* was the throne of kings.

Our first hosts however, could not have been more kind. Geoffrey* and Doris Burton, both from Yorkshire, met us and housed us for several days in a manner which we have not forgotten. He was then in a senior post in the provincial secretariat. He stayed on beyond the normal retirement age throughout the war, in the capacity of Adviser to the Governor after the dissolution of the Congress Government at the beginning of the war in 1939. It was a matter very much to be regretted that there were not many more British officials and wives of their calibre in Nagpur.

This does not mean that all were bad. Some were very good. But of the European official element there were far too many for whom adultery and bridge were the main amusements; and for many of whom their official duties, often conscientiously performed, were in no way a vocation. Even the club retained the objectionable feature of not admitting Indians as ordinary members. Only a few honorary members were admitted. Naturally very few Indians indeed would accept in such insulting conditions. And yet at this time a full half of the ICS officers and many police officers were Indians, while recruitment of British officers to such services as the Public Works Department, and the Indian Forest Service had been discontinued altogether by the Government of India Act 1919.

My first 'boss', the Deputy Commissioner, was C H Trivedi, whose career in the ICS was to be most distinguished. In Nagpur he had already

* He was knighted before his retirement.

handled political unrest firmly and ably and was about to meet his final trial before being promoted to the Government of India Secretariat in Delhi. This was the actual day of the count of the 1931 census. The local Congress Party were to stage hostile demonstrations and to disrupt the count. My instructions, in my capacity as a Third Class Magistrate, were to be on duty at a large police station in the city. I did not, of course, after a very few weeks' service, have much idea of what I should do if anything happened, nor indeed of what might happen. I armed myself, therefore, with a revolver and a detective story. With both boredom and excitement thus catered for, I sat down on the verandah of the police station and admired the barbed wire and sandbags which surrounded it on all sides.

About 3.00 pm it seemed as if my vigil was not to be in vain. Out of the street to the south a really terrible noise suddenly broke out: the crash of drums, wild, high-pitched cries, trumpets braying savagely in a musical idiom unknown in the west. I could see that action was imminent. I was wrong. The authors of the noise came round a corner and marched past the police station revealing themselves, apart from the musicians, as about a dozen small children, most of them girls. They were manifestly enjoying themselves under the conductorship of a mild-looking, middle-aged man in the saffron robe of a Brahman. So they passed by. There were no further incidents.

The province was created in the early 1860s after the dispossession of the Maratha ruler, the Bhonsla Raja of Nagpur. Its system of land tenure was various and the law which governed it was very complicated. To the east and south-east of the province the land was mainly owned by the Government – the *Sarkar* – and those who farmed it were tenants of the *Sarkar*. This was a simple system, whose legal name was *raiyatwari*, meaning a system based on tenant cultivators.

Elsewhere, however, the 19th century administrators had produced something more like a tessellated pavement than a clear pictorial mosaic. These administrators were recruited from a wide field to be the members of the Central Provinces Commission. The Chief Commissioner was the head of the administration. The head of the judiciary, even in my time, was the Judicial Commissioner. Junior officers in many instances were military officers on secondment. The Government of the time was of the view that it would be beneficial to the stability of the country if a class of landowners could be established: the Scottish laird, the English squire and the English yeoman were the models in their minds.

Hence was devised the system called *malguzari*. The word means one who processes, ie collects, the land revenue and passes it on to the treasury after the deduction of his commission. It is purely Persian, as were nearly all the technical terms of the legislation which governed the system. Some indeed had a very sound and commendable origin in the land administration of the Moghul Emperor Akbar and his Hindu Minister Raja Todar Mal in the 16th century. To study it was for me at first a penance. Twice I succeeded only in passing my Revenue Law by the lower standard instead of the higher standard required. There were so many other things to learn, and in which to be examined while still doing a day's work in one's court as a magistrate and an assistant commissioner. The languages required were Hindi and Marathi by the higher standard. For these the *munshi* – ie tutor – came six mornings a week to one's house at 6.50 am for an hour.

Otherwise one was on one's own; but it was not very difficult to build up knowledge of a language if one listened to little else in court for six days a week from 11.00 am to 4.00 pm. There was still the necessity of passing by the same higher standard examinations in Criminal Law, the Law of Evidence, Civil Law in certain aspects and Civil Procedure. Less exacting, but nonetheless insisted upon, were a written examination in Audit and Accounts and what may be politely called a field test in Survey. It was no surprise that, when I at last was liberated from Nagpur, I still had not passed my Revenue by the higher standard. I had passed the rest.

In September 1931 I was transferred to Chhindwara district, eighty miles north of Nagpur. The Deputy Commissioner, P G Brée, and his wife were very kind and good in every way. This was our official posting for the next two years, my designation being Assistant Commissioner, and once I had passed the higher standard in Revenue Law in March 1932 I became fully qualified as a district officer. My wife went back to her home for the birth of each of our first two sons, which meant that I was alone from May to December 1932 and again from September 1933 until I became eligible for leave in 1934. This was sad but prudent in a country where dangers to health were not compensated by adequate medical services. Our eldest son indeed, in the period December 1932 to September 1933, was almost continuously ill and did not recover until he and his mother got back to Chicago.

The life as a whole, however, was pleasant. At full strength there could be as many as twelve Europeans in the station, man, woman and child. The place possessed in fact a vague classification as a European station. This was helpful since our Indian friends, so far as purely social life was concerned, were too different from ourselves to make association easy. To be quite honest, much the same remark could be applied to some of the Europeans, but at least my wife could speak English to them, which to Indians she could only do with very few. Later on in our Indian years she defied her shyness, grasped the nettle and forced herself to speak

Hindustani to Indian ladies. At this time however, Mr Dewhurst and the Devanagri script were fading into the past and family matters occupied the foreground.

Shortly before we went to Chhindwara my wife had bought an elderly mare called Julie for Rs 100, approximately £7.50. In the bargain were included two saddles and bridles, grain for a month and the wages of the *syce* (groom) for the same period. The lady from whom the purchase was made was expecting a baby and, while having no wish to ride, could not afford to pay for an idle horse and groom. Very soon my wife found herself similarly expectant, and at this stage never rode the mare at all. For me this was most fortunate. From this time until the end of 1935 Julie and I were almost constant companions. A rather insignificant third party was an undersized fox terrier bitch, which also belonged to my wife.

Norval and Mary with baby Bill and the terrier, 1933

During my months of grass widowerhood in 1932 I was frequently touring under canvas, travelling on horse-back. On such journeys, although only one servant came with me in addition to the *syce*, I thought it only right to take the poor little dog so that we might bear one another company. She seemed to enjoy the experience. The pace at which Julie and I covered a stage of a tour – say twelve miles – was no strain. The stops at villages, where the village dogs showed strong hostility, were not easy for her, but she became skilful in remaining under a directly central point of Julie's stomach not only at the halt but also at quite a brisk trot.

Julie occupies a large space in my memory. She was said to be thirteen years old when she joined us, but she did not look it, as they say. Her last three owners had been women, all of whom I knew. Two of them said she was a brute of a horse. The third, from whom she was bought, had said nothing. She had the reputation of having been a pig-sticking pony, which may well have been true. She was very sure-footed, had numerous scars, and was very sly. Most mornings in Chhindwara I would get up at 6.30 am, have a cup of tea and be off on horseback to inspect a variety of places round the outskirts of the town for which I had responsibility. As I mounted, Julie would betray every symptom of foundering from fatigue. When we emerged onto the metalled but un-tarred road which passed our house, she would stumble over every piece of road metal which protruded as much as an inch from the surface. If this failed to arouse anxiety or evoke sympathy, she would heave a deep sigh and change to a trot, or plod, which for current purposes suited me very well.

But I came to understand these idiosyncrasies. She hated the bit, however gentle. Any touch on the curb was intolerable, the snaffle odious. I found, however, that there was no vice in her. So long as I neck-reined with one hand and used voice and heels quietly, she would be wholly obedient. There was one occasion on tour at this time when she frightened me. I halted for two nights in the same camp, and I used the intervening day to ride a circuit of villages, returning to my camp in the late afternoon. Julie accepted this departure from normal routine with a form of cautious suspicion. Somewhere about 4.00 pm, however, I mounted and made some such remark as 'Well, now we can go home'. This was no matter of the horse understanding either the words or their sound. In fact I spoke in Hindi, which at that time I often spoke to the exclusion of English up to three weeks on end.

No, she simply knew what I meant. We were not more than three miles from the camp, but about one mile of this was round the skirts of a hill with some very nasty screes. At first she just leapt into a gallop. And after all the gallop of an elderly pig-sticker has little relation to the speed of a steeple-chaser. Then we hit the screes. She was still going at her maximum pace. It seemed to me that any touch on the controls might be disastrous, so I sat back and committed myself to Julie and our Maker. My confidence in the terrestrial sphere was justified. She was puffing a bit when we got there; but she knew, as surely as any animal knows, that she was among friends and was due for a grooming, a drink and a good meal. There was not a thread of blood on her pasterns.

She came down with me to Nagpur when I went back there again in October 1934. I was very hard up and tried to sell her, and for a short time she went on approval to a Parsee gentleman. In anticipation of the price I bought a bicycle, and it was on this machine that I was riding home from the golf course one evening when I came up behind him mounted on her. We exchanged courtesies. I asked him how he liked the mare. His answer was, in effect, not at all. He would mount and leave his house, and thereafter there was nothing which he could do to make her break out of a walk.

Meanwhile she had recognised me without being prepared to admit it. I pedalled slowly up on her nearside and told her to trot. She did so, and was still doing so as I directed my bicycle ninety degrees away from that route. But apparently not again. Finally she spent the eight months of my leave in 1934 as a sort of paying guest with a police officer friend of mine. Early in December of that year she accompanied my family from Nagpur to Nowshera by train, a matter of twelve hundred miles or so. She then began to make her name on the Frontier. It was not a very glorious name but rather one of how cunning a horse can be. When one went on tour on the Frontier, one was entertained very lavishly at every village. Some villages were very poor; but Pathans could always produce green tea and iced cakes. Julie knew this. When we reached a village I would dismount, knot the reins on her neck, and make a clicking noise indicative of my wish that she should follow.

This was quite superfluous. She would follow me and wait in a rather noble manner until I sat down before the tea and the iced cakes. Her head would then be politely but firmly pushed over my right shoulder. Delicately but accurately she would take up an iced cake in her lips. Thereafter she would stand quietly until I had finished my business. At the end of 1935 she was getting past hard work, so I gave her to a Sub-Inspector of Police. He was a small man of pleasant disposition, and thus not likely to be a burden to her in any respect. She did die in a tragic way however, in the course of that winter. Some idiot tied her up one night with a rope round her neck. She fell into a panic when the rope tightened under pressure and in her struggles she strangled herself.

In Chhindwara, I was busy learning my trade as a district officer. The district included the sub-division of Seoni, which had been a district itself until its status and staff were reduced in 1931 as part of the economies necessitated by the worldwide financial crisis. I held charge there three times for a few weeks at a time during temporary vacancies; and I was interested among other things in the fact that the scene of Rudyard Kipling's *The Jungle Book* was a forest some eighteen miles south of the town. It was in this forest that I managed to lose myself one very wet September evening in 1932.

Accompanied by a head constable of police, who carried my 12-bore gun, I set out at 4.00 pm with my .500 double-barrelled express rifle to seek a good chital stag. I did not find one. I dallied a long time instead while I worked on the curiosity of a sambhar doe and fawn, and brought them up within ten yards of me. This is an easy trick. You bark from time to time like a deer. You wave a handkerchief or a rifle. But you must not move your feet nor, if possible, show your body below the waist. It was on this occasion a mistake. Darkness came on very quickly; and although I was on a road, I did not know that the fork road which I had known previously, and which would have taken us back to the forest bungalow, had been abandoned and had become overgrown. An attempt to take a short cut through the forest due west soon foundered in the darkness. And so the head constable and I spent a very uncomfortable night with our backs to a rock while the rain came down steadily.

When we decided to go no further, he remarked that I was only wearing a vest, a sleeveless shirt, shorts, stockings and shoes. I must therefore have his waterproof cape, which was rolled up like a sausage and strapped to his belt at the back. I protested of course, but it was no good. He pointed to his uniform of strong cloth and a sweater under it. We were both soaked, but I had no insulating garment. I yielded. I even slept a little, putting my face down inside the cape and creating some warmth with my breath.

Daylight came about 5.00 am, but unfortunately the clouds were down at treetop level. I had intended to get a bearing with my watch on the sun, but now this was not possible. I decided however, that we must keep moving, and so we did. There was no suffering from thirst: there was water everywhere. Likewise there was no sign of a track or path so we plodded on. About 7.00 am I began to feel shaky, and the head constable promptly relieved me of the heavy rifle. I tried to get it back but he stuck to it. At 8.00 am the sun came through the clouds, I got my bearing, and we started off confidently south, where I knew we would hit inhabited country.

Quite soon we came to forest which had clearly been grazed by cattle. Then there was a path. And suddenly we were in a cleared area which I recognised as a forest village. These villages were a means whereby the Forest Department kept a labour force always available. They would be established on *rayatwari*, or similar tenure. The villagers farmed their assignments of land, but also owed certain service in respect of forest work. In this case it was the village cattle which had facilitated the last mile or so of our walk.

We picked our way along the *bunds*, that is, the low holding walls between the rice fields, towards the thatched houses. There were no people in sight, but when we were inside the village I called out and a woman of thirty or thirty-five came out of a house. She was an aboriginal. My companion and I presented a sorry appearance. His uniform was almost unrecognizable. My topi (pith helmet) looked like a plum pudding under the rain. My forearms and legs were covered with red ticks. I said to the woman that I was the sub-divisional officer who had lost his way. She said firmly that there had been no notice that the SDO would be touring in these parts.

Then I realised that she was rather frightened, and I drew from her the information that all the men of the village were away working. I then said a little more in explanation, but what really touched her heart was when I said that we were very hungry owing to our own stupidity. We wanted food but she would have to trust me to pay later. These aboriginals lived very close to hunger themselves. At that moment, she said, there was no prepared food in the house. I suggested milk. Yes, now there was something that could be done. She picked up a little brass vessel called a *lota*, hurried outside the village to where a buffalo was grazing, milked her into the *lota* and offered it to me.

I offered the head constable the first swig. He refused. He was a Brahman. Under no conditions of hunger, thirst or fatigue could he accept such pollution. I drank gratefully and then asked the road westward to the main road. This she pointed out and we resumed our walk, which turned out to be something over three miles, aiming at a particular police station. On the way we fell in with some men of the village, and I took the opportunity of asking them what I could do to reward them for the woman's kindness and their services as guides. They had little hesitation in asking for a licence for a gun for crop protection. These were issued by officers of my grade to individuals nominated by villagers whose crops were especially liable to damage by wild animals. There was the additional benefit (although this was never mentioned) that the holder of the licence could supply a variety of meat fairly regularly to a small community whose lack of protein in their diet set up a strong craving for something more than rice, pulses and vegetables. It was pleasant to be able to grant the request forthwith, rather than await a stamped written application, which would have to go through the police for a report. I had also had an experience at close quarters of the simple kindness of some of the most humble people on earth.

We reached the police station on the main road about 11.00 am. To my shame it was situated some ten miles south of the point whence at 4.00 pm on the previous afternoon we had started walking north. So much for the effect of inattention, darkness and morning mist. A friend of mine, who also happened to be staying at the Forest Bungalow, had alerted the police station that I had not got back on the previous evening, and, being confident that I would emerge in due course onto the road, had asked the sub-inspector to expect me and give me something to eat. The sub-inspector complied very willingly, and I was offered an excellent meal. It was still obligatory, however, that the head constable should be fed. In the absence of a Brahman cook at the police station he stoutly refused to eat. Fortunately my friend arrived in his car quite soon, and we were able to transport the head constable to his house without delay. There he stood to attention and saluted as we drove away. I thought that he came very well out of it as compared with me.

As regards aboriginals, the first I met in India were dwellers in the disgusting slums round and about the railway station and marshalling yards of Nagpur. They were called Gonds. In those early months of my service I only knew them as voluntary litigants in cases of assault in the court where I sat as a Third Class Magistrate. Section 323 of the Indian Penal Code dealt with the offence of simple hurt, and since the offence was not cognizable (ie the police could not arrest without a warrant), nearly all the cases were the result of private complaints. They were in a way a sort of bad-tempered, vindictive game. Sometimes they were in pursuance of an ancient feud, sometimes only the result of a drunken brawl.

There was only the one invariable element, viz that no one ever deviated into truth while giving evidence. Consequently for my first six months I acquitted all accused persons, being incompetent to discern where the truth lay. I was greatly helped by one personal involvement. One afternoon I was driving home after the closing of the court when I saw a single man with his back to the iron railings of the grounds of the Legislative Council. He was clearly taking a very nasty beating with *lathis* from some six other men, while others cheered them on. I stopped the car, got out and as quickly as I could put a stop to the one-sided affair. It was then that I recognized the victim as a man whom I had that same afternoon acquitted of a similar charge.

Some weeks later I was summoned as a witness in the court of a colleague. I was required to testify on behalf of the same man. When I had told my story to counsel for the complainant, I was asked if I could identify any of those in the dock as having been among the assailants. After a careful scrutiny of their somewhat coy faces, I had to admit that I could not. This taught me that the witness who was supposed to be disinterested, and who so often came into court fluent, bland and presenting a persona of wide-eyed innocence, must be lying. There were also, as one sat hour after hour, day in day out, month after month, unexpected but regularly repetitive indications of when a witness was or was not telling the truth. After a time I found it possible occasionally to convict.

Unfortunately the so-called Gonds were always in the drunken brawl category. At that time I could only observe, I could not interpret. When however, I had sloughed off Nagpur, and when I found myself in charge of two sub-divisions or *tahsils*, namely my first 'child', Amarwara, and my second, Chhindwara itself, I moved much closer to the questions of where aboriginals stood in India of the 20th century. For me there was not yet to be an answer. I knew that an ancient breed had sunk into degradation in Nagpur. Then I knew that in Chhindwara district there were many more of these people not confined by railway slums. Obviously there was much more to learn.

Chhindwara district and the neighbouring Betul district to the west included within their northern borders the Satpura Mountains. In the middle of the mountains was the well-established hill station for the Central Provinces Government, Pachmarhi, nearly 4,000 feet above sea level. The British made themselves very comfortable there, and it was so beautiful that a whole guide-book would be needed to describe the surrounding mountains, the deep ravines, the surrounding forest, even the golf-course (as hard as a billiard table), and the sunsets which were liable to be such a sweetly aesthetic prelude to the routine adulteries.

But there were no aboriginal inhabitants of this European spa. The main road from Chhindwara climbed gently for about a thousand feet over nineteen miles to a point called Tamia. From that point the road went winding down again into a forested flat area before winding up once more to the highest points of the Satpura range where Pachmarhi had been established. At Tamia there was a rest-house from which one could look across the wooded country below for ever and ever until vision died in the haze of trees and mountains fifty miles away to the north. Even here there were no aboriginals, at least so far as the ordinary passer-by could see.

One summer day in 1933, however, I left my car at the bungalow and started walking eastwards along the edge of the escarpment. Walking was the only means of penetrating this part of the country; bullock carts could not negotiate the steep, stony, afforested mountain sides; a horse could barely have done it but would have caused me anxiety for the horse. So I went accompanied by my servant Ithu (who did not like walking) and a galvanized iron bath-tub. This held all my requirements for ten days or so. A bamboo pole was thrust through the handles and so the burden could be carried on the shoulders of two men – eager local volunteers for the job at four annas per trip. The trip might be ten miles. This allowed time at each one-night halt for the work which accompanied every day on tour – mainly checking of annual and quinquennial land records. Word had been sent ahead asking for branch shelters to be built in which I might bathe and sleep. All these facilities were of course, paid for. Finally, if time were left in daylight, there could be perhaps two hours at the end of the day for shooting.

In the previous cold weather I had penetrated these mountains and forested valleys by an easier route. Sixty miles or so to the east the main road from Nagpur to Jabalpur passed through the fringe of the Satpuras. From this road it was possible to travel west on horse-back with a bullock cart to carry some comforts. The two tours between them were designed to investigate complaints of the oppressive conduct of the landowners known as the Chhindwara *jagirdars*. *Jagir* is a Persian technical term, first employed by the Moghul emperors, for a grant of land to an individual. In these remote mountains the 16th and 17th century Moghuls had never had much interest in acquiring and administering territory. They found it more convenient to make grants of hundreds of square miles to the acknowledged chiefs of the aboriginal inhabitants. These were confirmed by the British when the Central Provinces were established.

In the first of my visits I travelled in a semi-circle west, north and then east back to my starting point on the road. In the second it was a case of dropping down the *ghat* eastwards, turning north and then west to meet the main Nagpur–Pachmarhi road some twenty miles north of Tamia. There my car was waiting by arrangement to take me south again, out of the valley, up to Tamia and back to Chhindwara.

I would have visited these remote villages and forests as part of my normal duties even without any special reason. There had however, been vague but numerous complaints reaching my ears for some time about oppression of the aboriginals by their landlords and by minor officials. These had to be investigated both as a matter of principle, and also because the special conditions of the area made oppression there more than easy and grievous. It was easy because supervision of landlords and corrupt minor officials was for physical and geographical reasons very difficult. It was grievous because the people for whom district officers were responsible were so poor, so timid and so helpless. Ultimately I found no incriminating evidence against the *jagirdars* themselves, with one possible exception of a bizarre type. On the first visit one *jagirdar* put an elephant at my disposal. I could not in fact use it, but it had some small value since, going ahead of me during my day's journey, its *mahout* could tell the people of each village how long it might be before I arrived. I was as usual riding and stopping at each village to inspect land records and investigate complaints. Thus I might alternately fall behind the elephant and catch it up again. Every time he heard me coming he would perform an embarrassed shuffle, agitate his hindquarters, look back over his shoulder and in general behave in a very nervous manner.

Later I commented on this to my companions, who told me the explanation. The *jagirdar* had, when young, been full of fun all the time and (as in later life) full of drink most of the time. One of his amusements was tent-pegging, that is, picking up a small piece of wood from the ground with a spear from horse-back while galloping at full speed. This is never easy. In a bemused condition induced by alcohol it is impossible. The *jagirdar* therefore, a man of an ingenious cast of mind, lit on the idea that a greater measure of success – and with success, satisfaction – could be achieved by using a larger target. What more readily available and suitable than the ample rear view of the family elephant? The poor beast, with its proverbially good memory, naturally associated hoof-beats in the rear with pain.

I could then acquit the *jagirdars* themselves, but the evidence of intimidation and extortion against their employees was both distressing and abundant. It would be very tedious to retail all that I was told, especially after sunset round the fire at my camp. But one such instance has stayed vivid in my mind through subsequent years. It was on my first visit, when I enjoyed the luxury of a tent weighing about eighty pounds. One thing these poor people did not lack was firewood, and on that winter night at three thousand feet the fire was very generous. Tobacco and cigarettes had been distributed. Then I asked whether the people had any complaints to make specifically against the Government or the *jagirdar*. I explained that I wished to make no bones about it. Vague complaints had been reaching me. There had been nothing specific. It was my duty to go further, and it was my hope that such matters should be brought into the open and dealt with.

After a short silence one of the older men said that a certain Lotan Singh, who had been very badly treated by officials, should tell his story. The name could mean 'the lion in his lair' or 'couchant'. Lotan Singh himself was a small man of mild appearance. His story was a long one. He needed money for a daughter's wedding. Three times he went to the market at Parasia, a full thirty miles on foot, to sell a bullock or two to raise money. Each time, on his return home with the money, he was met by petty officials (who knew all about what was going on) and blackmailed into giving up the money. One was actually a Forest Guard, who was prepared to lodge false charges in the distant District Court if Lotan Singh did not pay up. Another posed as a *chaprasi* (ie orderly) of the Excise Department who said he had found illicit home-made liquor in the house during Lotan Singh's absence. And so on.

He paid over all his money. He never did tell me how he paid for the wedding. The predicament in which he found himself was easy to understand once it had been told; Chhindwara, where the court was, for him was an alien and frightening world; he was helpless at home in the face of dishonest employees of the Government; in Chhindwara his helplessness would be supplemented by extreme fear of the unknown. It was better to pay up.

Naturally I was very angry. This was far worse than Edwin Montagu's 'pathetic contentment' of the Indian peasant. It was a frightened acquiescence in oppression. For the first time in my service I began to perceive how easy it could be to pass departmental examinations, dispense justice in court, and still be ignorant of the people for whose welfare one was responsible. For good measure I made a very foolish remark. I rather pompously explained to all those present that this was a classic example of how difficult it was for officers to protect people, since those people themselves did not have the courage to stand up for themselves and to lodge complaints.

The man who had originally suggested that Lotan Singh should tell his story stood up and told me straight that it was unfair to impugn his courage. Not long before, Lotan Singh had been cutting firewood in the jungle. He had taken his small daughter with him, and the child was playing a short distance away while he plied his *kulhari*, a light, winged axe. Suddenly a tiger charged from a thicket, seized the child and made off with her. Lotan Singh went in pursuit, beat the tiger over the head with his axe, made it drop the child and then laid her on the ground. She was almost unhurt, but the tiger had torn off her sari and was playing with it (at this point Lotan Singh interpolated quietly that it was only a young tiger). But by now he was really warmed up. He lit into the beast until it dropped the sari. He re-clothed the child, took her home and then returned to his work.

I am sorry to say that none of the prosecutions which I initiated (I could hardly try the cases myself) were successful after these two tours. These were heard in Chhindwara during the rainy season of 1933. One afternoon a small party of the people with whom I had been associating in the preceding months came to my house, which was nearly a mile outside the town. In effect they had come to apologize. They wished to tell me that they knew that I had tried to help them. They had, however, come all this way, leaving their homes and fields unguarded, to be met by *vaqils*, ie pleaders, representing the accused persons. They were not very precise about what ensued, but it was beyond doubt a combination of intimidation and petty bribery. I was grateful for their thoughtfulness, but I was bereft of hope of what could be done for them.

In addition to the aboriginal Gonds, there also lived in these mountains a tribe called Bharias, described as semi-aboriginals. I do not know what this means, but certainly they did not speak a Dravidian language, as Gonds do, but a rather inelegant dialect of Hindi. At one village there came to my camp a very old man indeed. Such longevity is almost unknown among forest dwellers. Disease, malnutrition and toil do not permit it. Yet this man, they said, was a hundred years old. Moreover he was carrying a child of two or three which he had begotten. An Indian official working in the area told me that the latter point was almost certainly true. This meant that the actual age must be exaggerated, so I asked him as nicely as I could a number of questions. He was cheerful, he still had a few teeth and he was all there. On the subject of how many wives he had married, he said three. Of children there had definitely been seventeen sons; but he was vague about daughters and about how many children had died.

Then I asked him what his earliest memory was. He said that he could remember, when he was about seven, being taken by his father to a Government office (perhaps Amarwara) to change Bhonsla rupees, which were no longer current, for Company rupees. This obviously bore no reference to the defeat at Sitabaldi (a hill near Nagpur) of the Maratha forces of the Bhonsla Raja of Nagpur in 1817. But the mention of Company rupees places the date before the Mutiny of the Indian Army in northern India in 1857.

Finally, I asked him when he first saw a white man. This was an easy one. Not that he could say how old he was at the time, but one day a white man (he was careful to say a sahib, not a *gora*: a gentleman, not a paleface) had come to this very place where we were sitting. When people collected he spoke. At this point the old man produced standard Hindi in place of his dialect. The sahib said, 'Now the rule of the Company is finished. The rule of Victoria Maharani has begun. And so will you learn to sing with me like this'. And the old man put his head back, clapped his hands in time, and sang three verses in rhyming Hindi about Prabhu Jesu, the Lord Jesus. He withdrew amidst applause and laughter. He must have been well over eighty.

My two years in Chhindwara drew to an end. I had been lonely for much of the time but never at a loss for how to spend my time. On days when the courts were closed I could mount the old mare, use one hand on the reins, with the other carry either shot-gun or rifle across my shoulder, and make off northwards into the countryside in search of sport and food. There would be some money in my pocket. If I were to dismount anywhere, the people who were not too busy would volunteer as help. I might be after duck or snipe or partridge; or there might be a blackbuck. Once it was a hungry panther which was working its way through all the village goats and dogs.

Whatever the bag might be, I, as a grass widower without a deep freeze, would keep as much as my servants at home and I could eat in the next twelve hours or so. All else went to the helpers plus a small amount per person in cash and a certain weight of crushed cane sugar from the village shop. I hoped, as I rode home of an evening, that they had enjoyed the day as much as I had.

In the compound I kept a female *chinkara*, a small antelope sometimes called a ravine deer. Normally she grazed, tethered to a post on a long rope. But she would follow me when I was riding, if allowed to do so, and enjoyed literally running circles round us. When I was about to depart, I took her down the road one evening and presented her to the little daughter of the Divisional Forest Officer. I was about half way home again when she overtook me, trailing her rope and making a noise like the mewing of a cat.

I have always been fond of animals and birds, but seldom so well situated for keeping them. I was, however, transferred from the end of September to Nagpur, and my odd collection (of which it would be tedious to give details) had to be dispersed and left behind. The pea-hen was an exception. She had often disturbed our sleep; she always ate up the garden; ultimately we ate up her. My wife returned to Chicago for the second time and for our second son in mid-September during one of the brief spells when I was posted in charge at Seoni. I feel that a story which I first heard at this time should conclude the account of this period. The facts were undoubted. The context was that of the changing India and its effect even on these peaceful and, I am convinced, genuinely contented villages and towns.

There had for many years been in Seoni a Presbyterian Mission staffed from Canada. It did much good in the service of the people. When I was there the head of the mission, Mr Macneil spoke better Scots than I did and had a fame which had spread far and wide. He took advantage of certain provisions of the Land Revenue Act to establish a new village in a forest area, and he had himself appointed as the official headman. Conversion to Christianity was not a condition of becoming a tenant of land in the village, but the pressure to be converted must, by example rather than precept, have been strong. Certainly he gave his life to the development of the village and the physical and spiritual welfare of its people.

I went there once. It was a paradise, whether in the Greek sense of the word a park, or in the derived sense connoting the happiness of another world. One day he came close to giving his life in another sense. He was walking round the fields with two or three cultivators when a panther sprang from cover on the last man in the line. Our friend was carrying a very light .22 rifle, useless for most purposes as he knew. So he quickly went to the panther, put the barrel against its ear and shot it.

Politicians became active in Seoni and elsewhere in the years just before and just after 1930. Their ultimate objective, the Independence of India, was one which any man would respect. Their methods were, however, often misconceived, and sometimes downright disingenuous. So it was in the case of what a junior member of our friend's mission did. He was not even a Canadian, he was a very simple and recently ordained minister from Scotland. Moreover he had recently acquired a camera and went about taking photographs of anything which might have local colour in the eyes of his family and friends at home. One day he was snapping away happily at a number of women washing clothes at a tank. It was the wearisome task which Mark Twain was so unkind about when he wrote that in India he had actually seen a woman trying to break a stone with a wet shirt. Not unnaturally the women wade into the water for this work, tucking up their garments above the knee.

A political acolyte saw this young minister. In no time at all he had given the information to the local chairman of the Congress Party, and the poor young man received a summons, in a pastiche of legal form, to attend a religious court in the temple of Ram in Seoni on a certain day and hour. The charge, almost verbatim lifted from the Indian Penal Code, concerned the outraging of the modesty of the women concerned.

The young man wisely went to his superior officer. The latter told him to forget all about it, and himself appeared at the temple of Ram in answer to the summons. He was greeted quite courteously and asked to sit down (of course on a stone floor) since the chairman had not yet arrived. As he himself told me, he waited patiently for upwards of an hour. Then he stood and told the 'court' that he was a busy man and could wait no longer to give evidence. But (he said) 'I did testify. I preached to them the Word of God on the subject of women for three-quarters of an hour by the clock; then I took my leave.' No more was heard of the matter.

My transfer to Nagpur was to the post of Under Secretary in those departments of which the Chief Secretary was the head. These included Law and Order with the police; Appointments, Promotions and similar matters connected with personnel; and the wide-spreading word, political. I did my best to earn my pay, but things were quiet in the political world of the Province, as in India as a whole. In my capacity as a personal assistant to the Chief Secretary I was hardly called upon at all. He was N R Roughton, a large bear of a man with a kindly disposition, a first class brain and a very quick disposal of work. Our office hours were 11.00 am to 4.00 pm. In my five to six months' tenure of the post I can only once recall taking work home.

This in one way was very good for me since, whenever a really fat file appeared on my table (sometimes with several volumes), I could read every page of it at leisure, and so learn many things of importance – not least how to write a minute or an official letter. Noel Roughton left the office at 3.50 pm and was on the so-called golf course by 4.15 pm. As was fitting, I was exactly ten minutes behind him. Darkness fell about 6.00 pm in the cold weather. He would be playing bridge in the club, bathed and in a dinner jacket, a few minutes thereafter. So would I. It was the morning hours from, say, 6.50 am onwards, that were not accounted for. I suspect that, before the office officially opened, he had already disposed of a great deal of work. Certainly his *chaprasis* had a lot of stuff to carry out of his car. No such burden weighed me down; and only twice was the even tenor of my way disturbed by earth-shaking events.

The first that I remember was literally that, namely the disaster of the earthquake in Bihar early in 1934. It was felt in Nagpur. Sitting in my cool, dark office one day, genuinely concentrating on something so that my conscience would acquit me of sloth, a strange vibration set the floor moving under my feet. My God, I said to myself, Roughton is having a fit next door. His heels are drumming on the floor. In a flash I was through the door of my office which led via the verandah to Roughton's office, only to meet him coming out of the corresponding door of his office in my direction. I was somewhat put out when he sharply asked what was that bloody noise in my office; but hot feelings were quickly chilled when in quick succession the keystones over the arches of our respective doors cracked noisily, and it was manifest what had happened.

The second crisis of those months hit me in the first instance. It was one of my responsibilities to decipher or decode any telegram which did not reach the office *en clair*. One such telegram was on my table one morning. The cipher was a numerical one of the type which requires a fat tome filled with groups of numbers as the key. You subtract the groups of numbers in the telegram from certain groups of numbers in the tome. You then check the product of such subtraction with that number in the later pages of the tome. The answer will be a word. But it need not necessarily be the right word.

In the case which I am quoting the date had been included in the message, so that it began with a group of numbers which not only made nonsense when applied to the key, but also made nonsense of all that followed. It took me three hours to discover what was wrong. I took the correct message into Roughton's office and went back to my own office. I picked up the daily paper, which until now I had been too busy to look at. There as the main headline was a report of a very important speech delivered the night before at a dinner by the Viceroy himself in Hyderabad. It was verbatim the same as the message which I had so proudly offered to my boss.

There seemed to be a much more pleasant atmosphere in Nagpur than there had been in 1930–31, largely, I think, because there was a new Governor. Sir Hyde Gowan died untimely in office, and his career, confined entirely to the Central Provinces, was not very distinguished. He was bluff and, in an engaging way, rather pompous. But he knew all about everyone in the Province; and certain lines were drawn which everyone had to toe. I was occasionally asked to play auction bridge with him of an evening in Government House. His ADC would be one of the four, together with anyone else of a fairly submissive nature whom he could rustle up. He had one rule for his partner: if he, the Governor, opened the bidding and the partner held five of a major suit, then regardless of any other consideration the partner must call two of that suit. Thereafter His Excellency would take over the bidding. This convention led to some interesting contracts.

He was very devoted to his old college, which was New College, Oxford. An instance of this occurred one evening before we sat down to play. He began in this manner: 'Well, New College seems to be just about running India at the moment. I'm here, and then there are . . .' and he ran off the names of a number of people in high places. 'Now, young Mitchell can Balliol match that?' I tried to convey by my manner that I was deeply impressed by such brilliance. Nonetheless Balliol must be defended *in partibus infidelium*; so in a rather small voice I pointed out that at that moment at home the Archbishops of both Canterbury and York were Balliol men. His Excellency flinched noticeably, and then asked who these men might be. I said Cosmo Gordon Lang (York) and William

Temple (Canterbury). Then he really showed his mettle. 'What? Billy Temple an Archbishop? Ho! Ho! Ho!'

In spite of the lack of office work, there was plenty to occupy one's time. In 1932 I had been commissioned in the Nagpur Regiment of the Auxiliary Force, India. Its headquarters were in Nagpur, but not so the majority of its officers. It had at one time been called the Nagpur Rifles, and its single crowded hour of glorious life had occurred during the 1914–18 war when an under-strength company had fought the Germans in East Africa. Our commanding officer was Lt Col Wilfred Shoobert, an officer of the ICS, who had served in the Rifle Brigade during that war. He had not led an easy life. On one occasion he addressed the officers of the battalion for some reason, and, although we were a very motley bunch, I am sure we were all impressed when, monocle in his eye, back very straight, he said words to the effect that 'At any time when things are going badly for you, remember that you are a rifleman and square your shoulders'. His last service to the Central Provinces was his brilliant report as Census Officer for the 1931 census. He left the province to go on deputation as Postmaster General in India. He was knighted and, one may hope, reaped some reward for earlier steadfastness.

For me as an officer at headquarters there were a few minor tasks done in company with the adjutant, who was always a regular officer on secondment. The major task was to attend the periodic dances at the regimental institute, with a view to putting at least some curb on what usually turned into a saturnalia. There were in theory no Indians in the regiment. It was intended to be recruited from those whose mother tongue was not an Indian vernacular language, and this in practice opened the ranks to British members of the various administrative services, to Anglo-Indians in general, to Goanese, and apparently to Indian Christians. At least this is my only explanation for an occasion when the adjutant sent a message asking me to go to the orderly room, where one Bugler James was on a charge. He only spoke Marathi and I was required to interpret.

I attended the annual training camps, and I must have been on the very brink of promotion when I left Nagpur. Thereafter I was never posted in a place where there was a unit of the AFI to which I could be transferred and so pursue my military career. While India and Pakistan were becoming independent in 1947, I was confidently able to claim that I was the oldest second-lieutenant in the sub-continent. I met with much kindness and friendliness during these months.

I remember especially an invitation to join the Christmas camp of six people whose ages were all over forty. This meant that they were as much senior to me as a battalion commander is to a subaltern. It is not easy to describe how grateful I was. Without such an invitation I would have had to spend the long Christmas break in Nagpur, where there were hardly any people of my own age whom I knew. Even the 'reformed' Nagpur was a dusty and rather disgusting place; and my quarters were so infested with mosquitoes that I could never sit there after sunset. Yet here I was about to have ten days' holiday in a place called Chikalda. For good measure a cable from Chicago brought the news that our second son had been successfully born on 21 December, 1933. I was bicycling to a football game when the telegraph messenger stopped me to hand over the cable; and the start of the game was delayed while, in a somewhat silly way, I conveyed the news to the other players.

This news must have moved fairly fast. Next morning a senior clerk in my office came in to see me. He was, on the side, a professional *jyotishi*, that is astrologer. He offered to produce a complete horoscope of the babe (for a fee), and did so in a document which still survives and has been proved accurate beyond probability. Of course he was handicapped by the fact that I could not provide the precise hour, minute and second of the arrival. He was obviously however, a virtuoso when it came to improvisation. He offered to produce (for a fee) a complete horoscope of the previous babe, born in September 1932, even more heavily handicapped by lack of detailed information owing to the lapse of time. He did so. The product has again proved to be uncannily accurate. It is moreover, wrong that I should be more than gently ironical. He was a charming, middle-aged Brahman; and for all I know he knew the secrets of the stars.

Chikalda was an enchanting place. My wife and I had spent a few days there in the hot weather of 1931 as the guests of the Deputy Commissioner of Amraoti and his wife, Mr and Mrs John Stent, Chikalda being in that district. We had never imagined the contrast between it and Amraoti itself. In our second-hand Overland Whippet car we drove the ninety miles west to Amraoti at an average thirty miles per hour, the heat being tolerable at 6.00 am when we started and severe at 9.00 am when we reached there. We then turned north for Ellichpur, where we arrived at 10.00 am and halted for breakfast.

Already we were emerging from the dust and unrelenting heat of the tree-less black fields of the cotton-growing country. Ellichpur was slightly higher than Amraoti as the land sloped upwards towards the range of mountains called the Melghat. It had been a military cantonment in its earlier days, and has been very well depicted by Colonel A R Glasford in his two books, written more than thirty years apart, *Rifle and Romance in the Indian Jungle* and *Musings of an Old Shikari*. As I drove along what must have been called the Mall – the main road through a cantonment was always the Mall – there were the military officers' bungalows with their deep verandahs, their low overhanging thatched roofs, and thick walls, most of them by then sadly dilapidated. Experience from elsewhere suggested that those bungalows also had the usual canvas ceilings, filled with the intriguing scamperings and smells of the civet cats which inhabited that limbo. Colonel Glasford says that before he went up into the Melghat on a shooting trip he would have his ears syringed to improve his hearing; and he would give up smoking to improve his sense of smell. He does not say (what must have been the case) that these measures would greatly improve his awareness of the civet cats on his return home.

Most impressive to me was the deep shade of the great mango trees, the nim, and above all the pipal (*ficus religiosus*) with its faculty of dropping roots down from its branches like stalactites and creating large areas of shaded ground not unlike a Gothic church. There was a feel about this almost dead habitation which gave me what in Scotland is called a 'grue'. This is something very far beyond sentimental imagination. Indeed it is something which seemed very liable to occur in India. In our own experience there was the matter of the inscriptions on tombstones in Nagpur and the cantonment of Kamptee eleven miles to the east.

Very soon after my arrival in India I was told (in a devious way) by the Governor to collect such inscriptions in pursuance of a survey which the Commissioner of the Jubbulpore Division had undertaken. My wife and I embarked on the task, which may ultimately have provided pabulum for back-room historians, but for us would have been the ultimate in boredom had we not been improving our technique in taking rubbings of what was otherwise illegible. There were not even any of those exquisitely quaint things for which people earn small sums of money if they send them to the appropriate periodical.

As the early months of 1931 brought me the imminence of examinations and for my wife the burden of the heat, we had to give up the work. It was taken over by the wife of the military chaplain in Kamptee, Mrs de Saumarez. I should mention that Kamptee was, as a place, very similar to Ellichpur, but the latter was abandoned; Kamptee, with a battalion of the Indian Army and one of the British Army, was very much alive. One day Mrs de Saumarez told her husband at lunch that she had just recorded a very sad little inscription of a child which had died in Kamptee in the middle of the last century. He checked this with the church register and the death was there recorded. In the evening they went out to look at the gravestone and there was nothing there.

From Ellichpur the road began its climb from the average one thousand feet above sea level of the Berar plain to the four thousand feet tops of the

Melghat. From the beginning of the ascent the forest also began. The narrow road, even in the desolation of the hot weather, wound its way under trees and into re-entrant angles where tiny streams flowed through culverts under the road. All the time the air became cooler until, unexpectedly, small bungalows began to appear at the side of the road, barely visible through the trees. Then the road suddenly levelled off and ran so until coming to an end. One cut off the engine of the car and there was silence, until people, Indian and European, emerged with words of welcome from the trees.

On that first visit my pleasure was complete when I shot my first panther, although I was aware of some untidiness in the process. The animal had been doing great damage to cattle. After he was dead he measured just over eight feet from nose to tail, which so far as length goes, though not in the matter of bulk, would be reasonable for a small hill tiger. On the night preceding our arrival he had killed a doe sambhar. My host, John Stent, offered me the opportunity to sit up over the corpse and the loan of his .577 express rifle (double-barrelled). My own only rifle at that time was a .405 Winchester, which I had not brought with me, and which I have always regarded as a sort of academic instrument rather than one for close quarter shooting in thick jungle.

It is all too easy for one or other of the leaves of the back sight to become elevated. In such circumstances an animal one hundred yards away will glance upwards with a wild surmise as a bullet passes high over it on a trajectory which might register a bull's-eye five hundred yards further on. There was also always the risk of the bolt and the magazine not agreeing with one another. Such a jam can lead to a tragedy. The .577 express however, gave two quick chances. On this occasion I sat in the *machan* (a platform of branches in a tree) which the local people had made for me in a tree on a very steep slope. It was so steep that the corpse of the sambhar was very little below the level of my eyes. On the rifle I had fixed a form of torch designed for night shooting: it was called a Roddalite. It would shine a beam on the foresight and then on to the target. So I sat on the *machan* and waited.

Just before dark I saw the panther come over the sky-line at the top of the hill, but he must have been very suspicious because it was nearly half an hour later that I heard him start his evening meal some twenty yards away as the crow flies. I was, being a novice, in a state of great excitement. I did however, raise the rifle in the darkness and prepare to shoot. Unfortunately the Roddalite failed to light. There was therefore, nothing for me to do but sit back and wait until the panther had finished eating. This took about one and a half hours. The cracking of bones and attendant noises were alarming. At last however, there was silence and, after a prudent interval, I blew my whistle. My local friends came along with lanterns and shouts; and I was just in time to slip as unobtrusively as I could into dinner at 8.50 pm looking as little as I could as if I had been shooting.

I did get the panther the next night. There was still some light when he came on over the hill and he was shot. The recoil of the .577 sent my topi over the back of my head, held on only by the chin strap. The cloud of smoke from the black powder in the still air made it impossible to see where the shot had gone. The darkness increased and during lucid intervals I fired two more shots. In due course the whistle was blown. The voices and the lamps came up, and all was well. On our way back to the house in the car a large boar crossed the road in the headlights of the car. My aboriginal friends urged me to shoot. I refused. I would be happy to pay cash for the value of the boar in terms of food; but a fourth shot from the .577 was more than I could tolerate in one evening.

At the Christmas camp in 1933 I did a lot of walking in the jungle at dawn and in the evenings. Most of the 4,000 foot mountains have plateau tops, with quite sparse forest, which provide easy walking. Between them are very steep gorges, their slopes tree-clad, leading down to streams many hundreds of feet below. As one watches the sunset, these gorges fill steadily with shadow which at first is of a deep violet colour. Then the violet changes to black as the sun disappears below the edge of the plateau. In winter it becomes suddenly very cold. In the darkness before dawn the verges are filled with rolling mist. As the sun emerges above the eastern rim of the plateau, the mist is quickly drawn up by the warmth and it is possible to greet the sun as a friend, unlike the pitiless enemy of summer in the plains. I did not shoot much, except in so far as I was required to keep the party in meat. This meant mainly pea-fowl, jungle-fowl and perhaps one of the smaller animals such as the four-horned antelope. It was a holiday of silence in a natural paradise.

With the advent of 1934 my first tour of duty was coming to an end. Nagpur remained consistent so far as its beastly climate was concerned, the temperature reaching 100°F on 28 February. I left on leave in the second half of March with a very deep feeling of relief. Before that time however, my affairs took a new turn. One day in January there appeared on my table a letter from the Government of India inviting applications for recruitment to the Foreign and Political Department. This became the Indian Political Service when the Government of India Act, 1935, came into force in April 1937. My length of service fitted one of the requirements. I took advice and permission from my superior officers, and put in an application.

Then in February I was summoned to Delhi for interview. As far as I remember there were not less than five interviews, culminating with lunch at the Viceroy's House. After lunch I was steered by an ADC to sit beside Lord Willingdon on a couch, and there for fifteen minutes or so did my best to make sensible responses. He looked very much as a good Anglican bishop should look, and he spoke kindly. I was (or so I gathered later) fortunate not to have to be interviewed by Lady Willingdon. The stories about that masterful lady are very numerous, but the one which I most hope is true concerns an officer of the Indian Medical Service who held the post of Surgeon to the Viceroy. After some six months in the post he applied to be relieved. He was sent for by the Viceroy, who liked him well, and asked his reason. He said straight that he found Lady Willingdon very difficult. Lord Willingdon was said to have answered that he was surprised at this surrender after six months, when he himself had undergone the same difficulty for a life-time without complaint. She was undoubtedly well-meaning, but she was more energetic than sympathetic.

Lunch had been for me rather embarrassing. Placed, as was proper, at the very bottom of the table next to the most junior ADC, I was happy enough. He and I were of an age and we got on well. Opposite however, was the Nawab of Arcot, a title famous in the 18th century. The precedence of the holder had been greatly lowered in later times, which explains why he was sitting where he was. Also he was clearly very hungry. Dish after dish vanished like magic. Between dishes he was silent. For some reason the ADCs not only thought this very funny, but also had difficulty in containing their mirth. Not for the last time in my life I kept my eyes on my plate and tried to keep pace with the Nawab. After all it was a very good lunch.

I returned to Nagpur, but it was not until I was on leave some months later that I received the news that my application had been successful. This meant that I would never again serve in the Central Provinces. In retrospect over forty years I cannot recall any regret, but in justice certain things should be said both in favour and otherwise of the province. From the purely personal point of view I have to admit that my first year in Nagpur was as uncomfortable mentally as it was physically. To be working in India as a member of the ICS was the achievement of my early life's ambition. Like most young men I was possessed of a limitless enthusiasm. Everything in that year tended to kill that enthusiasm as in my old age I see the autumn frosts in my garden blackening the leaves of summer. Of course I survived and later revived.

So clouded has been my remembrance of Nagpur that I had almost forgotten that my first introduction to the Indian jungle took place while

The family with David added, 1935

I was there. A friendly Divisional Forest Officer called Carr took me to a block of jungle to the north-east of Nagpur. It was called Totladoh, which to my ear has a certain trochaic liveliness. It means 'parrot spring' in the Gondi language. After my time in Chhindwara and the Satpura country, these were my last six months in Nagpur. During that time I rounded off to some extent my training in the administrative field, and likewise my knowledge of the depth and extent of the administration. In them were exemplified both the strength and the weakness of the civil administration; and in my view there could ultimately be only one conclusion, however unwelcome, namely that no civil service is properly equipped to govern a country beyond a certain point in that country's development.

To say such things in India in Civil Service circles in those days and long after would have been, professionally speaking, suicidal. Once, even after 1945, I ventilated this type of opinion to a man who was both friend and colleague. He was deeply angered. I learned too late that his father, a member of the ICS, had devoted himself to the service of India and suffered great damage to his health. For me to suggest that not only the ICS, but the British administration as a whole, had outlived its mission was in his eyes a form of betrayal.

What I thought then, and believe now, was that as the 20th century drew on the British mission in India had been completed so far as was humanly possible. I would never retreat from my belief that the British did have a mission in India. A Kashmiri pandit, who was Diwan, ie chief administrative officer, of Keonjhar State in the Orissa States Agency, mentioned this point one evening in 1943 when I was visiting the state. He was aged between 55 and 60. He told me that his father had always told him that he must take service with the British because God had sent them to rule India for India's good. It may be doubted whether other Kashmiri pandits would have agreed. I am thinking particularly of the Nehru–Haksar nexus.

It is not usually easy, moreover, to say that the territorial acquisition of India by the British showed signs of divine guidance and protection. The fact that has impressed me is this: the British acquired India mainly by force of arms. In terms of 18th and early 19th century thought there was nothing very wrong in this. Indeed much of the early conquest was achieved by joining with an Indian ally and ultimately celebrating the joint success with a mutually satisfactory distribution of the proceeds. The British on the whole showed a very high standard of courage and endurance. Their Indian soldiers lost nothing by comparison. It has to be accepted however, that while there was an occasional element of chance, deliberate policy was the main factor in the acquisition.

India, following the Mutiny in 1857, came under the Crown. The flag had tended to follow trade, which in itself is implicitly a tribute to the qualities of the men of the East India Company. Now the flag flew over one and three quarter million square miles of wholly alien country. Whether the men who had inherited this property from their predecessors, either in the field or the council chambers, wished it or not, they had inherited with the property the responsibility for endowing it with an administration.

Macaulay wrote that the British had in India taken over a civilization in dissolution. There was a truth in this. Hindu civilization suffered terrible destruction from the early Mongol invasions. There is a strong similarity on a larger scale to what the Danes did to Ireland in the 10th century. The Hindu revenge came from the Marathas who, from a spiritual home in Satara, spread north and east until they stabled their horses in Cuttack in Orissa and were only just halted by fortifications on the outskirts of Calcutta. Today it is unlikely that the Marathas would claim that they contributed significantly in the late 17th and in the 18th centuries to the welfare of anyone except themselves. Civilization was in dissolution in India in 1860.

Into this situation there entered the so-called Secretary of State's Services in India. The mission was not in any sense to repudiate what had been done before or to cast shame on those who had no memorial but who had died serving. It was to take over the responsibility which, consciously or accidentally, the East India Company and the British Government had incurred. Considering, as I have been doing, the Central Provinces, I have already referred to the administration of the land. This was so meticulous and just that Raja Todar Mal himself could not but have approved.

The Indian Forest Service in its rehabilitation of so much of the country could hardly have been more skilled or more devoted. The Public Works Department, for all its tedious duties from day to day in the maintenance of buildings and roads, was very efficient; and in its irrigation branch, seemed to bring technical skill and human sympathy into harness together. For the police (or so it seemed to me) there could be nothing but admiration for their discipline in dangerous situations and their efficiency in other fields such as the Criminal Investigation Department. The Medical Services were starved of funds but still very good.

How then can I say that the depth and the extent of the administration were inadequate? The answer is that the administration, with all its merits, did not in the main aim at development (provinces varied considerably in this respect; but differences were on the whole of degree rather than kind). One of its strongest convictions was that a light burden of taxation, combined with the availability of justice and peace to all, was an end beyond which it was not necessary to look. The result could be, and often was, economic stagnation and the perpetuation of poverty.

The population of the Central Provinces in 1931 was something over 18 million. The area was roughly the same as that of England, Wales and Scotland, being about 85,000 square miles. The available revenue was just over four *crores* of rupees or £3,000,000. Three shillings and four pence of contemporary British money per caput of the population. The inferences are obvious. Wages and salaries were extremely low. A head servant would receive Rs 30 per month, £2.25. The lowest grade of servant was paid 60p per month; my court orderly 90p; a clerk, often a university graduate, would start at £2.25 in Government service.

It was often argued that food was cheap in proportion. This was true at that time. A man might buy 40 lb of rice for 8p. This would ensure for him personally very nearly 1 ½ lb a day for a month. But if he had a wife and two children the situation would be very different. And rice, or wheat, or any other food grain, were only the beginning of a human being's needs. At the risk of emphasizing the obvious, there may be mentioned vegetables, eggs, perhaps meat or fish, salt, clothes.

As often is the case, an instance can tell more than many figures. One day a man came into my court and accused one of my clerks of demanding a bribe for a service which it was his duty to give. I immediately enquired into the matter and absolved the clerk, against whom there was no real evidence. Later however, I called him in privately and told him that I strongly suspected him of being guilty, and he had better mend his ways. No, he said, he was not guilty. I had done right to dismiss the complaint. The fact was that not long before, when his salary was Rs 30 per month, he had regularly taken petty bribes. Otherwise his family would have gone hungry. Quite recently he had reached Rs 45 per month, and he could afford to be an honest man again.

There were myriads of low-paid public servants who lived on their illicit receipts with varying degrees of cruelty, rapacity or (as in the instance which I have given) weakness under pressure. The whole misery ultimately fell on the primary producer, the worker on the land. He and his family, over very large areas of India, lived always on the very verge of starvation. Moreover, if he had an attack of malaria, of bacillary or amoebic dysentery, if bilharzia struck, if hook-worm were endemic, there would not be the money in the Government budget to provide the medicines and the medical services that might relieve him.

I have inspected many dispensaries, so-called, in rural India. I recall that in one year in the Mandla District of the CP the whole financial provision for medicine in the headquarters hospital was Rs 8,000. Yet I never saw a dispensary which did not include in its equipment, among other instruments of purely surgical use, an unused, well-greased pair of Lane's forceps. One of my colleagues however, who had very ably carried out the land revenue settlement of the same Mandla district, gave it to me as his opinion that it would be quite wrong if the district was 'over-administered'. It was mainly peopled by the aboriginal Baigas, who were painfully poor.

The summary of the administrative policy of the Government of the Central Provinces was finally this: taxation must be light. This was on the whole the case, although the land revenue, to people so poor, was not a negligible burden. The consequence of this, namely shortage of funds, must be accepted. Provincial Governments were not permitted to incur public debt for development. There was, therefore, no development originating from the Government. Such as there was – eg coal at Parasia, manganese at Ramtek – came from private enterprise. For most of such enterprise the capital came from Britain. Naturally the profits went back there, but it is only fair to say that the companies concerned did not overpay their alien staff and did provide quite well for their Indian employees in terms of wages, housing, public health and medical services and so on. Nonetheless, in an area which was not well endowed with natural resources, the general effect was stagnation. The people were not apparently discontented, at least in the rural areas.

Then no sooner do I write that than I remember one of the main rice producing areas of the Central Provinces, the Chhattisgarh Division to the east. Here the normal basic diet of the cultivators of the land was boiled rice with a few herbs in the evening and, in the morning, a long drink of the water in which the rice of the previous evening had been boiled. When this was happening the British had been giving peace and justice to the Central Provinces for more than seventy years. It seems that integrity and efficiency had over-ridden imagination; or that at least imagination was not informing integrity and efficiency.

Whatever the explanation may have been, the responsibility rested with the British Government at provincial level in the first instance. How far the responsibility extended to the Government of India I cannot with certainty say; but my later experience has led me to believe that the deplorable policy which led to so much hardship was, from the provincial aspect, wholly the fault of the Central Government. Instances will occur later in this narrative. At this point I would only cite by way of example a matter from my own experience as Financial Secretary to the Government of the North West Frontier Province.

The Government of India subvented the Province. When Sir Otto Niemeyer in February 1936 conducted his special enquiry into the financial needs of provinces, some small increase of the subvention was granted to what was recognized to be inevitably a deficit area. But the amount still remained so small as to preclude any significant development.

In Chapter 11 I have given an account of the new concept in 1943 of post-war development. The underlying motif from the financial point of view then was 'the sky's the limit'. Such a change of policy had not been dreamed of previously. Who conceived the change I do not know. It was not any Indian politician of the majority party, the Indian National Congress, because they had all resigned from office in 1939, had rebelled in 1942, and were many of them in prison. It may have been of British origin. In any case it seemed rather meretricious; and as a justification of government by civil servants it came far too late. The time was overdue for the statesmen to take over.

Chapter 5

> Some feeling of permanence, some consistency between past and future, is essential to the confidence a soldier needs; he must feel that what he dies for will not end with his death.
>
> Philip Mason: *A Matter of Honour*

My leave was spent partly in England, partly in the United States as the guest of my wife's parents. Among many interesting experiences in America there was an invitation to address the association of commercial and professional men called the Kiwanis. It is similar to Rotary International or the Round Table. The invitation was due to the influence of my younger brother-in-law, who was active in the organization. I was to speak for fifteen minutes, no more and no less, after lunch, to an audience of my elders and betters, who were in a hurry to get back to work. I would not do it now. Yet then I thought that I had something to say which might interest them; and something from India which I wanted to tell to Americans. My title was 'The Silent People of India'.

It was the story of two tours in the Chhindwara district. One took place in the early autumn when the fields were green with the burgeoning of the *rabi*, that is winter, crops. The other took place in early spring when a savage hail-storm had devastated thousands of acres of ripened crops. I tried to tell them what this meant to the people and how the imperialists, through their local representatives, dealt with the situation. I hoped that they would see, in one typical instance, what we were doing over there. They were so courteous that I shall never know whether I really made a fool of myself or not.

My second experience was to visit, as a guest, the so-called Chicago Wheat Pit. What I especially remember, apart from the ceaseless activity on the floor as seen from the gallery, was that wheat prices were moving round ninety-nine cents a bushel, approximately 20p. This was very cheap, and was only made possible by bad farming methods in the wheat-growing areas of the United States and Canada. These methods were leading to the creation of the 'dust-bowl' phenomenon. This was simply wind erosion of the surface soil on a disastrous scale. I had actually seen it happening. My journey to the United States had been by Canadian Pacific liner from

Southampton to Quebec. There my wife and her younger brother met me, and we drove by stages to Chicago.

One stage was from Buffalo to Toledo, Ohio; the next from Toledo to Chicago. For both these days the sun was obscured by wind-borne clouds of dust coming from the west. A daily paper in Toledo showed a photograph of a horse drinking-trough which had completely silted up between dusk and dawn. Incidentally I learned that the production of wheat per acre in this most favoured country from the climatic aspect was very little higher than in Chhindwara, where my poor Indian friends could not even supply fertiliser or manure to the starveling soil.

We returned with our two small sons to England in early September, 1934, and after a short stay in a rented house in Parkstone, Dorset, reached India again at the end of November. In Nagpur we organized our migration to the North West Frontier Province, where I had been posted as Assistant Commissioner, Nowshera, in the Peshawar District. First however, I had to recruit a head bearer (servant), since our previous, Ithu, had died while we were away. Through his family I let it be known in the appropriate circles that there was a vacancy.

Interviews would take place at a certain place and time. Twelve men turned up, to whom I explained that I was now a Political Officer and wanted someone who would go with me anywhere. Several dropped out. Then I said that, since I was a junior officer with a family, I was hard up and could only offer the current rate of Rs 30 per month plus *bhatta* (travelling or field allowance) when admissible. This reduced the field to three. Having considered references and asked questions, I ultimately selected a tall, very dark, thin man called Chandu. He was also more than usually ugly. I had made a most fortunate choice, and he shared our vicissitudes (mainly my vicissitudes) until he too died while I was on leave eleven years later.

Stories about the loyalty and sometimes very moving devotion of Indian servants are two a penny. All those which I have heard or read have carried conviction of their truth. There is no call to add to their number. I would only wish to record that Chandu seemed to be a rather cheerful fellow with a strong sense of responsibility. He must at some time have been a Christian, but it was not easy to see how or when he practised his faith. He was manifestly a Madrasi and in one or two camps in the south of Bastar State (later) his native language, Telugu, came in useful. But on the Frontier, in the Province itself, he became Chandu Lal, which would seem to connote a middle-class respectability to which, in terms of the caste system, he certainly had no claim.

When he and I were serving trans-border in South Waziristan he briefly blossomed as Chandu Khan. This, I think, followed an incident in the bazaar at Tank (again more later) when I had travelled down with my usual escort of Mahsuds to see my senior officer, the Political Agent. Chandu and the escort wandered off to see what the bazaar had to offer; and the escort started baiting him (as a Hindu, which in religion he was not) and asking how he would like it if they, as Muslims, attacked him, He answered that he would not mind much if they only came two at a time. This sort of thing the Mahsuds really like. Finally, with me he would never speak anything but Hindi. With my wife, the children and even visitors who seemed to need help he would turn on some very fair English.

With this matter settled I started off ahead of the family for the Frontier. The intention was for me to have the house ready in Nowshera. So off I went one morning in December by the same Grand Trunk Express by which I had travelled to Delhi for my interviews in the previous March. I very nearly felt sad as the sleepy old train climbed slowly over the Satpuras. The forests of the Betul district, which lay immediately to the west of Chhindwara, looked so essentially the old and peaceful India where warring kingdoms never penetrated. It did not at all surprise me that the communication cord was pulled some fourteen times during this part of our journey, bringing the train abruptly to a halt.

Each time a mixed party of third-class passengers would leap down, draped with luggage, from the train and vanish into the jungle. The guard, poor fellow, would also in duty bound leap down, but his whistle carried no authority in this primitive Arcadia. He knew it. His green flag was his only weapon, spurring the engine driver to resume his journey, and I felt fairly certain that his reactions were intentionally slow. I like to think that he had a measure of sympathy for the poor people who probably never wanted to travel in the first instance, and who could not tolerate the idea that, if they alighted at the appointed station, they might have as much as fifty miles to walk home.

We reached Delhi twenty-four hours after leaving Nagpur. There I spent a dull day in the station waiting for the Frontier Mail which ran from Bombay to Peshawar. To those interested in trains it was in a way delightful. From Bombay to Delhi it travelled very fast. From Delhi to Peshawar it was very slow, its average speed being twenty-five miles an hour for the six hundred miles or so involved. But it was very solid and comfortable, with long stops during which one might saunter to the dining-car (along the platform, it was not a corridor train), and have drinks and a meal at extreme leisure before sauntering back to one's compartment at the next long stop. Moreover every station was teeming with Indian life.

When the next morning came we were well into the Punjab. From latitude 22 at Nagpur we had reached roughly latitude 32. In December it was fine but very cold, with a great difference, sometimes as much as 50°F, between day maximum and night minimum temperature. The country was on the whole flat; but that morning I found myself looking at very high, remote, snow-covered mountains to the north. As that day wore on my recollections of the Central Provinces fell away. All my thoughts and feelings were aroused and directed towards the future. The Frontier Mail rolled slowly into Peshawar as darkness was falling, and I became the guest of the Deputy Commissioner, A D F (later Sir Ambrose) Dundas, under whom I would be working. I ultimately reached Nowshera a week or so later and was joined by the family in good time for Christmas.

The North West Frontier Province had been brought into existence for strategic reasons by Lord Curzon in 1901. The British had first reached the Trans-Indus districts after the first Sikh War, and had taken them over in 1849. From then until 1901 the administration had been in the hands of the Government of the Punjab, and it was the view of Lord Curzon that this channelled form of administration, in which the Central Government could only have remote control, was not capable of maintaining either the peace of the area or the safety of India.

The new Province consisted at this time of five settled districts. From the Babusar Pass in the far north, leading into the Chilas area of Kashmir, it extended to the district of Dera Ismail Khan in the south. The most northerly district, Hazara, lay to the east of the Indus, the remainder between the Indus and the mountains of the so-called Tribal Territory to the west. The political and administrative border had been settled when the area was taken over from the Sikh Government. The tribal territory formed a buffer area between Afghanistan and British India, the western boundary of which, the so-called Durand Line, had been settled by agreement with the Afghan Government. Demarcation began in 1893. The total length of this frontier was about 450 miles, and the average depth of the tribal territory from Peshawar District southwards was about forty miles. It was almost uniformly mountainous, rising to over 25,000 feet in the case of the mountain called Tirich Mir in the north. Only occasional fertile uplands gave scope for agriculture. Deforestation had led to severe erosion and the timber line had retreated so rapidly, as the result of the demand for timber for building purposes in the settled areas, that by the 1930s there was very little vegetation below 5,000 feet and no trees below 6,000 feet.

To the north of Peshawar District lay the vast, mountainous area where the Hindukush and the Karakoram meet, divided at its extreme northerly point from Chinese Turkistan (Sinkiang) and Russia by only a narrow strip of Afghan territory. In this area lay the estates of Dir, Swat, Chitral and Amb; and east of the Indus, the lands of the sundry tribes of the Black Mountain country. From the north-west of Peshawar District southwards, in order of their respective territories lived the Mohmands, the Afridis round the Khyber Pass, the Orakzais, the Shia tribesmen of the Kurram Valley, the Wazirs of North Waziristan and in South Waziristan the Mahsuds, and the Wazirs of Wana, bordering on Baluchistan.

Until 1932 the province was governed by a chief commissioner and enjoyed no representative political institutions. Its record for turmoil prior to 1901, with a high watermark of revolt in every tribal area except that of the Mahsuds in 1897, was reflected, even after the creation of the province, in the similar disturbances of 1915 to 1917, and 1919 to 1926. Sir George Roos-Keppel, who had shown himself a masterful and able frontier officer in 1892 when the Kurram Valley, at the request of the Shia* people, was brought under British protection, and who had also been for some years Political Agent in the Khyber Agency for the Afridis, became Chief Commissioner in 1908 and succeeded to a remarkable extent in holding the Frontier under some measure of control through the uneasy years of the 1914–18 war.

Indeed he was able to write in his last Border Administration Report for 1918–19, 'In a world at war it is curious and pleasing that the North West Frontier has no history in 1918–19'. This was undoubtedly true; but there were constant occurrences, excursions and alarms during the ten years which were part of the history of India. Of these the so-called Third Afghan war of 1919 was the most serious. It is no part of the object of this book however, to produce a précis of history. Those who served in either the military or civil services on the Frontier came to know the facts as the background of their work. Those who did not will find the facts in very many individual and official publications.†

1930 saw the rise of the so-called Red Shirts in the Frontier Province and the trouble which involved the arrest in Peshawar of its leader Abdul Ghaffar Khan on 23 April.‡ Lord Irwin had been forced to act strongly,

---

* The Shia Muslims were always regarded with hostility by the more orthodox and more numerous Sunnis.

† I suggest Major Edwards' *Year on the Punjab Frontier* for the origins of British intervention; and Major-General J G Elliott's *The Frontier 1859–1947*, Cassell, 1968. The latter reveals the remarkable degree to which the history of the Frontier was its military history. Sir Olaf Caroe's Preface is brilliant. Caroe's *The Pathans, 550 BC–AD 1957*, Macmillan 1953, is a standard work. Sir Terence Creagh Coen's *The Indian Political Service*, Chatto & Windus, 1971, recounts all that one needs to know of the service up to the time of its publication. For further information about the Afghans there is the Oxford University Press' 1972 new edition of Elphinstone's *Kingdom of Cabul* (1814), also with an introduction by Caroe.

‡ It was at this time that the Indian Congress Party became a political force on the Frontier.

and on 4 May Mr Gandhi himself was arrested. The inauguration of the first Round Table Conference on 12 November was not an encouraging occasion. But Lord Irwin's decision to release Mr Gandhi on 25 January 1931, followed by nine meetings between the two men, changed the atmosphere to one of relative calm. The so-called Irwin-Gandhi Pact emerged therefrom and was an outstanding example of statesmanship on both sides.

My own arrival on the Frontier came at an interesting point in the constitutional development of the Province. The provisions of the Government of India Act 1919 had been extended to it in 1932. The Governor* was, therefore, functioning with an Executive Council consisting, in view of the small size of the Province, of two members. For those portfolios which comprised what were known as the Reserved Subjects the Executive Councillor was Mr George Cunningham. He was soon to be knighted and to be himself Governor from 1937 to 1946. For the Transferred Subjects, the Minister, nominated by the Governor, was Nawab Sahibzada Sir Abdul Qaiyyum.

Nowshera was the smallest of the sub-divisions which made up the Peshawar District. The district itself was very roughly circular. To the west there lay the Khyber Pass into Afghanistan and the Tirah, the homeland mountains of the Afridis. South-west also were the lesser mountains through which went the Kohat Pass, these representing a salient of Afridi territory into the so-called settled districts. These mountains continued south-eastwards and eastwards, crossing the actual Frontier on their way, until they dipped down to the Indus, which formed the eastern boundary both of the district and of the province. To the north-west lay the Mohmand country.

Most of the district was very fertile and there was extensive irrigation. Poor unfortunate Nowshera had only a small share in this. The Kabul river, emerging from the Afridi mountains, ran eastward through the sub-division, and certainly provided water, but its use for irrigation had not been developed; and most of the country was stony and unproductive. The area extended beyond the mountains to the south to a large valley of scrub and stones. Normal access was by the Grand Trunk Road eastwards to the village of Attock. There the road and the railway are carried across the Indus by an impressive bridge over a gorge. The touring officer must break off southwards along the right bank of the Indus, travelling on an unmetalled road to a small village called Nizampur. This is what I did in February 1935.

---

* Lt Col Sir Ralph Griffith KCSI, CIE.

At that time my mare, Julie, after a long tour in January, was showing her age. So I went all the way to Nizampur, where there was a police station and a *dak* bungalow, by car. There I borrowed a mare from the Sub-Inspector in charge for my journey west again round the spur of the mountains running up towards the Kohat Pass. This spur held at its highest point the small military hill station of Cherat at 4,000 feet. On the first day I went hawking on foot with one of the local khans. He and his men handled the hawks. I carried a gun. The prey was the *sisi*, a species of small grouse.

The ground was uniformly rocky and clothed with *acacia arabica* and other bushes which can survive in poor soil and low rainfall. The hawk would sometimes flush a bird, kill it, and start to eat it. The party would catch up, breathing hard; the hawk would be hooded; and the bird would be put in the bag. Sometimes the *sisi* would seek refuge in the dense branches of a bush. Then the hawk would perch in a stern attitude on an upper branch until the party came up. With the hawk once more hooded, the party would smite the bush and utter loud cries until the *sisi* flew out. It was then my job to shoot it. I can think of many more sporting ways of procuring one's supper.

One of my happiest memories comes from this tour. We all went back to Nizampur after the hawking; and I did my job of inspecting land records till evening. Then next morning, on the borrowed mare, I rode off to see the valley up to the point where it began to rise to its junction with the hills of the Afridis of the Kohat pass. The total distance in a straight line was some twelve miles. At one point on the right of the valley (there was no road) and at the foot of the hills there was a shrine – *ziarat* in Pashtu – commemorating a local *pir* or holy man. It shone white in the sun.

As I approached, the mullah in charge of the shrine was standing before it. He asked me to stop. I did so and dismounted. He invited me to enter the shrine. I explained that, as a Christian, I would much wish to do so and to pay proper respect; but I was wearing a very tight-fitting pair of polo boots which would take forever and a day to take off and put on again without the necessary tools. He smiled gravely behind his white beard; produced a cloth and with it dusted the soles of my boots. We then entered the shrine and prayed for some minutes.

The calendar year 1935 was very disturbed at the northern end of the frontier. In his youth Sir Winston Churchill wrote a considerable book, *The Story of the Malakand Field Force*. In the first nine months of 1935 there were events which, by his standards, could have provided material for several books. And yet there was nothing unusual in this. Early in the year the Nowshera Brigade under Brigadier the Hon H R L G Alexander* operated in that same Malakand area, which lay trans-border to the north of the Peshawar District. The Political Agent, Major Best, was among those killed.

In April the extremely serious earthquake in Quetta called for strong efforts from district staff to raise funds to help survivors. In my case it gave me my first experience of public speaking in Pashtu. In the summer there was serious communal rioting in the Punjab over a building in Lahore called the Shahid Ganj mosque, which was claimed by both Muslims and Sikhs. This spread to Peshawar District. One day in July I returned to my house at 1.00 pm after a short holiday in the hills at Nathiagali about 140 miles away. As I stood under a shower I was called to the telephone and learned that the Hindu quarter in Nowshera city had been set on fire by Muslim agitators. I was on the spot in fifteen minutes and, seeing no other course, proceeded to act in a high-handed way.

First, I arrested all Hindus and Sikhs seen bearing arms. A desperate minority such as they were could spark off their own massacre. When the Peshawar Fire Brigade arrived, some Muslims tried to cut their hoses with axes. It was a pleasure to clap them too into jail. With confidence in British impartiality thus established, the next move was facilitated. An admirable subaltern of the Royal Engineers, urgently indented for on the telephone from Brigade Headquarters, agreed with, and carried out a proposal of mine to blow up about twenty houses downwind of the fire. Since another twenty in the very congested city were already burning out of control, a fire-break of this size was not excessive. I got to bed at midnight. The disturbance had died down, but with a shade temperature of 115°F one could have done without a fire.

At thirty minutes past midnight the usual sentry woke me at the garden gate with a telegram. The Hindus were very angry with me (I could hardly blame them). They had come to the gate to say so, but he had turned them back because I was again under the shower. So they stirred up the postmaster and sent telegrams to every authority that they could think of, with a copy to me for information, impugning my conduct. No one in official circles either approved or condemned what I did that day. The Frontier was a violent place. A man had to be extremely good or abysmally bad to attract even departmental attention. I am happy still to have with me an address which the Hindus gave me when I left Nowshera. In it they thanked me for the way in which I dealt with the fires of discord. I was transferred at very short notice at the end of August to Peshawar as a minor

* Later Field Marshall Viscount Alexander of Tunis.

administrative adjustment consequent on military operations against the Mohmands.

The Mohmands were regular contributors to the chronic unrest of the Frontier. From the autumn of 1916 to August 1917, following an incursion into Peshawar district, they were blockaded, electrified wire being used over a wide front. In 1935 the trouble followed a similar course so far as the provocation was concerned. The basic cause in all such troubles was the passionate devotion of the Pathan tribesmen, living across the border of the settled districts, to their own, utterly independent way of life. They would call it freedom.

No modern European could agree with that word. For example the prevalence of the blood feud meant that anyone of any importance lived in constant danger of assassination. They did not live in fear. They were brave men and hardly knew fear. But they did live in a type of house which was essentially a fort and bore a remote resemblance to the peel towers of the Scottish borders. Whenever they went abroad they were in danger. The manner in which retaliatory murders were committed would be regarded by us as cowardly. There lay a paradox which English people might find inexplicable. It would not be strange to the same extent for any Scotsman.

The history of the Scots, those 5th century immigrants into an almost empty country over against Ireland, bore a very strong resemblance to that of the Pathans. The clan system and the tribal system, with mutual hostility as a permanent feature of life in each case, were very similar one to another. The Pathans had a longer history by at least a thousand years. There were Pathans, and more specifically Afridis, in the army of Xerxes which invaded Europe in 480 BC. But clans and tribes had in common such features as the odd combination of bravery, savagery and treachery on the one hand and humour, hospitality and a sense of fair play on the other. One may reasonably ask what kind of freedom it is in whose ambience one lives as a hunted creature always in danger of death; and in a country where (as in the case of the North West Frontier mountains) neither agriculture nor forestry can support the people.

My posting, which continued for two months, was as an Officer on Special Duty under the Deputy Commissioner. The fact was that his whole time was taken up with the Mohmand war; and I was required to interview all his visitors and to deal with all his revenue and criminal cases. Fortunately I had already been gazetted as an Additional District Magistrate while I was in Nowshera. In other matters however, the provincial Government had neglected to specify my powers; and it was necessary for me to pass scores of orders signed (illegible) 'for Deputy

Commissioner'. I assumed that what people wanted was a just and clear decision. It did not at that stage matter who 'illegible' was.

It was in the field of criminal law that the most striking event of those two months occurred. I went to my court one morning and found that the first case on the list, falling under a section of the Foreigners Act, was Rex versus the King of Bokhara. The clerk of court could not explain it. The section quoted merely meant that the police prosecutor wanted me to expel the royal person from India – presumably signed 'illegible', ADM for DM. I called the case at once. The parties came in. The accused, to adapt Virgil, *verus incessu patuit rex*: he bore himself as a king. He was several inches over six feet in height in his shabby sandals. His back was as straight as a guardsman's. His hair, his beard and his eyes were brown, his cheeks light brown suffused with red. He made a gesture of salute with both hands, and I saw that they were hand-cuffed. We had the hand-cuffs off very quickly. He was mildly pleased. His whole appearance, however, was one of composed detachment, completely devoid of arrogance as it was of servility or fear.

The police prosecutor could tell me no more about the case than what was written in the charge sheet. The accused was an undesirable alien who had entered the country by way of the Khyber Pass. I adjourned the case briefly and telephoned a friend in the Government of India Intelligence office. I asked for guidance, for background information. Was I expected to be a latter-day Pontius Pilate and let the law take its meticulous course? One of the good features of the official machine in India was that one could ask questions like this and receive an honest answer. The answer was that the accused was indeed as described. Years ago he had sought refuge in Afghanistan. Then Russian influence in Kabul had led to pressure on the Afghan Government to hand him over. He escaped to India; but we were bound by treaty with the Russian Government not to harbour those whom they alleged to be their enemies.

The case was resumed. The King and I discussed various routes by which he might be deported; I first suggested that he might go back up the Khyber. Surely the Afghan Government would not reject him. He bent down to the floor and picked a small piece of fluff off the carpet. He placed it in the palm of his left hand, puffed it off and said, 'So is the Government of Afghanistan before the power of the Russians'.

I offered him one route after another by which he might leave India to the west. We even got down to Gwadar on the coast of the Gulf of Oman. All were wrong either because of the danger to him or from him to the local authorities. At last I hit on a solution. Was I not right in supposing that he was not a Haji, that is, he had not performed the pilgrimage to

Mecca? I was right. Would he not wish to do so? He would. He was sent off accordingly by rail to Karachi and ship to Jeddah, certified by me as being entitled to first-class accommodation at government expense. I never knew the end of this story. There was, however, a sequel in 1940.*

There were other interesting events in progress. I was fortunate to be allowed to spend one day watching operations against the Mohmands and saw Brigadier Claude Auchinleck (later Field Marshall Sir Claude Auchinleck) conducting a battle. He had the Nowshera brigade, in addition to his own Peshawar brigade, and to a civilian the speed and precision of the advance on a very broad front in rough, hilly country was astonishing.

Cis-border the Shahid Ganj mosque agitation continued to give us trouble. Gradually however, matters simmered down and peace supervened. My next two years were spent in the Provincial Secretariat. From October 1935 to February 1936 I officiated as Financial Secretary. Then I became Under Secretary until April 1937, when the Government of India Act 1935 came into effect. Finally I officiated until December as Home Secretary. I thought then, as I think now, that at this stage of constitutional development in India full dominion status in terms of the Statute of Westminster should have been conferred by this Act.

In retrospect it is possible to argue strongly that much ill would thereby have been spared. Independence was in fact conferred ten years later when the only substantial change in the situation was that the United Kingdom no longer had the power to do anything else. Since I was in junior posts during the years of the sessions of the Round Table Conference (1930-35) in London and during the passage of the 1935 Act through Parliament, I could not know, and have never known, what may have gone on behind the scenes or what underlay the main decisions which the Act embodied.

It was however, an instrument with which I soon came to be as familiar as I was with those Codes or Acts comprising the Civil, Criminal and Revenue law which every officer was trained to administer. I can, therefore, advance the opinion that it was an intricate and possibly disingenuous method of appearing to concede much without in fact conceding anything of substance. Provinces had since 1921 been allowed to administer the so-called transferred subjects. This in a sense was grudging, since finance was not a transferred subject; and without some power over money the ministers administering those subjects were somewhat restricted.

Now, in 1937, there was granted 'provincial autonomy'. This was, so far as it went, a clearly defined delegation of legislative and hence

---

* See also page 122.

administrative authority over matters set out in a schedule to the Act. But the schedule also set out matters in respect of which only the Central government might legislate; and there was a cunning little cuckoo in the nest, namely a list of matters wherein both Central and Provincial Governments might legislate. The structure of the Central Government still left the Viceroy presiding over an Executive Council. This was the result of the provision in the Act for the establishment of a Federal Government and Parliament in which both British India and the States would be represented. I have written more of the latter below.

The federation never came into existence, and the detailed proposals are now no longer of anything but academic interest. The Viceroy might, therefore, as Linlithgow, Wavell and Mountbatten did, appoint political leaders to his Council; but these bore no resemblance to the formation of a party government in Westminster. This was not wholly bad. It did at least ensure the presence of a representative of Hindu India's sixty million untouchables, Dr Ambedkar, in the seats of the mighty.

Provincial autonomy was, likewise, not wholly meaningless. The provinces had full powers over the administration of their finances and within certain limits full power to impose taxation. The limits however, such as the exclusion of income tax, were very restrictive; and the revenue available from other sources often trivial. For example, in the hot weather of 1937 there was imposed for the first time in the NWFP a system of motor vehicle taxation. As Home Secretary I was responsible for the implementation of this Government decision to have effect from 1 July. As part of the task I visited each of the districts in turn in order to explain the legal position and the type of administrative machinery needed. In a way it was ridiculous. There may have been ten thousand vehicles (excluding military vehicles) of all types in the province. Whatever reasonable tax might be applied – suppose for example, it were Rs 25 per annum – the yield before deduction of the cost of administration could not exceed £15,000.

Finally, there were reservations in the Act which gave great offence to Indian politicians of whatever party or complexion. Of these the responsibilities of governors were the most important. For this particular subject I may quote the summary given by R Coupland in his pamphlet 'Britain and India':*

> Each Governor was expressly instructed to act, as the King acts in Britain, on his ministers' advice, subject to the observance of what were called

* Longmans, Green and Co Ltd Madras, 1941.

> 'special responsibilities' or in common parlance 'safeguards'. On certain matters, of which the most important were the maintenance of peace in grave emergency and the just treatment of minorities, the governor was empowered to override his ministers and to take the steps needed to carry out his decision on his personal responsibility.

Coupland writes moderately. In doing so he abbreviates the list of 'safeguards'; and one omission, namely the protection of officers of the so-called Secretary of State's services from action by provincial governments, represents a matter of special adverse criticism. Those officers were under the aegis of the governor.

In effect, provincial governments had been since 1921 in control of a substantial part of the administration of their provinces. The extension of those powers and functions by the 1935 Act was, in terms of quantity, considerable. I have shown, however, that they were not complete. Part of the powers not conferred were those which were to rest with the Central, or Federal, Government, and included defence and foreign policy. These in fact, even under the federal scheme, were reserved to the Viceroy, himself responsible to the Secretary of State. The list of federal subjects was long even without them; but there was no Federal Government. One may understand how hostile reaction might arise. Perhaps these reservations had some merit. Thus a provincial government could not on impulse call out the army to help its mode of government against discontented voters. The police must suffice.

In my own experience one potentially horrible situation arose in 1947. In the Frontier Province it was normal procedure to issue rifles for the purpose of village defence. The rifles were usually old .303 Lee Enfields. They were especially needed along the Mohmand border; but wherever the area might be, the whole point was that the village concerned might be able to repel raids from trans-border. The men of substance in each village stood surety for the weapons. One day the Chief Minister, Dr Khan Sahib, told me to recall all these rifles. He wished to re-distribute them to his party militia, who were alleged to be quite trustworthy in the defence of public safety. They were in fact the Redshirts, the *Surkhposhan*, who, however loyal to Dr Khan Sahib, were notorious for the subversion of law and order.

I think that this order more than any other matter decided that I could never serve Pakistan after the by then inevitable partition and independence. A senior official was being ordered to divert the legitimate weapons to the private army of a political party. I did not in the event do so. I procrastinated. Any reader of this may wonder why I was so treacherous to my employers and why I did not do the honourable thing and resign. I can only say that at that time I had to make my own analysis of what was honourable.*

To return to the 1935 Act, I regarded all that was new in it as mere constitutional juggling.† Such measures were understandable, even necessary, in the 1919 Act. At that time those Indian and British officials who were serving the civilization in dissolution had by no means finished their course. By 1935 however, there had been great changes. First, what was known as local self-government had now a history of fifty years. Partial autonomy at provincial level had fourteen years. The history of education at all levels was approaching its centenary, and that is to take no account of education by ancient indigenous systems. In the Indian Army Indian officers had been commissioned for fourteen years and had reached field rank. In certain administrative services there were hardly any British officers left. Everything was poised for the achievement of dominion status.

What actually emerged seemed to be designed to keep ultimate control in British hands. It is impossible to assess how far this was due to the influence of Winston Churchill. He was wholly opposed to the grant of independence to India. In the fifth volume of Churchill's official biography Martin Gilbert, the author, draws full attention to this opposition, which extended over five years up to 1935. He speaks of Churchill's passionate sincerity, urging that he was in fact concerned throughout with the future welfare and unity of India, and worried about the social and political difficulties which would be created by the dominance of the Congress Party.

Above all he seems to have been concentrated on the need to keep India within the Empire. He argued (and rightly) that the federal scheme contained in the Bill would only stimulate demands for full independence, which the Government itself, from which he was excluded, rejected and which they hoped to avert. His own wish was to see full provincial autonomy established, with safeguards for the minority rights, for example, of the Muslims and the untouchables. The retention of India in the Empire was, in his mind, an essential element of British security in the

* I do not wish to imply that Dr Khan Sahib was anything but honourable himself. He was in some degree saintly. He saw nothing wrong morally in having a private army because it was to him his band of fellow idealists. He was quite ready to believe that the lion would eat straw like the ox in his type of Utopia. His Redshirts were so called in every day life. In the party their name was Khudai Khidmatgaran, servants of God.

† One new matter which was not dealt with either in the 1919 or in the 1935 Act was the question of whether, and if so by what means, the tribal areas beyond the North West Frontier might be integrated with India.

war with Germany which he foresaw. These are all serious arguments. What he does not seem to have appreciated was that India was already demanding full independence, though many moderates might qualify this by invoking the Statute of Westminster as the framework of their demand. No velvet glove could conceal from Indian nationalists the existence and the purpose of the mailed fist which the Bill represented.

There was also perceptible in Churchill's arguments an attitude towards Indian social structure which had something in common with Kipling's doctrine of 'the white man's burden'. It would be very inconsistent of me if I were to say that this was both ludicrous and wrong in view of how much there is in this book about Hindu intolerance. I have, for example, been bitterly angry to see caste Hindus in Deccan villages refuse to allow untouchables to draw water from Hindu wells when their own had gone dry during a period of drought. Leading Hindus, and especially Mr Gandhi, were however, equally conscious of this scandal. And such major concepts as that of political independence cannot be discouraged or put to shame by lectures on social reform. Mr Churchill, and those who with him resisted the 1935 Act, simply do not seem to have appreciated the spiritual and emotional issues involved.

A fundamental part of the Indian problem, which the Act was designed to solve, was the existence of the Indian States. There were some seven hundred and fifty, more or less. I came to know something less than a hundred. They varied, from small but obscurely privileged estates to the dominions of the Nizam of Hyderabad, similar in area to France. He was said to be the richest man in the world. He may well have been. The Nizam, who was contemporary with my service in India, not only inherited vast treasure but was, not to put too fine a point on it, a skinflint and a miser. For example, his presence at weddings in socially prominent families was greatly prized. For this condescension he would charge a fee,* perhaps one lakh of rupees (then £7,500). For this the parents of those being married received the personal attendance for the short time of a small man in the simplest of robes, the exchange of a few greetings and something to tell their descendants.

Between the one extreme and the other there was the main body of the princes. They owed their survival as such to the favour and the respect of the Moghul emperors; and to the similar attitude of the British not only towards those whom the Moghuls had admired but also to those who, when the Moghul Empire was breaking up, established themselves as independent rulers. In this century their dominions comprised about one

---

* In Urdu *nazar*. It means 'sight'.

third of the area of India and about one quarter of the population. In the course of my experience I formed the opinion that one fifth of the rulers were the salt of the earth, but four in five were ignorant anachronisms. For the constitutional development of India they had to be federated, as mentioned above, with an independent Government of India if there was to be an India which was a unity.

No progress towards this end had been made by 3 September 1939 when the second great war of the century started. After a hesitant approach in 1937, governments of the Indian Congress Party had agreed to co-operate and to take office in those provinces where they commanded a majority. With the outbreak of war the Viceroy pledged the loyalty and support of the whole of India to Great Britain in her fight for freedom against Nazi tyranny. The view of the Congress Party was that they had not been consulted and that they saw no reason to support the United Kingdom in a war which was not their war. On instructions from the Working Committee all Congress provincial governments resigned; in effect this meant all provincial governments except Bengal, the Punjab and Orissa.

Worse was to come, as will be seen in due course. For the moment the faults in the Government of India Act 1935 had resulted in most of the Act being inoperative. The constitution of the Central Government persisted, and its work continued in a manner beyond praise. For eight provinces representative government was in suspense; governors and their civil services governed in accordance with Section 95. And so India functioned for nearly three years.

In the NWFP the course of events had not been the same as in other parts of India. The government which emerged from the elections following the introduction of the Act in April 1937 was not a Congress government. A coalition emerged with Nawab Sahibzada Sir Abdul Qaiyyum as Chief Minister. The Ministry included one Hindu; and the Congress representatives led by Dr Khan Sahib were left in opposition.

This was in many ways an excellent start for the reformed constitution, since Sir Abdul Qaiyyum, who had a long and distinguished career both in government service and as a minister under the previous constitution, had both the ability and the prestige to lead a government although he was by no means *persona grata* to the land-owning classes. The Ministry did not, however, last. The constituent elements of the coalition began to fall apart. At the session of the Legislative Assembly on 3 September 1937, a motion of no confidence in the Ministry was passed by 27 votes to 22.

The Congress Party led by Dr Khan Sahib took office on 7 September. The new Chief Minister had been, at one time, a Medical Officer attached to the Guides (Punjab Frontier Force) in Mardan, but, with his brother Abdul Ghaffar Khan (the Frontier Gandhi), he had for more than ten years been a leader of the Congress Party in the Frontier Province. Like his brother, he had served his share of imprisonment, and had taken part in the Redshirt movement of 1931.

After the swearing in of the Ministers, they held a meeting of all Secretaries to Government and Heads of Departments; and immediately a friendly atmosphere was created. Dr Khan Sahib made something of a hit, while speaking of the budget, by remarking that they would be able to save on CID expenditure now that the main target of that department's work was running the province. The Governor, Sir George Cunningham, with his remarkable combination of courtesy, sympathy and strength, established a relationship of trust with the Ministry.

It was always a feature of Dr Khan Sahib that he did not allow his political views to affect his social activities more than he could help, in contrast with the normal rigid refusal of the Congress Party to participate in anything which might give the impression of collaboration with the British Government. He and his wife and his Education Minister, Qazi Ataullah, even dined at Government House on 19 November not dressed in their conventional *khaddar* and Gandhi caps. All the other guests were much impressed by their friendliness. This smooth and friendly inauguration of a new regime was of great importance to the future of the province.

As the year drew to an end the political situation in the settled districts was most reassuring. I could never, however, feel that the 'permanence, some consistency between past and future', referred to in the text at the head of this chapter, were inherent in the 1935 Act. My loyalty, which in youth had been comprehensively attached to a number of ill-defined ideals, was still wholly at the service of the people of India. I felt no confidence now, however, in the political integrity of the British Government; and for the future I saw nothing but change, violent change. One character in *A Modern Symposium* by Lowes Dickinson is made to say: 'Force is the midwife of society; and never has radical change been accomplished without it.' I had never accepted this thesis. To me in 1937 it began, so far as India was concerned, to seem inevitable.

Chapter 6

Haec olim meminisse juvabit
(Some day these memories will bring happiness)
Virgil

MY SECOND LEAVE FROM INDIA is a period on which I look back with both pleasure and sadness. I look back with sadness as I still look back on a day on a hill or a loch simply because it is over. I look back with pleasure because then I did many things which I wished to do, at rest in my conscience because I could pay my bills and had worked hard to earn the money.

My family, which now included three children, had travelled to England in October and were staying with my mother in her house, The Leigh, near Cheltenham; I arrived in London at 6.00 am on 18 December

Norval with daughter, Genevra, aged 3 in Peshawar, 1939

travelling through an empty London to the Berners Hotel where my wife was to meet me. I had forgotten what an English winter was like; but, having just come from a Frontier winter, I felt no hardship in the cold. Rather I could enjoy even the smells of London in the humid air. This enjoyment was enhanced when we reached Gloucestershire next day. By that time I was the owner of a heavy tweed overcoat which my wife had made me buy at Austin Reed in Piccadilly. It cost seven guineas. It went with me for over twenty years until I gave it to a Belgian refugee from the Congo who came to our house in Lusaka in 1959. Fortified by it, I drove my mother's car to Winterslow taking presents to my aunt Sara and her husband, Jacob Seaward. While there I walked through the December woods which had so much appealed to me during my years at school and at Oxford.

Christmas was very much a children's affair, and after the New Year we settled to a quiet life for a while. I did much cross-country running under the excuse of exercising my mother's spaniel. I bought a Hillman Minx car, which was to go back to India with me. My cross-country running was abated somewhat when I began to find myself being chased by bullocks, who enjoyed the pursuit and hated the dog. Walking was for a time substituted, and it was on one of these walks to the Severn that I went into an inn for a pint of draught beer. There was no one else in the bar, and the landlord and I conversed uninterrupted. I must have done my share of the talking because I remember him interpolating at one point the question, 'Then are you one of these 'ere pro-consuls?'

In early spring I visited Shrewsbury, partly to see my friends again, partly to determine whether the school was as good as I thought it to be in earlier years. All my friends said yes. These included my friends D S Colman and D J V Bevan of Bedford School and Balliol, both of them inspired appointments of Canon Sawyer. There were also those who had been masters in my own time at the school, especially J M Street, S S Sopwith and J M West. The first taught me the classics. The second gave me my first appreciation of English prose and poetry. The third gave me my first insight into what young men thought and felt as they went to war in 1914. Jimmy Street and Sidney Sopwith, the former with an allegedly weak heart (he was beyond measure indignant); the latter with deficient sight (he was turned down eight times even when he had paid good money to those who could give him the charts to memorize) taught me much of the meaning of service which could be devoted and beyond price even when inconspicuous.

I was introduced to the headmaster, H H Hardy. On being told that I was interested in entering two of my sons for the school, he insisted that

I must stay with him at Kingsland House. This was a change from my time. The headmaster now lived in a house of his own, and not in part of the School House as he had done before. I protested that I wished to stay for three nights in Shrewsbury and would not wish to trespass on his hospitality to that extent. He insisted and I accepted. It was on my last night there that the subject came up again of entering two sons for the school. When I told him how old they were, roughly six and five, his demeanour became frigid.

He had not expected anything so remote in terms of dividends. I think that I must have made it clear that this was not my fault; and as the port circulated he paid me the implicit compliment of being indiscreet. I must understand, he said, that the public school industry was insolvent and on its way out. He mentioned one ancient school (even today I will not betray his confidence) which would be winding up and closing down within a year. It did not do so, but I learned elsewhere that his information at that moment was correct. Why, then, should I be so bothered about my sons? Nonetheless they were entered. In due course a third was also.

But in that spring I moved on to Oxford and introduced myself to the Balliol College Boat Club. The result of this was that I was invited to share the coaching of the First VIII for the bumping races at the end of May – 'The Eights'; the other two were John Lascelles and Bob Sherriff. J H Lascelles, a New Zealand Rhodes Scholar, had been at Balliol after my departure for India. He was a very distinguished oarsman, who had the misfortune to row in an Oxford crew which broke the record for the Putney to Mortlake course in the race itself, but still finished second. He had what used to be called a good war, which, I should perhaps explain for later comers, means that he again distinguished himself, acquiring a wound in Greece. His later distinction is in the rarified altitudes of the commerce in copper.

R G Sherriff was the man who wrote *Journey's End*, among much else. He went to Oxford relatively late in life and even so only missed a rowing blue by misfortune. Both these men were fine coaches. Since they were busy men, they could not always be on the job; and I was very happy to take on the work in their absence. During my fifth and last year at Oxford, in the summer of 1930, Balliol had for the first time for many years made enough bumps to emerge from the second division (of the three into which the races were then divided) and finish in the first. From 1931 to 1937 the college had moved steadily up, and in 1938 the crew was a good one.

The racing was of a high class with its climax for us on the fifth of the six days on which racing took place. We moved up to second behind New

College, who had started Head of the River. Balliol had last been Head in 1879. Telegrams and cables from all over the world were coming in to the Boat Club with eager and encouraging messages. Unfortunately an extremely good Trinity crew had been moving up behind us; and on that Tuesday evening the question was whether Balliol could catch New College (which they had until then failed three times to do) before the Balliol crew itself was caught by Trinity. If they could then they were Head. Trinity would have to spend the sixth and last night disposing of New College.

I am glad to say that justice prevailed. Trinity were better than Balliol. In the first minute of that race Balliol rowed forty-eight well completed strokes. For a brief moment their bow overlapped the New College rudder. But no bump was made and Trinity, the better crew, moved in and made their bump. I know that we would not really have been happy with any other result; and of course Trinity went Head the next day, which was right.

It was during these weeks of early summer that I was doing what the Ancient and Modern hymn calls 'knitting severed friendships up'. I must have made considerable efforts to get in touch with contemporaries whom I had not seen for eight or more years. Today I would hesitate to take such an initiative with all its possibilities of incompatibility and embarrassment. Then nothing of the sort supervened. I lunched as a guest at the Carlton Club and at the Junior Carlton. It was at the former that my host (my contemporary) told me how naughty Anthony Eden had been to talk so loudly at that table over there about his differences with Chamberlain over Mussolini. Very soon I learned how at that time things of which most of us in India knew nothing could be common coin in those circles in London.

On another occasion I was a guest at the Australia Club dinner on Anzac day. The Duke of Gloucester was the guest of honour. We were arranged for dinner at round tables for eight people. My host was on my right. At my left was a middle-aged man in military mess kit with many miniature medals, who turned out to be Brigadier General Scanlon, Air Attaché at the American Embassy. We seemed to be congenial even in the matter of the speech of His Royal Highness. I thought that it could not well be better. So did Scanlon. Only in the matter of Bourbon whiskey did we disagree. I liked it. He did not.

When the dinner was over he invited my host and me to go with him to his quarters in the American Embassy so that we might test the validity of our views on this important question. For him rye whiskey was what really mattered. A friend had, however, recently given him some allegedly

The barber, 1939/40

good Bourbon. Having arrived at that imposing place by taxi, we reached his quarters, I at least being already in a somewhat elevated state. He produced glasses and bottles from a cupboard and, having asked me to excuse him for a moment, gave himself in a wineglass the equivalent of two double whiskeys. He swallowed this neat with a graceful gesture and then said no, he had been right, he did not like Bourbon and would try something else.

While we were discussing matters in general the wife of the American Ambassador, Mrs Joseph Kennedy, came in and joined the conversation. It was about midnight, and after what I had lived through that evening nothing surprised me. I do not remember what we talked about, and I never did know why she came in anyway. But she was an extremely handsome woman with classical features and an appearance of that combination of youth and maturity which I have always associated with Pallas Athene. It was hardly credible that she was in early middle age and had already borne the many children who have made the family famous. Moreover she was kind without being condescending.

This very happy time was nearly over. I was (in common with millions of other people) quite aware that war with Germany was coming again only twenty years after we thought that we had seen the last of major wars.

The grain seller, 1939/40

The cloth merchant, 1939/40

The tea shop, 1939/40

Some weeks before, my wife's mother had come to England and we had jointly rented a pleasant house near Eastbourne. There were the sands and the swimming at Birling Gap.

By this time it had become known that our fourth child would be born in the following January. There could be no confidence in the obstetric skill of the doctors who might be available in India when the time came. We had once before lost a child through what (we were later advised) was simple incompetence. We decided, therefore, that we should rent a house in Parkstone. I would return to India alone while my wife would be in the care of the staff of the Cornelia Hospital, Poole. She would follow in due course.

So that summer faded. We moved into the Parkstone house. It was there that our admirable German governess, Else Lohlbach, listening to the radio one evening wept uncontrollably as the strident voice of Hitler instigated his people to war. From there I drove the Hillman Minx first to my mother's house in Gloucestershire; then to stay one night with my friend Kenneth Irvine and his family in Corwen, where I had stayed more than once in more carefree times. Then on to Bootle, where the car had to be delivered for stowing on the Anchor Line boat with which I would a week or so later make my rendezvous at Marseilles. That day I went back by train and taxi to my mother's house; and next day, using her car, I drove away. I was not to see her again from that September day in 1938 until April 1945.

The time before I left was spent in Parkstone. Then my wife travelled to London with me and at midnight of the last night we emerged from a cinema to find newspapers selling with the news of the Munich agreement with Hitler. Next day I left London in the afternoon for Marseilles.

Chapter 7

What a record of futility it all is.

Quoted by Sir Evelyn Howell, *Mizh*

MY TRUSTY FRIEND Chandu was waiting for me at Bombay; the car had survived its journey from Bootle, and was quickly swung ashore; and I spent the first night of my return in the rather cheap Ballard Pier hotel. Next morning we left early on our journey by road to the frontier. The first day was interrupted by mechanical trouble, which made it difficult to ascend the Western Ghats as far as Nasik. There however, a garage mechanic corrected what no mechanic in England had been able to correct, and this in the brief space while I had lunch in the Nasik club. By the method of driving from 6.00 am till noon, halting for three hours and then continuing till 6.00 pm, we reached Peshawar in five days.

I stayed briefly with my friend Sir James Almond, Judicial Commissioner, and visited many people both officially and socially. Then we turned south once more to join my new post of Assistant Political Agent, South Waziristan. Through the Kohat Pass, Kohat itself, Bannu, Dera Ismail Khan, then west to the remote outpost and sub-divisional headquarters called Tank. This was also the headquarters of the Political Agent, South Waziristan. The agency itself lay entirely beyond the border of what was then called British India. I was to be in political charge of the Mahsuds. I had a colleague, Captain Hasan, whose headquarters were in the south-west corner of the agency at Wana, where he performed similar duties in respect of the Ahmadzai Wazirs. My headquarters were at a fort some twenty-two miles into Mahsud territory called Sararogha. The word means 'cold plateau'. The plateau lay at an altitude of 4,000 feet. In winter the wind whistled from the north week after week at a temperature of about 26°F. In summer the wind died away, the maximum temperature reached 104°F and the stone-built fort became, at the opposite extreme, very uncomfortable. But the first thing was to learn what I was required to do.

South Waziristan was the southernmost of the Political Agencies into which the so-called tribal areas, which lay between the Frontier Province and the Afghan border, were divided. Unlike North Waziristan, which was homogeneously populated by Wazirs, South Waziristan was not only the home of the Mahsuds, but also of Wazirs in the south and south-west. My duties were exclusively connected with the Mahsuds and fell roughly into two parts: to command the seven hundred and fifty Mahsud *khassadars* (levies, paid by the Indian Government); and to act in a very junior capacity as the Government's agent in maintaining some semblance of law and order in a country where British law did not either *de facto* or *de jure* prevail. Only on the main roads and immediately round the Scouts' posts did the Frontier Crimes Regulation apply; and that differed from British-Indian law as chalk from cheese.

The lesser part of such responsibility rested on encouraging and promoting embryonic administration. Since the country was politically free, anything smacking of administration could only be promoted by the consent of the Mahsuds themselves. So it was that there was a school in Kaniguram* in the middle of the country. Or I might, with the agreement of the Medical Officer of the South Waziristan Scouts, offer his services from time to time when he came with me on one of my almost daily journeys of inspection of the *khassadar* posts along the roads. In a very small degree agricultural advice was available. Most of this however, was not called for. Cash grants were offered for minor improvements; and a visit and a recommendation by me would suffice for those.

In the ultimate analysis however, control over the Mahsuds depended on money. The tribal chiefs, *maliks*, received stipends from the Indian Government. In return they were required to be responsible for the behaviour of the tribesmen. Their emoluments were increased by the grant of contracts: perhaps the mail bus with the royal cypher on its sides; perhaps the supply of potatoes to the military cantonment at Razmak. Failure to fulfill responsibility would incur either direct fines or, indirectly, the withholding of pay or allowances to an amount decided by the Government. In extreme cases of delinquency the result was war. Then the political control of the tribal territory concerned might be transferred from the Governor (in his capacity of Agent to the Governor General for the tribal areas) to the military authorities.

This is of necessity a simplification of what was a very complicated structure. Fortunately there is available to historians the masterly monograph *Mizh* by Sir Evelyn Howell.† This was printed by the Government of India Press in 1931 as a confidential document, and seems to have been published in 1960. It was then reviewed in the *Journal of the Royal Central Asian Society* by Sir George Cunningham. It covers the period from 1848

---

*I once 'inspected' it at the request of the Urmar inhabitants.

†See also Caroe, op cit ch XXIV.

to 1930. The record up to that time was one of recurrent war and variations of policy. Some might say that the use of money as an instrument of pacification was mere bribery. This would be to misunderstand the basis of that policy.

The grant of allowances, subsidies and contracts was primarily aimed at the relief of poverty and the buttressing of the authority of hereditary chiefs. Obviously no policy could be more jejune than, as it were, to throw food to the wolves pursuing the sleigh. Nothing could be more constructive than to build, even if it entailed spending money. A possible alternative policy was that labelled 'close-border'. This at its most extreme would entail absolute occlusion of the border. It could only be a policy of complete sterility at its best. At its worst it would be calculated to perpetuate the chronic poverty of the Mahsuds and to lead to ever more complex reasons for their hostility . . . to say nothing of throwing them into the orbit of Afghanistan. The model of the Roman *limes* seems to have occurred for consideration from time to time, only, quite rightly, to be discarded. The Romans found the method very costly across northern Britain, with little return financially and no guarantee of impregnability. The final solution, that of 'peaceful penetration', was what I found in operation when I joined my post in October 1938.

Up to the end of my time in India the Mahsuds were raiders of the settled districts. Yet Cunningham, reviewing Howell's monograph, put his finger on several paradoxical features of the Mahsud character. He speaks of their grisly record of looting, kidnapping and murdering in the settled districts. There was nonetheless 'something fine in them'. The Brigade Commander of Razmak in my time, Brigadier Lewis, told me that, as a young man commanding in East Africa during the 1914-18 war, he found the Mahsuds (some of them still going in my time) the bravest of the brave.

The controversy about how to deal with the problem may well have abated in the years since 1947, although a friend of mine was murdered outside Sararogha only a matter of weeks after he had joined the service of the new state of Pakistan. The Mahsuds, with all their cleverness, their bravery, their acute sense of humour, even their sense of what we call fair play, often contrived to weaken the good will of those who sought to serve them.

Since 1931 there had at first been a period of peace in Waziristan. Officers from the cantonment of Wana in particular were able in safety to shoot in the surrounding country. In April 1936 people in general first heard the name of Mirza Ali Khan, the Fakir of Ipi. This man was a truly worthless agitator who managed to impress himself, and impose himself, on the somewhat unwarlike tribe called the Daurs. They lived trans-border to the west of Bannu with, as their neighbours, the powerful Tori Khel Wazir clan of which the Fakir was a member. He clearly found the adoption of a religious calling among an ignorant, superstitious and timorous people more materially rewarding than his original employment, which was as an overseer in the provincial Public Works Department. He was a clever opportunist who achieved prominence by exploiting an unhappy affair in Bannu.

In that year there was in Bannu a young Hindu girl who was an heiress in her own right to a small fortune – about £2,000. She fell in love with a young Muslim, eloped with him and, having become a convert to Islam, was married to him according to the rites of that faith. She also received the new name of Islam Bibi. Her Hindu family were outraged. A complaint to the police led to the prosecution of the young man for kidnapping. He was acquitted; but an appeal to the High Court resulted in the reversal of this judgment and an order, among other things, that the girl be returned to her family.

The arc lights were switched to the Daur country. There the Fakir raised the cry of Islam in danger. At the head (as the saying is) of a *lashkar* of Daurs, infused with the bravery of their religious convictions, he moved cautiously across the border. The Bannu brigade at once moved out in his direction. This was enough. They all went back across the border and it appeared that the matter was ended. I was not at that time sufficiently senior to be in any degree involved in the policy which then prevailed. At this interval of time I can only say that in retrospect the policy seems to have been mistaken. It involved breaking the peace of the southern part of the Frontier which had prevailed for some ten years. Be that as it may, the Government of India were persuaded that the insolence of the Daurs must be punished.

There was the additional reason that the Tori Khel Wazirs were apparently unable to control the Fakir, who was conducting a general agitation against the British. The *maliks* asked for military support. The decision was taken therefore, to make a show of strength. The Razmak brigade was to march down the Khaisora River eastwards and join the Bannu Brigade at a place called Bichhe Kashkai in Wazir territory west of Bannu (the full details are given by Elliot).* This operation gave rise to fierce fighting, and sporadic fighting continued into 1937, the war covering areas in both North and South Waziristan. Even in 1938–39 there were what Elliot describes as 'a few small operations'.

---

* See footnote, p73.

The last serious battle took place at Taudah Chineh (warm spring) south of Razmak on the main road on 7 December 1939. Of the Razmak brigade, the 5/8th Punjab Regiment suffered eighty men killed, including their commanding officer. It was my good fortune, since this was in my area as Assistant Political Agent, to have been transferred some six weeks before. The Political Agent, Major J A Dring (later Sir John), described this as a disaster the more serious because of its effects on both the Mahsuds and Wazirs and also because the degree of its seriousness affected vital work in connection with the war with Germany.

I must, however, revert to my arrival at Tank at the beginning of October 1938. I stayed for several days in the *dak* bungalow trying out an ingenious camp bed with attachments for a mosquito net which I had bought very shortly before in the more plush conditions of Austin Reed in Piccadilly. It worked very well, as it did later on operations with the army but it did make me feel rather homesick in the Tank *dak* bungalow with the inevitable smell of the civet cats in the roof, and a shade temperature during the day of 106°F. In due course I travelled up to Sararogha.

Many an area in the world is described as a hell on earth. So far as my experience goes, each one deserves the phrase; and I unhesitatingly apply it to the area round Tank and on either side of the road west and north into South Waziristan. The heat, apart from a few weeks in winter, is extreme and merciless. The so-called Gomal wind, named from the Gomal pass to the west of Tank, each year begins to blow in spring. It shrivels the scented and fertile gardens overnight as if it were a flame-thrower. Into the holocaust go the sweet and delicate little flowers which occasional winter rains from Persia have enabled to carpet the desert. Village women must bring water from many miles away in the height of summer as water-courses and wells dry up. Strings of stunted donkeys, appearing to walk in a stupor, carry each a goatskin of water on either side. The women must have great endurance, but little pleasure in life what with poverty, hunger, thirst and child-bearing. Then slowly the ground rises as the road crosses the border to the country of the Bhitannis, and my own first stop was Jandola, the headquarters of the South Waziristan Scouts. This was a very well conceived oasis (apart from its military importance on which I neither was nor am qualified to speak).

I made my duty calls on the Commandant and the Adjutant and the officers' mess, and then finished my journey – some twenty miles to Sararogha. My room and bathroom on the second storey on the eastern side of this stone fort were my home for the next thirteen months. My own activities during that time were of no importance except in so far as

I gained an intimate knowledge of one so-called tribal area which was of value when I occupied a more senior post later.

On my first evening I heard several shots in the river-bed far below the east side of the fort. Since they did not appear to have been fired at the fort, I was not much interested; but at breakfast next morning Captain Babington, the commanding officer and the only member of the officers' mess besides myself, told me what they were. A local householder had killed his wife for infidelity. This, by almost general Pathan custom, was more a matter of honour than a mere venial crime. It is understandable in a barbarian community and is not unknown in civilised communities. I had not however, been an ear-witness to such an occurrence before – an occurrence which in trans-border society excited no more interest than would the shooting of a useless collie by a shepherd in the Scottish borders.

In time I came to have great admiration for the Mahsuds in many respects. This was the usual effect on British officers of the Indian Army, of the South Waziristan Scouts and of the Political Service. Yet it was a feeling which held me as it were in spite of myself. They were brave. They had great physical endurance. They could enjoy a joke. They were very shrewd and could debate like lawyers. In many cases they were completely, and indeed devotedly loyal not only to their own faith and tribal law but even to insignificant individuals like myself.

To illustrate the last point first, in the summer of 1939, contrary to all orders, I gave a lift to an army officer from Razmak to Jandola. He was extremely anxious to get down into the settled districts. Unfortunately 'my' road – south from Razmak to Jandola, whence it led beyond to Dera Ismail Khan – was closed to all military traffic. The stipulated exit from Razmak was eastwards to Bannu, and for that the road had to be 'opened' by the posting of army and militia pickets along its entire length from Razmak to the border. My friend did not wish to wait for a 'road open' day; so he and I took a chance. I delivered him at Jandola in mid-afternoon and got back to Sararogha before 5.00 pm.

Next morning one of my visitors was a *khassadar* of the rank of *havildar.* He embarked on a laboured story of some villainy which had been plotted for the day before. Whatever the villainy, it was clear that he had been party to it, otherwise he would not have known about it. Since it had not reached fruition he was now, as in duty bound, reporting it. For this he could expect Rs 5 from my allocation for informers. I suggested that this was the case. He agreed. He then told the truth. He had been one of a gang who had laid an ambush on the road in the hope of bagging a British officer. At this point he became quite excited. The miscreants heard a car coming. They rose from their supine positions and took up positions behind rocks above the road, a car came into view and a groan of disappointment rose, 'It is only the *chhota*'. That was me, the junior. As Mahsuds they would not shoot a sitting bird unless there was some profit involved. So they relaxed. I gave him his Rs 5.

The Mahsud men were, however, very treacherous on occasion and very cruel. There were some very nasty occurrences in the fighting of 1919 and after, which I prefer not to specify. These provoked some atrocious reprisals. Of the women I cannot speak. I never spoke to one or even saw one unveiled. The little girls were extremely pretty. Some evidence of the women's nature came to me from two Hindus who were kidnapped from Dera Ismail Khan district in the summer of 1939. They were held for some weeks (unknown to me) in a village near Razmak. A military intelligence officer in Razmak, who spoke no Pashtu, discovered this and was good enough to tell me. Before any action could be taken on this information, the Hindus escaped one night and reached the south gate of Razmak cantonment before daylight. We took statements from them, and among other things they said that the women had been kind to them in their captivity.

Of the cruelty of the men there could be no doubt, although in my time I never heard of any torture. Of an insensate lust to kill however, there was ample evidence; and also of killing in a callous, cold-blooded way designed to achieve a particular purpose. An outlaw called Sher Ali – and that means that he had placed himself beyond the protection even of Mahsud tribal law (*riwaz*) – kidnapped three Hindus in Dera Ismail Khan district in 1939. I knew the man. He belonged to the Manzai section of the Mahsuds, and at one time early in 1939 he went down to Tank to have an interview with the Political Agent and make his peace.

As chance would have it, I was also in Tank at the time and offered to give him and a companion a lift back as far as Sararogha. They accepted; and of course it was very interesting to me to be able to drive fairly slowly and talk at length to such desperate characters. By chance a water-course between Manzai and Jandola was in spate as the result of a thunderstorm higher up. I tried to drive through and failed, with the plugs flooded. There was nothing for it but to walk the remaining three miles to Jandola. The question was how to play this awkward hand.

Quickly I told my orderly that he and I and Sher Ali would do the walking. My orderly had his rifle. Sher Ali had his. I took the rifle in a firm manner from the colleague, and somewhat to his mystification gave him in exchange my pistol. This, I said, was a weapon wherewith to defend the car if any Bhitannis were to approach with evil intent. More than that, it had belonged to my father, which was quite true. It was a very nice little .38 Smith and Wesson with an ebony grip. I expected it back as soon as he was relieved of his responsibility.

All went well. Sher Ali, Maule Khel the orderly and I arrived not long after at the gates of Jandola, I weighed down by an outlaw's firearm and the ammunition for it in a belt. A breakdown lorry soon brought the car. After lunch we resumed our northward journey. My pistol was back in my pocket. Sher Ali and colleague were set down at a certain point and I never saw him again.

I did not derive much benefit from our meeting. Later in the summer, when Sher Ali kidnapped the three Hindus from Dera Ismail Khan district, it was only to find that, in accordance with government policy he was to get no ransom for the captives. He brought the three unfortunates down onto the main road near Sararogha under cover of night. He sat them in the catch-water drain on the east side of the road and shot them. I was elsewhere at the time, but one of my staff told me that these decent merchants were clothed like coolies and very thin.

The blood feud, called *badi*, which also means 'badness', was endemic among Pathans. In this century most people, including most Pathans of the settled districts, would regard this as a barbarous anachronism. Nowhere was it more virulent than among the Mahsuds. I have lost friends through its operation. Much Mahsud savagery may have been due to inbreeding. It can hardly be a matter of chance that tribal vendettas were formerly so similar a feature of the clans of the Scottish highlands, where inbreeding was general. Only when such mountainous and thinly populated areas are opened up, not only to the dubious benefits of civilisation but also to the manifest benefits of exogamy, do the people seem to become more kindly in their social relations. I have looked on trusted men with revulsion when I learned that they had fresh blood on their hands. If I sound self-righteous, let me admit that on one occasion I was delighted with the working of this evil thing. Matters went as follows.

There was in my time a notorious outlaw named Khonia Khel of the Kikarai sept of the Shaman Khel clan. They were the least civilized Muslims whom I ever met, and the least aware of their disgusting smell. I attended a *jirga** of Kikarai at Sararogha on one occasion, where my senior officer, Major Abdur Rahim Khan, was conducting the annual distribution of allowances to the *maliks* and hearing the general petitions of the sept. I was puzzled by two things. First, he did not hold the *jirga* in the special hall built for the purpose at some distance from the fort, he held it in an open veranda inside the walls. Secondly, he was bearing a

* A tribal gathering; or in legal disputes a tribal jury or panel of assessors.

handkerchief sodden with eau-de-cologne. I soon regretted that I had no such protection. In vain I smoked cigarettes throughout the proceedings. The unwashed warriors wearing, in the hot weather, insufficiently cured sheep-skin waistcoats with the wool on the inside were the stronger.

Khonia Khel was one of these. I later came to the view that he was a homicidal maniac, this being the result of meeting him face to face. After his biggest success, the ambush of a military convoy in the Shahur Tangi in April 1937, he had been able to boast of nearly one hundred and twenty deaths to his credit including ten or eleven officers of the British and Indian armies. Apart from his sporadic paramilitary exploits and his personal blood feuds, he took up as a profitable sideline the profession of hired assassin.

One of his exploits was perhaps typical. A certain Wazir from North Waziristan approached him and offered him money to kill any member of the family of another Wazir with whom he had a blood feud. Khonia Khel accepted the offer. In due time he arrived one day at the house of the man who was to be the target. He begged protection. He was, he said, in a desperate situation owing to his various blood feuds, and for the moment he must beg to be accepted as a *hamsayah*.* The request in Pathan society is irresistible and it was granted. A few days later, while Khonia Khel was lounging about outside the house, it happened that all the men were away about their business. He took his opportunity. There were two small children playing near him. He seized them in turn by an ankle and beat their brains out on the ground. When the men returned he was several miles on his way to his home in the Kikarai country.

As time went on it seems as if he found murder to be rather hard work. He made indirect advances to the political authorities therefore, with a view to making his peace with the Government; and in no time at all, in accordance with a policy in which I could never see any sense, all was forgiven. Not only that, but he was brought on to the Government payroll with minor rank in the *khassadars*, the right to nominate two or three, which meant his relations, and so on. It was this creature whose hand I must shake when he thought it appropriate to visit me at Sararogha. I resented this deeply; but I found a horrid fascination in looking at him.

He was something under six feet tall, well proportioned and lean. His complexion was of the light brown shade always described in 'wanted by the police' notices as 'wheat'. His eyes were dark brown marbles with the whites showing all round. They were never still. Nor was he. He could not, of course, bring his rifle into a personal interview, and without it he

* One who lives in the shade of another's protection.

clearly felt uneasy, especially if we were meeting (as I always tried to do in the case of Kikarai visitors) on an open verandah at ground level. Small arms would be of no use to him in the event of an ambush, and he would hardly be bothered at that stage to conceal a knife or a pistol with a view to shooting or stabbing me. His honeymoon with the authorities was still simmering. So he would sit looking this way and that, the hands restless without the butt of a weapon to clamp on, exchanging meaningless remarks until I could tactfully end the nonsense.

It is with satisfaction that I record that he died at Sararogha. I was absent at the time and can only write what my *tahsildar* told me when I returned. Khonia Khel had been down to Tank and was returning to South Waziristan by the lorry carrying His Majesty's mails. He must alight at Sararogha and complete his journey by many miles on foot to the north. As he got off the bus, some friends told him that three blood feud enemies were awaiting him in the bazaar. This was the collection of small, stone-built huts on the western side of the plateau where travellers might buy tea, cigarettes etc. Most men would have returned to the mail bus and taken a safer way home. Khonia Khel fell into a cold fury. He went from shop to shop with his rifle at the hip and his finger on the trigger. Soon he came to the low door inside which the three avengers were sitting. They shot him dead before his eyes had adapted themselves to the relative darkness; and they accomplished an awkward escape in a most nimble manner.

Unfortunately they had committed this venial crime in an area where the law applied, namely the environs of the fort. It was my responsibility, therefore, to summon them for trial by *jirga* under the Frontier Crimes regulation. They pleaded guilty, which made the verdict of the *jirga* a formality, and I fined them a few hundred rupees each. They paid up, but they were very cross. In all the circumstances I sympathized.

As a final example of savagery I would mention an event of the summer of 1939. The Mahsuds described what was done as a *khai*, a word which I never heard before or after. It seems to imply extermination. A small number of inter-related men – men of no possessions – conspired to acquire by inheritance the house and land of another branch of the family. To this end they lay in wait one night outside the *burj** of their kinsmen, which was of course bolted and barred. Soon after dawn a door was opened and a woman came out. Her they knifed, and then rushed the house and murdered by rifle or knife every man, woman and child therein, numbering some eight or ten. One woman far advanced in pregnancy,

---

* Towered house.

contrived to slip away while the enemy were setting fire to the *burj* and still debating the manner of her death.

The men in Ladha Fort saw the smoke of the burning *burj* as the sun rose. They were puzzled at first. Then the news was brought to them, including that of the woman who escaped and who had been given asylum by a clansman living over a mile away. She must have been strong and brave to outwit the enemy and outstrip them over the loose shale and through the *chert** bushes which clothe those steep mountain-sides. And then a few weeks later she gave birth to a son. The child became the heir to the property, so that the crime was committed in vain.

In justice I must record that no single Mahsud to whom I spoke had anything but condemnation for what had been done. The fact that they had a word for it seems to indicate that, at least in the past, it had a place in their social organization. In 1938, however, a tribal *jirga* not only condemned the deed and decreed that the culprits should not benefit from it, but also outlawed them in much the same sense of the word as applied to it in mediaeval England.

In December 1938 my first chance occurred to accompany a military column on active service. The Razmak brigade moved out of its cantonment on a progress intended to impress upon the Mahsuds in general and the Manzai *maliks* in particular that the Government of India would not tolerate the activities of certain outlaws. The brigade first moved south along the Razmak–Jandola road, and reached Sararogha on the second day. There had been no substantial opposition, but the wild and precipitous nature of the country south of Taudeh Chineh had provided Mahsud sportsmen with an irresistible chance to practise their musketry. No harm was done. My superior officer, Major Abdur Rahim Khan, the Political Agent, accompanied the column as far as Sararogha. There his feet gave out, and to my delight he ordered me to take his place for the remainder of this flag-showing campaign.

First it was necessary to work out what baggage I needed. Chandu radiated disapproval when it was explained to him that we must travel light. Yes, one camel must carry all. Even so my tent was of 160 lb weight, which was about twice the size of the Brigade Major's; and my spare clothes were contained in a wardrobe suitcase from Austin Reed. It was accompanied by the camp-bed which would at each camp be sunk in an excavation equal to itself in dimensions. The soil so excavated would be piled all round the edges; and so one could sleep in complete safety from snipers.

---

* Similar to holly.

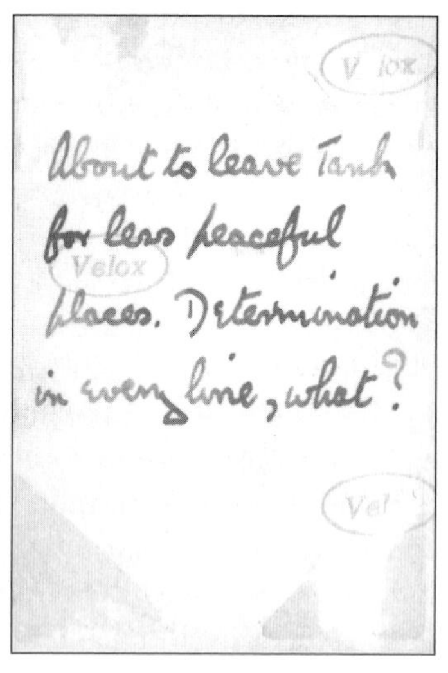

Norval ready for patrol

My military colleagues knew nothing of these solecisms on the first day when I rather timidly reported to Brigade Headquarters. I was an inconspicuous figure, or so I hoped. Like all British officers on active service on the Frontier with Indian troops, my head was nicely crowned with a *safa* (a length of khaki muslin) wound round a *qula* (a conical cloth cap). Below that was a face weathered to much the same colour, descending to the normal Frontier Corps uniform of grey *mazri* (woven cotton) shirt and knitted khaki sweater. At the other extreme were sandals called *chaplis* worn over khaki stockings supplemented by grey socks rolled down over the ankles.

It was the part in between which caused me a measure of anxiety. During most of the year it would have been covered by immaculately laundered khaki shorts. Winter in Waziristan however, is perishing cold. This point had flashed into my mind some months before when, walking along The High at Oxford, my attention had been caught by something in the window of Burton the Tailors: this was a pair of plus fours at five shillings to clear. I bought them. They did me well. The cloth was hard and difficult to identify. They were more plus ones or so than plus fours. But they were warm and no one seemed to notice.

That day the brigade moved some eleven miles south, still along the road, to a small post called Kotkai. This was usually occupied by a company of *khassadars*, but was taken over for the night to house Brigade HQ. The progress was quiet until the rearguard, spread out on the level straight mile which was the end of the journey, came under heavy rifle fire from the east across the river, the Takki Zam. A picket on the slopes above the river-bed was strongly attacked, and the rearguard itself was held up.

In the middle of this Chandu arrived. He had insisted on my escort lorry leaving Sararogha during the morning with my equipment (a she-camel with her owner was waiting at Kotkai). Finding the column held up by what he regarded as irrelevancies, and since he was on good terms with my driver, they simply went on, blowing the horn. He spotted me standing on a knoll by the roadside. The lorry stopped. He emerged, manifestly put out, and came up to me quite fast. In this hand he held a packet of sandwiches, in that a flask of milk. We knew one another pretty well, and he rather brushed off my thanks. 'But', I said, 'You have had a dangerous trip.' 'Dangerous? Oh! Yes, you mean that fellow in front of me. Yes, he got a bullet in his thigh. But there wasn't any more than that.'

Shortly after that, the picket mentioned above signalled that it was in serious trouble, and the Brigadier sent in a company of Gurkhas to relieve it and bring in the casualties. He also told me to convey orders to a mountain battery, which was stationary a short distance up the road, to open fire on the enemy beyond the picket. These were, according to my information, some fifteen men ensconced in a dry water-course. The officer commanding the battery, a subaltern whom I knew, was delighted and proceeded to shout terse and rapid orders. First however, he told me to stand by. Thereafter, with the guns firing as fast as they could just beside us, conversation was impossible.

In dumb show the wireless mule, an enormous beast loaded with two very heavy-looking panniers, was called forward. One pannier undoubtedly contained radio equipment. A sepoy was standing beside it, earphones in place, with an aerial vertical beside him. The other pannier was different. Under the deft hands of an unmistakable mess servant (his field uniform was all wrong) there first appeared two light folding chairs; then a table on which two cups and two cans of beer were set. A three-course lunch from tins followed, which gave the mess servant plenty of time to prepare the coffee. The guns were still raising hell as I left, gesticulating my gratitude. Later my friend explained that officers and men of the Royal Artillery were enjoined to regard the battery as their home, and it was a duty to put this into practice. Two lunches that day made up for the fact that there was no afternoon tea served at Brigade Headquarters.

Soon after I had again taken up my post at Brigade HQ (ie lurked some ten paces to the rear), the Brigadier decided that he would walk back to the rearguard to hurry it up a bit. A young officer of my acquaintance had first been sent with a message of some sort (I did not hear what). For the purpose he borrowed, God knows where, a white horse on which he clattered away at a strong canter. Later he confided to me that he hoped 'to get something' for this feat. This asinine remark consoled me and warmed my feelings towards him. There was one man in the column who was a bigger fool than I was.

In due course Brigade HQ moved back northwards along the road. By now the gunnery had died away. The very brave sepoy in the picket, who had for several hours, though wounded, continued his semaphore messages under fire without intermission, had been relieved with his companions and evacuated by the ruthlessly efficient Gurkhas. As we drew near to the central point of the attack we began to pick our steps, and slither somewhat, on a carpet of expended .303 cartridge cases on the tarred road. A section of armoured cars provided the clue to the origin of this prodigality. The Brigadier barked an enquiry to the effect that he wished to know what had been going on. A prosperous-looking English sergeant stood, visible from the waist upwards, in the turret of his armoured car, saluted and said, 'Just spraying the 'ill-side, sir'.

It would be pleasant to finish the account with that sort of idiocy and to pass quickly over the dead and the wounded in the fight over the picket. I still remember however, a Gurkha with his jaw shot away at close range from a *burj* as he was on his way to relieve the picket. Then as the sun went down word came to me from a picket of my *khassadars* which I had placed on the high ground far away to the east. The intention was to prevent exactly what had happened in the matter of the holding up of the rearguard of the column, that is, infiltration by the enemy to a point where they could be dangerous.

My men had failed. They may have not even tried, being Mahsuds. But they really were unlucky when an Indian Air Force plane, which up to that time had been swanning around at an altitude which made army co-operation impossible, dropped a bomb unerringly on the picket. One dead, three wounded, was my message. The Government paid full compensation. I was undeservedly given some credit for this by the Mahsuds; but the death and injuries were to no purpose.

Next day we turned west up a stream to a place called Ahmadwam (*wam* means a junction of streams). This time there was no fighting and I had time to watch the efficiency with which the Royal Engineers (with their Indian equivalents such as the Madras Sappers and Miners), the RIASC, and the staff officers in general, set about their business. There was, for example, the necessity of providing water and fodder for 1500 mules. Water came gushing from pumps into great storage tanks which until then had been folded waterproof material. The fodder came as loads on camels.

Too late I discovered that it was issued in three days' rations at a time. All that night I drowsily listened from time to time to my she-camel munching. It was only the next evening that an indignant staff captain told me that the pampered jade (or words to that effect) had consumed her three days' allocation between dusk and dawn. The whole operation in most respects was perfect. Only two things went wrong. Towards sunset an aircraft flew over and dropped a small container attached to a small parachute. This was understood to be messages for the Brigadier. I did note however, that confusion was caused by the breaking of a bottle of gin on landing.

The second mishap occurred in the realm of the occult. 'I tell the tale that I heard told' said A E Housman (*A Shropshire Lad*). Likewise do I. Some Gurkhas elected to sleep in a Muslim cemetery. Interested parties of another faith gave warning against such disrespect for the dead, and indeed they were justified in the event. In the early morning hours one of the Gurkhas sprang from his lair and ran about in circles swearing in *Pashtu*.* Next morning he was still feeling poorly. His shelter had been the tomb of a Muslim *pir* – a holy man.

Now we turned north. From Razmak to Kotkai had meant a drop from 6,000 feet to about 3,000 feet. The rest of the march would be uphill over country never very fertile and in mid-December stony, barren and colourless. The camp was to be near a village called Karama at about 5,500 feet. At this village my orders were to supervise the burning down of the houses of three of the specially troublesome outlaws whose activities had, among other reasons, led to the operations of this column. The punishment, a recognized tribal one, had been agreed with the *maliks*. One of these was Colonel Shah Pasand, Langar Khel, a very prominent man, who actually lived in Karama. He enjoyed, with a handful of' others, an allowance of Rs 100 per month from the Government of India and received his due share of military and civil contracts.

At this time he was of mature age, tall, rather stout, very strongly built, with rosy cheeks, hazel eyes and brown hair. His military rank came from the Afghan army. He was one of the many Mahsuds who, in 1929, supported Nadir Khan in his successful campaign to achieve the throne of Afghanistan. No doubt he was (like many other Mahsuds, Wazirs and Afridis) also receiving something from Nadir Khan's successor in 1938. He

* ie the soft southern form of Pakhtu.

once showed me an exquisite jewel, without explaining how he came by it. It was the star of an order of nobility (not recently polished), with a Persian inscription, which he had acquired in those days. When I met him he seemed to be a man who honoured his contracts.

When I reached Karama (the camp), smoke was ascending from houses in the village about three-quarters of a mile away to the east. This could quite well have been coming from bundles of straw, and I clearly could not carry out my orders by observing smoke from where I stood. I had at the same time to bear in mind what my superior officers on the Frontier had many times hammered into me, namely that no one cared tuppence if I personally got myself killed through neglecting elementary precautions. What people in authority really resented was the clearing up of the consequences of a British officer being killed.

I reported to the Brigadier, therefore, that I now proposed, if he approved, to go over and see that the job was being done properly. He approved. I then asked whether he had any orders to give about an escort. He did not like the idea. He remarked, quite rightly, that I was supposed to be going on safe conduct under the protection of the *maliks*; and I was content with this. I had covered my tracks. At the last minute however, he said that I had better have a platoon of South Waziristan Scouts. I saluted, moved off to find my friend Captain Farquharson and asked him if he could provide a platoon. This young man not only did so but also insisted on bringing it himself. I never saw or had news of him again after 1939; but then he lived up to his name – a cheerful, fearless Highlander, somewhat irresponsible but, alas, no trace of the Highlands in his speech.

We had to make haste as the winter afternoon was drawing on. At the last moment a subaltern of the Royal Signals came up and asked if he might come along too. I did not know him well, but he was clearly a man of character, probably having had as little to do on this journey hitherto as I had. So he came. And off we went at about 5 mph. On the outskirts of the village we were met by Shah Pasand and the other *maliks*. They were understandably firm that the escort platoon should stay outside the village. This was fortunate. I would not have dreamed of taking some fifty riflemen into the narrow lanes of a Mahsud village, dominated by the high houses of which each was a fortress, but I was spared the necessity of saying so. I saw that the houses of the three miscreants were indeed burning nicely, and I was in the act of taking my leave of Shah Pasand and his colleagues when he insisted that we three officers should partake of his hospitality.

Refusal was out of the question, but by now I really was uneasy. The lanes were congested with Mahsuds armed with rifles and knives. They looked very cross, which was understandable. And now we had to go through a door into a courtyard, through the courtyard and up several steps onto the verandah of the house. The angry-looking men followed us in, sat down and filled the courtyard. There were more outside as the smoke from the burning houses wandered about in the windless air. Shah Pasand's household began handing out, without actually revealing themselves, the delicious green tea, the iced cakes and the conventional hard-boiled eggs. We were sitting ducks, and I literally thought that we would very soon be shot. I asked the Signals officer in a whisper whether his revolver was loaded. The cheerful answer was no.

Farquharson was too far away to hear the whispered question, but I could see that in fact his .45 Colt was loaded but his holster was buttoned up. It really did seem as if we were for it. I treated the audience to a few words to the effect that it gave the Government no pleasure to insist upon tribal punishments on outlaws . . . and so on while I cracked hard-boiled eggs on my knee and peeled and ate them. The third egg was not hard-boiled and made a serious mess on my knee on impact. This raised a loud laugh which relaxed all tension. Shah Pasand had not apparently been conscious of tension anyway; and away we went, after the proper exchange of courtesies, back to the camp. Some desultory sniping of the camp closed the day.

This happened on 18 December 1938, my thirty-second birthday. The following day's march was uneventful and the night undisturbed. We marched next morning at what the army called first light, ie in pitch darkness, after a very cold night. I slept in my clothes under blankets. One of my colleagues was made of sterner stuff. He was a young RAF officer attached to Brigade HQ as Air Liaison Officer. His duties, like mine, occurred occasionally and sometimes simply did not occur – in a snow-storm for example. As I went to my tent he was standing in the light of a hurricane lamp stripped to the waist and performing thorough ablutions in cold water.

As the light came it was possible to see the column converging on a narrow re-entrant valley into the mountains to the north. We were to ascend from 5,500 feet to 7,000 feet, and descend again to 5,500 feet. We would camp that night at Ladha, where there was a newly-built fort of the South Waziristan Scouts. It was country which I knew to some extent then, and which I came to know better, as the result of frequent *gashting* (patrolling) with the Scouts.

Of this category of exercise I remember clearly a *gasht* led by Lt Neville Williams, commanding Ladha fort. Clearly the men must be kept fit, but that day I came to understand how fit. In four hours, starting at 9.00 am, we moved south and climbed straight up to the top of the 7,000 foot ridge. There we turned west for a matter of eight miles in a straight line, but with several ascents and descents in order to cross breaks in the line of the heights. Then came the final descent to the stony river bed which led eastwards back to Ladha. Estimated on a point to point basis we had covered sixteen miles. There had been a twenty minute halt at one point, when I recall eating raisins. There had at no point been anything but very rough and steep ground and the air at that height is thin. The Scouts were fully loaded as riflemen on active service. I was carrying a pistol and a walking stick. Williams led all the way. My hand-picked *khassadars* fell out very early on. I brought up the rear with the more or less middle-aged *Subehdar.* He was at least still smiling.

This could not be said of me on that morning of 20 December 1938. I did not know what measures the Brigadier had taken to guard our flanks. It must have been an acutely difficult tactical problem; but the ground was so steep that the problem was almost certainly more difficult for the potential enemy. We were soon marching along a track about twelve feet wide worn out of a mountain side by the feet of men and pack animals. On our right the ground fell away almost sheer for several hundred feet. On our left it ascended likewise.

At one stage the whole column came to a standstill and the Brigadier went forward to find out the reason. An unfortunate camel had died on the ascent. This I might have passed over lightly but for the fact that protruding rearward over its rump was a rather nice suitcase, black, with my name inscribed on it in prominent white letters. Chandu seemed to have the situation in hand; so I, having heard the Brigadier (lucid as always) order the carcass to be thrown over the edge, walked delicately backward and joined the rearguard. I did leave information with the Brigade Major as to where I might be found,

When the baggage train reached the top of the col, my embarrassment was soon forgotten in watching hundreds of heavily laden mules embark on the descent. The ground was still steep, but not so precipitous as to require the type of track by which we had come up. The mules, accompanied rather than controlled by their sepoys, slithered down at an exhilarating speed on their hind-quarters. Everyone in the train was hilarious; and it was as well for the enemy that they had not taken up any positions on the way. Nothing can stop a mule train when it really gets going. The brigade bivouacked outside Ladha Fort. I spent that night in my quarters in the fort itself. This was not from fear of Brigadier Lewis but because I wanted a bath, not having had one since leaving Sararogha.

Nor was it much warmer in the fort than outside where, during the night snow began to fall heavily. 'First light' was an even more than usual misnomer next day. Cracking rather feeble jokes with the guard who let me out of the fort at 5.00 am, I found my way in pitch darkness back to Brigade Headquarters. Off again we went, along a road this time, and also this time with the Brigadier leading the column. We reached a point east-north-east near where the road joined the main road from Razmak south to Sararogha, Jandola and British India. There he took stance on a small eminence to watch and ensure that the column went through on the final day's march to Razmak.

There we stood for several hours in steady snowfall. Some of us tried to sing Christmas carols, which much amused the Gurkhas as they went past and to which the Brigadier did not object. When the rearguard arrived we joined it. Visibility all day was not much more than fifty yards, which made the normal tactical posting of pickets impossible; and one could only hope that any potential enemy would regard an attack on a closely ordered column as a waste of time. This seemed to be so.

Nonetheless when we reached the main road to Razmak the Brigadier led us off the road eastwards and down into a watercourse some forty yards wide with thirty foot banks on either side. Up this we marched, sometimes calf-deep in snow-water, for the few remaining miles to the south gate of Razmak. When I was released and reached my quarters, Chandu was there, a fire blazing and a bath and high tea ready. Never one to consider anything but his duty as he conceived it, namely my comfort, he had the previous evening telephoned my office in Sararogha from Ladha. He called for the presence of my escort lorry, complete with escort, at Ladha at a certain hour. While I was paddling up the river, he had bowled past in the lorry along the main road and preceded me by several hours.

Not all columns were so fortunate. My next experience was in March 1939 in the valley of the Shaktu river in North Waziristan. I would much like to forget it; and certainly I would not wish to record its details even thirty-seven years later. I saw at a distance of a few feet eleven tribesmen, who had surrendered to me on terms, bayoneted to death by a guard from a proud regiment of the Indian Army.

This brigade had been particularly unlucky from the start. It was the 1st Infantry Brigade, stationed normally at Abbottabad in the north-east corner of the Frontier Province. It did not, therefore have any comfortable quarters to which it might return as was the case with, say, the Razmak or Bannu Brigades. When I was ordered to join it, it had been snowbound for several weeks in its perimeter camp in the upper reaches of the Shaktu valley. My journey to join it entailed travelling north from Sararogha to

Razmak, then north-east on the steep descent towards the border and Bannu district. On this road stood the Tochi Scouts' post of Dosalli. Here I was to take off again southwards to the Shaktu river.

For three days the snow confined me to the fort. My orders were not to go on foot by the unmetalled road among the hills. I was to await a section of armoured cars which would escort me and my lorry to the column. After three idle and comfortable days in Dosalli I was very ready to face the open-air when the armoured cars arrived. An armoured car led, my lorry came next and an armoured car came last. It really was unnecessarily pompous for a junior political officer doing much the same as he did every day of his life except Sundays. That it was also not very helpful was soon shown.

The leading armoured car came to a stop at a point where the narrow track had been carved out of the gently curving side of an almost sheer mountain. Silence fell. My four Mahsud orderlies and I got out of our lorry and walked forward. From the closed turret of the armoured car came nothing but unintelligible voices. That however, was immaterial. Plain to see was a barrier of stones about two feet high across the road. While guns traversed in a menacing way through 180° from the armoured cars (the other 180° were too steep for that sort of thing) we five, reinforced by Chandu, disgusted as usual, proceeded to dismantle the barrier by hand.

Quite soon one of my orderlies announced that he had found what we had all expected, a primitive land-mine two or three pounds in weight. The man was not conspicuous for quick apprehension. He was like a small boy showing a half-pound trout to his father. Had I not been quick he would have passed it to me. He took the point when I said that it would be better to throw it into the abyss. With a cheerful cry he threw it and was answered by a rather dull boom.

Soon afterwards we reached the camp-site. The armoured cars were able to turn round and go home, and my lorry had to go with them. This would not have mattered were it not for the fact that the Brigade, taking advantage of a fairly fine day, had disappeared. It was clear however, that it could only have gone down stream, that is, eastwards. Desultory shooting, as when sportsmen walk up partridges through root crops guided us. Moreover my luggage was very much more austere than it had been in December. We were fortunate to pass through the rearguard without casualties, and about noon I reported to the Brigadier.

The Brigade spent several nights in this next camp, though not wholly voluntarily. On the day after the arrival there the Brigade began what was intended to be a substantial advance down the course of the Shaktu. Fighting started as soon as light permitted. The Brigadier, unable to walk owing to kidney trouble, was completely unperturbed as he rode on a white horse (always a white horse!) with bullets whistling about his ears from time to time. Then we reached a point in the river bed where there was a rock formation involving a three-foot drop. The column included some three hundred heavily loaded camels. These wretched animals could not negotiate it.

I do not know whether anyone had ever thought of this unexpected obstacle. It was not marked on any map available to me; and in any case North Waziristan was not an area in which I had set foot more than a few days before. The Brigadier was, however, inclined to question my competence in not having obtained this information, especially since it necessitated putting the column into reverse early in the afternoon and returning to our previous camp. It was this move, unexpected by the enemy, which led to the unhappy matter of the slain prisoners. They were cut off in a deep and narrow watercourse.

A British officer and two men of the regiment concerned had been killed in an attempt to dislodge them, and their bodies were lying in full view. The battalion commander sent a runner to fetch me so that I might negotiate for the return of the bodies. His regiment was not one where Pakhtu or Pashtu was spoken. I made the suggestion, which turned out to be an unhappy one, that I might negotiate for the surrender of the enemy as prisoners of war. He agreed, since this would also ensure the recovery of the bodies.

Negotiations proceeded and the enemy emerged led by one of my Mahsud orderlies who had been my go-between. He was assisted by a *lance-naik* (lance-corporal) of the regiment, who happened to be a Pathan, in carrying the weapons of the prisoners – rifles and knives. I took the precaution of holding my pistol in my hand, and my orderly and his colleague shed the motley collection of weapons to one side. The prisoners dropped the wounded man they were carrying and ran to me crying for mercy. They clasped my knees. They did the ritual clasping of the beard. The point was that my guarantee of safety as prisoners of war was inoperative since the guard, drawn up on the other side of the watercourse, was about to kill them.

The prisoners were right. The guard drew in with bayonets fixed. The leading prisoner turned his back on me, drew a knife from his clothes somewhere, ran on to the leading soldier and killed him with a blow inflicted with his right hand striking over the left shoulder and backwards into the heart. The same prisoner turned in his tracks and found himself faced by the Colonel who had jumped down into the watercourse intending to stop the killing. The Colonel felled him with a right hook.

They fell together. The Colonel's men leapt to his rescue and, since he was on top of his man, probed with their bayonets past him into the enemy. One bayonet went through the Colonel's left upper arm. Meanwhile the remaining prisoners were all killed by the bayonet. I remember very clearly how not one of them raised a cry; how the soldiers stood back and fired shots into the bodies; and, as the enthusiasm ebbed, ran their thumbs up and down their bayonets as they cleaned off the blood.

It was a relief when I was able to leave this column. A row blew up over the slain prisoners, but at the insistence of the Governor, Sir George Cunningham, fairly generous cash compensation was paid to the bereaved families. I was summoned to Peshawar, having been proposed, in my own interests, for posting to Charsadda sub-division; but this settlement made it safe for me to return to my post in South Waziristan. The Mahsud could sometimes be treacherous, but he had his own quite clear conception of what constituted a breach of faith. The prisoners were killed in circumstances which implied a breach of *itbar*, ie trust or safe-conduct. The Government of India had acknowledged this and played fair. The Governor was the main influence in this, but I had done my share.

The whole episode provided a useful example of Mahsud thinking – and indeed of Wazir and Bhitanni thinking, since one or two of them were among the dead. For me the whole thing finished on the afternoon when I went back via Jandola to Sararogha. At Kotkai some twenty armed men were drawn up across the road. My orderly, Maule Khel, said more or less, 'I told you so. They are here to thank you'. It did not for some moments seem so to me. I quickly decided to receive whatever was coming on my feet, so I stopped the car, got out and walked forward. In my self-centred anxiety I had not until then noticed that these men had their rifles slung across their backs. They came forward and embraced me, and I rather weakly sat down on the offside mudguard of the car.

There were not many weeks in either North or South Waziristan during that time when events of a surprising nature did not occur. I would only describe one more, and that because it related to one of the most prominent Mahsuds, *Subhedar* Major Mir Badshah, Mal Khel. He had conducted himself with distinction in France in the First World War. For some reason which I no longer remember, he came to loggerheads with the Political Agent, Major Abdur Rahim Khan. Information came to me that he would pay cash to the outlaw, Sher Ali, or to anyone else who would kill either Rahim or me. This sort of thing had to be taken seriously in Waziristan, and I arranged my journeys accordingly.

One morning, as I was about to leave Razmak for Sararogha, my Political *Tahsildar* came out and said that Mehr Dil, father of Mir Badshah, wished to speak to me in the office. He was very old and much revered. One does not in such cases do anything but be as courteous as possible. In fact he had absolutely nothing to say as his halting speech went on and on. This made me quite sure that he had been sent by Mir Badshah as a partial, perhaps psychological, alibi, for what was to happen on the road later.

When I took my leave of Mehr Dil I was even quite certain in my mind's eye where the attack would take place. It was a re-entrant curve of the road where a culvert carried off water from the catch-water drains above the road. I had often noted these drains as ideally suited to give cover for an ambush; and in this place the drain above the southern curve of the re-entrant was some four feet deep. In a rather cowardly way I made my escort lorry lead. I did this because it was in fact most unlikely that assassins would fire on their own brethren, while I, moving slowly behind, would be able to see the enemy as they rose to fire down on us. It was unfortunate that their range would be only a few yards.

I slowed down as we approached the left-hand bend and took my pistol in hand. The three orderlies with me in the car protruded their rifle barrels through the windows. And so the scene came into view, with the escort lorry just disappearing round the next corner. I sat back and cursed myself for being over-imaginative and over-apprehensive, for there stationary on the culvert was the car of Lieutenant Wingate, RE, Assistant Garrison Engineer. He was responsible, among other things, for road maintenance in this area. He had spent the previous night in Ladha and had clearly joined the main Razmak–Sararogha road from the west shortly before.

I drew up beside the car with a view to passing the time of day. He was not in it. The radiator and the windscreen were shot to bits. The main battery cable was severed by a bullet. The only occupant was a dead man in the back seat with six or seven bullets in him. (We learned later that he was a *khassadar* of the Urmar tribe. They are not Mahsuds, but live in Kaniguram in Mahsud country and are regarded with a semi-religious respect. They also occupy three villages in Peshawar District. This incautious killing cost the killers a lot of money under tribal law.)

Most men who have been exposed to this sort of thing know how hard it is to control one's fury and take appropriate action. So far as I remember, my escort and I did so. A *khassadar* was observed in the distance and tried to flee but was caught and brought to me. He was a youth substituting for the regular man on his road protection. He knew nothing except that there had been some firing. My crude anger evaporated as I saw his terror and I told him to go away, taking his rifle.

We had all (the escort lorry having backed up to join me) realised that, although we had a car and a corpse, we did not have Wingate's vanette with his escort. Probably things were less bad than we thought. So it proved. We brought the dead man with us down to Sararogha and there learned the rest of the story. When the volley from the murderers burst on Wingate's car he was lucky to escape with a glancing wound over one temple. His overseer in the back seat took one in the thigh. The Urmar was killed then and there. The half dozen *khassadars* in the following vanette however, were as staunch as they were competent. Tumbling out of their vehicle they joined Wingate and his companions, who also reacted coolly, and took cover under the downward wall of the culvert. Thence they fired and drove the enemy away. If this should sound somewhat run-of-the-mill, I would repeat that, with the car actually on the culvert, the enemy (about a dozen of them) were firing down at a surprised target at a range of only thirty feet.

I made it known generally that in my view I was the intended objective of this outrage and that Mir Badshah had organized it. This caused him much concern. Some days later he came down as far as the collection of shops on the west side of Sararogha Fort accompanied by some sixty armed clansmen. From there he sent in a message that he wished to swear his innocence on the Quran Sharif, but that he would not come inside the fort to do so.

The post commander, Captain Quigley, and I went outside to meet him. The meeting was cordial. By various quite cheerful lines of persuasion he was induced to come to my personal quarters. There one of my staff brought a copy of the Quran Sharif wrapped in a silk cloth and the oath was taken. His reverence for the Book seemed to be profound and I found myself believing him. I am glad that we parted on good terms. It could very possibly have been the outlaw Sher Ali who was the culprit, and I hope it was. Mir Badshah had many merits, and in the war which was then imminent he rendered further good service to the British Government as a recruiting officer, rising to the rank of Major.

I served for a further two months in South Waziristan after the war broke out on 5 September 1939. One more farcical event occurred. A message was sent to me from a battalion commander of a certain regiment of the Indian Army asking me to arrest about a dozen Mahsuds who had deserted. They had in fact been on leave on 3 September and had decided prudently to assess the merits or otherwise of becoming involved in someone else's war. I had, of course, no means of arresting them. Even if I had been able to send anyone to do so into their native mountains, those so sent would have been driven out with contumely and rifle fire. Incidentally I have no doubt that I would have been relieved of my post for being so irresponsibly provocative at a time of national crisis.

What I did do was to send a *khassadar* of the clan concerned with a verbal message. This told them of the colonel's 'request' that they would return, coupled with my own embarrassment caused by their failure to do so already. It never occurred to me that there would be any sequel. A few days later, however, as I was driving through the area in question on a routine patrol, I saw a line of very smart troops drawn up by the roadside. They were commanded by a *naik* (corporal) who called them to attention as I got out of the car and reported all present and correct. They had received my message. They were grieved to think that through pure inadvertence they had caused anxiety to their commanding officer and to me. Naturally they wished to put the matter right provided (and this was vital to their case) I would give them a personal letter to the Colonel.

I laughed quite a lot and so after a brief pause did they. I then sat down by the roadside and wrote some drivel, translating as I went along, which they knew quite well to be drivel. Such excuses as that their watches had stopped were unanimously rejected. On the other hand the absence in South Waziristan of calendars in the Pakhtu script seemed worth mentioning. I never met the Colonel, but a letter from him a week or so later showed that he had taken the point.

In early November 1939 I left Waziristan for a post in Peshawar. Even then I kept thinking of the remark which Sir Evelyn Howell recorded in the last chapter of *Mizh*, and which I have quoted at the head of this chapter. A distinguished colleague of his, having read most of the manuscript, said, 'What a record of futility it all is'. On this Sir Evelyn comments, 'The criticism is certainly pungent, but perhaps not penetrating'. His account takes the development of policy and the record of events up to a point only eight years before I went to the Mahsud country, and his summary of what happened in the preceding eighty years concludes with a look to the future.

He finally decided that the Mahsud 'must be trained to take his place in the federation of India. To that, as to Tipperary, is a long, long way to go, but it is the only (possible objective) to which our officers can worthily address themselves'. This objective has to a great extent been achieved in the turmoil of the following forty-five years, although partition of India in 1947 has meant that the Mahsud has dealt with Pakistan, not India as a whole.

So far as my contemporaries and I as Junior Political Officers were concerned, I think we saw the future in the same light as did Sir Evelyn. The 'forward policy', 'peaceful penetration' and other ideas aimed ultimately at bringing the Mahsuds into the economic, cultural and political life of the settled districts, were gradually being developed. Funds

A squad of frontier Khassadars

were meagre and progress in the provision of education, medical aid, agricultural advice etc, varied from agency to agency from the Malakand to Wana. The Mahsuds would not like me to say so, but in fact the fundamental objectives were civilization and peace. In 1939 it seemed fair to say of all the tribal areas *mens agitat molem* (a mind sways the whole mass). Yet the deep roadless valleys and the precipitous, forest-clad mountains of Shawal to the west of Razmak were, when I left India eight years later, still inviolate.

Chapter 8

I SPENT FOUR MONTHS of the winter of 1939–40 in the post of Senior Subordinate Judge in Peshawar. This was the highest court of original civil jurisdiction in the district and in addition exercised minor appellate powers. The cause list was an Augean stables. Some cases had been going on for years. In one case the cross-examination of a single witness had already been spread over eighteen months and was still unfinished. Mindful of the wholesale methods adopted by Heracles in similar circumstances, I decided to follow his example.

At the first hearing of the aforementioned case I announced that I would not permit the cross-examination to continue. In answer to protests I pointed out that it stood to reason that, if counsel could not extract in eighteen months what he wished from a witness, then it was in the highest degree unlikely that he ever would. In answer to further protests, I pointed out that I was acting well within the terms of a certain section of the Civil Procedure Code, which gave civil courts wide powers to act as they thought fit in the interests of essential justice. Finally, in reply to a request for an adjournment pending an appeal against my decision, I pointed out that this was a purely interlocutory order against which, by itself, in terms of Section so-an-so *ibidem*, no appeal lay.

The Peshawar Bar rather enjoyed this sort of thing and in time gave me great help. They knew that my main, possibly sole, objective was to dispense justice. Inordinate delay in the disposal of cases almost invariably entails injustice to one party or another; and accumulation of arrears in any court ultimately results in the complete denial of justice to litigants. The same result occurs if a court is unduly indulgent to perverse litigants.

There was one case where three brothers, members of that legal nightmare, a joint Hindu family, had applied to the court for partition of their property. This consisted largely of a garage, service station and motor sales business. A commissioner had been appointed to frame proposals for the litigants' acceptance and the confirmation of the court. I thought as I read the proposals before my first hearing of the case that they were very good. Two of the brothers also thought so. It then became clear that the sole necessity for the litigation lay in the character of the third brother.

Given time I might have been able to persuade him to be reasonable, but it did not seem likely as one looked at his bitter countenance.

When, after close questioning, he actually objected to the inclusion in one of the other shares of an old bicycle, lacking a chain, I appealed to the other brothers to agree to sacrifice this asset in the interests of quick disposal. They agreed. Then my elderly trilby hat was placed on the desk. The three shares as allocated by the commissioner went into the hat as numbers on slips of paper; but first the two brothers agreed that, if the third brother should again draw the share to which he objected, the ballot should be repeated until he did not. The first ballot sufficed. There was considerable amusement. Next morning the two, who had shaken off their incompatible brother at last, came to my house and offered me as a mark of their appreciation and respect free service of my car whenever and as long as I might be in Peshawar. Today we call that an open-ended liability. I called it bribery and, quite gently, told them to be off, which was anyway what they expected.

At the end of four months no case on the cause list was pending for more than two months. The volume of cases seemed at the time to preclude anything better; and I had done more hours' work in those four months than at any time before in my life. Yet the work had its own occasional special interest. One case in particular stays in my mind. It was brought by a man whom I recognized as the same man who offered the cash bail for the King of Bokhara in September 1935. He was a Bokharan, and he lived in Peshawar, practising as an expert in the assessment of the value of *karakuli* (Persian lamb) skins imported from Afghanistan. His case was brought against a client who refused to pay the fee of so much per skin demanded.

The case took its course. All the evidence was given in Persian with one of the court clerks acting as official interpreter, which I found both agreeable and interesting since in 1930, during my probation year at Oxford, I had taken an elementary examination in the language and had enjoyed the set books. Even Solomon would have found it impossible to reach a rational judgment. After hearing with close attention the diametrically contradictory evidence, I awarded the Bokharan gentleman a modest increase of fee above what his client offered and hoped that the slender arguments in my judgment would not be exposed to the appellate court.

Next morning the Bokharan gentleman was standing on my lawn. It was not easy to converse with him because I had not the necessary fluency in Persian and his Pakhtu was little better. It emerged however, that he was grateful for my decision and wished to present me with a book of which he was the author. It was in his hand and passed to mine with a rapidity which reflected his embarrassment. I read the title on the paper cover: *La Voix de Bokhare Opprimée*. It had been printed and published in Paris in 1921, having been prepared as a petition to the League of Nations and presented by the Wazir-i-Azam, the Prime Minister of Bokhara, who was at that moment taking my leave. The oppression referred to was the abolition of the kingdom of Bokhara by Soviet Russia.*

* Sir Creagh Coen in his book *The Indian Political Service* refers to Bokhara as 'A State whose status in Russia was surprisingly like that of Indian States in India'.

Chapter 9

O fortunatos nimium sua si bona norint.
(O greatly blessed, did they but know their good fortune)
Virgil

EARLY IN 1940 I was asked if I would like to be posted as Administrator of Bastar State. This was a name unknown to most people in the NWFP; and the offer had already been turned down by one who was senior to me. I had heard of it because the post in question had in the past been held by an officer from the Central Provinces. My wife had always agreed that obeying orders came first. The welfare of the family must be adjusted accordingly. We accepted. My acceptance, originally dubious, became a source of greater optimism as we corresponded with Mr E S Hyde, the Administrator at that time, and learned the advantages of the post. This applied especially to the health of the children, regarding which there was little anxiety in northern India, but which had always been at risk in the Central Provinces. In Bastar the Chief Medical Officer, Captain W P S Mitchell of the Indian Medical Department, and his department in general, represented all the knowledge, experience and devotion which anyone could wish.

We sold up most of our few effects. Our journey was complicated but mainly meant that my wife and I went by car while our governess, Else Lohlbach, Chandu and the four children went by train. In those days almost every move seemed to open a new life, and this was one such. The little Hillman Minx which had given me 8,000 miles of travel in England in 1938; which had then done its eighteen hundred miles from Bombay to Sararogha; which had done so many miles on the hilly roads trans-border; and from which I could never remove the blemishes caused by my Mahsud orderlies' rifles as they stuck out of the windows, now started one more journey.

Our first stop was at Lahore, the next in Delhi, where I had to make official calls. Then came the short stage to Agra. We had never seen the Taj Mahal, not having been tourists. We hoped that we would be able to do so under the most favourable conditions, and we were fortunate. No one, apart from ourselves, was there on that March night in brilliant moonlight to see this miracle of human art. The attendants were very affable. They illustrated the occasional echo and other such things as accompany ancient buildings; but they did not chatter in a meaningless way. In the moonlight the lower part of the building was barely visible. The upper part, and especially the dome, seemed to be floating white as fuller's earth against the darkness of the sky. As John wrote in the first chapter of the Book of the Revelation, I felt that 'I was in the Spirit'.

Next day we stopped at noon according to plan at a substantial hotel in Gwalior State. It had been built in a desert to cater for the earliest airmail and passenger service to India. The flying boats would alight on a large lake nearby and the associated activities would depend largely on the hotel. That had all been discontinued about two years before. The lake received no flying boats and the hotel, as the wind in the blinding sunlight blew sand through the rose bushes and up to its steps, saw very few visitors. As I got out of the car, I thought of R L Stevenson's eerie words, 'The wind blew widdershins and the sand-lice hopped between'. In fact I need not have worried. Two admirable servants were in charge. They were the usual cook and bearer and they produced the usual quite adequate meal in no time. We rested and resumed our journey with mutual felicitations. In the late afternoon we reached Bhopal State and the railway station of Bhopal.

Here it was necessary to cross the Narbada river; but, since there was no road bridge, one had to arrange for the car to be put onto a railway truck which would be attached to the rear of the next train. This may have been less a matter of routine than I had expected. Certainly when I went to the appropriate office I was received with some rudeness by the clerk on the other side of the counter. I think he was a Deccani Brahman, but my Marathi was not equal to tackling him in that language. Instead I asked in a half humorous, half humble manner in Hindi, 'Why are you rude to a poor traveller?' His reaction was sharp, 'What do you mean rude? Er, who are you anyway? That is, er, you are speaking Hindi. Who are you? And please sit down. Would you like some *pan* (betel nut for chewing)?' Nothing was too good for me. The orderly who was sent to fetch the *pan* was enjoined to get the kind enclosed in gold leaf, not silver. We conversed for a long time and we parted very good friends, but in spite of his insistence I never told him who I was. I remember him with warm feelings. I knew the stresses, caused by poverty and long hours of work, on railway staff. It was not surprising that they were at times acidulated.

So we were entrained, ourselves and our car, and crossed the bridge over the Narbada as the evening came on. This brought us into my old province once more, to Hoshangabad, headquarters of the district of that name. Next morning we met our family at Itarsi railway junction a few miles away and by one means or another transported ourselves to Pachmarhi, where I had rented a house. After a day's rest my wife and I went on. First there was a night in Nagpur, 160 miles south; then another in Raipur 170 miles east.

No one who has sympathy for poverty and malnutrition, without power to help, should ever look on this land. Our final day covered the stage south, 180 miles from Raipur to Jagdalpur, the capital of Bastar State. Some fifty miles from Raipur, a few miles south of the subdivisional headquarters of Dhamtari, we crossed the border into the small state of Kanker. It was a few minutes before we appreciated a change which we had seen at once. Here there were trees and grass, though very dry in March. This implied less dust and an end to the limitless plains of dry rice fields with the babul (*acacia arabica*) as almost the only verdure. The people seemed better fed. The town of Kanker itself was tidy and shady with mango and pipal trees.

Soon we came to an escarpment, called in India *ghat*, a staircase. We climbed this through forest for a thousand feet and emerged into a different world. Kanker had given us hope. Here there seemed to be fulfillment of hope. The people whom we passed on the road all seemed to be happy. One came to know later that they were poor, mainly illiterate and the victims of tropical endemic diseases. Closer scrutiny would reveal to the anthropologist the fears of the supernatural which haunted the animist. I mention these points in case anyone might think that my enthusiasm had blinded me to unpleasant facts. On a spring day in that year however, all over the land there was a generally content, well-knit tribal society. Field and forest provided all they needed except such items as cloth (of which they wore very little) and salt.

The state and its people have been the subject of two books of the type usually described as definitive. The first of these was *The Maria Gonds of Bastar* by W V Grigson ICS (Oxford 1938). He was Administrator from 1927–31. The second was *The Muria and their Ghotul* by Dr Verrier Elwin (Oxford 1947), the anthropologist closely associated with Merton College. I contributed two appendices to the latter, which were derived from my study of the local dialects. To attempt to summarize studies which cover so wide a field would however, be quite inappropriate; and this account will be confined to my own work in Bastar with a few historical facts to set the scene.

Grigson described Bastar State as 'an almost unknown backwater of the river of Indian history'. The ruling family, represented in my time by the minor Maharaja Pravir Chandra Bhanj Deo (aged 12), was descended from the Kakatia kings of Warangal in what became the domains of the Nizam of Hyderabad. The last king was killed in battle with Mohammedan invaders early in the 15th century. His brother fled north-eastwards across the Godavari river into Bastar, and from his time until well into the 20th century the country was without history and almost without contact with the world outside. The people were supposed to be cannibals. This was strictly speaking untrue. Yet even in my time human sacrifice, inspired by a dark combination of superstition and chronic ill-health, was occasionally practised. This reputation, combined with the absence of roads and the blanket of forest, daunted potential visitors. In 1940 communications had been very greatly improved; but even then, of the state's total area of 15,725 square miles, more than 11,000 square miles were under forest.

The administrative structure was based on that of British India. The area may be illustrated by comparison with the 11,755 square miles of modern Belgium. The population in 1941 was 634,912. In 1957 that of Belgium was over 9 million. On the western and southern sides the land is mainly about 1,000 feet above sea level. Within these limits the land is in the nature of a plateau with an average height of 2,000 feet.

Of the total population the vast majority, about 600,000, were aboriginals speaking Dravidian dialects, very closely related one to another and very inaccurately described by outsiders by the blanket word Gondi. The name Gond was applied to, and accepted by, the relevant aboriginals in the British provinces. I have no knowledge of its origin. The people called themselves Koitor. This is fair enough. It means 'men' or 'people'. In Bastar the main tribes, whose names really were names of remote origin, were the Murias of the north and north-east; the Marias of the north-west, west and centre; and the Dorlas of the south-west and south. The name Maria is unmistakably connected with a word meaning forest. Dorla means lowlander. There was little either ethnic or linguistic difference between any of them; but the Murias were of a very much lighter colour than any of the others. Elwin quite rightly records five other names; but those tribes were numerically small, and barely distinguishable from their cousins.

Apart from the Koitor there were perhaps 40,000 others in Bastar. The Halbas comprised nearly all of these. It is more than probable that they entered the state with the fugitive chief five hundred years before. Their speech was clearly a dialect of Marathi with a synthetic vocabulary of words derived, apart from Marathi, from Gondi, Hindi and Oriya. The rest were Hindus, Muslims, and Europeans in that order.

The first question which I asked of myself was what in the field of administration could I do to develop, as opposed merely to continue, the work of my three immediate predecessors.

W V Grigson (later Sir Wilfred) during his four years as Administrator gave all his considerable ability to the production of his book *The Maria Gonds of Bastar.* His view of the future of the aboriginal population was, in my view, negative. To put it very simply, they were to be protected from the outside world and preserved in their primitive happiness. If I do him injustice in this, I can only say that I never found any evidence to the contrary; and there was factual evidence to support my view. As a minor example, no lawyers from British India were permitted to appear in the courts except with the approval of the Administrator; and in the state itself only one pleader was licensed, he being an innocuous and incompetent Bengali resident. There was some merit in this arrangement. When simple people and hungry lawyers meet over litigation, in the history of the world only the lawyers have profited. So final a ban as this however, prevented any preparation of the simple people, and provided no inoculation against the inevitable intrusion, sooner or later, of modern civilization.

A more formidable barrier was his prohibition on entry to the area called the Abujh Marh. This was a mountainous, thickly forested tract, about one thousand square miles in all, on the west central side of the state marching with the Chanda district of the Central Provinces. The name is one applied by speakers of either Hindi or Telugu, which is to say that its origins are partly Sanscritic, partly Dravidian. It may perhaps be translated as the Unknown Forest, or even the Unknowable Forest; not, I would hope, the Ignorant Forest, which may be linguistically permissible. Grigson decreed that this area was to be a closed reserve for the Hill Marias who lived there. Only the Administrator might go in.

I would anticipate events at this point. If only the Administrator might visit a substantial area for which he was responsible, then it was essential for him to do so as soon as was feasible. This I did in the winter of 1940–41. The journey, which I started from the north, had to be done on foot. This meant that I started from the *tahsil* headquarters of Narayanpur in the north-west of the state, and walked some fifty miles due south to join the road which ran due west from Jagdalpur to the border of the Central Provinces. I took an elephant, Motilal, to carry my essential kit. The Marias built for me branch shelters at each camp, one for myself and one for the cooking. It was interesting to note that the cookhouse, whose necessity terminated while I ate my breakfast, was fed branch by branch to Motilal until he in turn finished his breakfast and was loaded up for the day's journey.

In this way I travelled through what should have been the Garden of Eden. It was for me a very sad experience. There was, first, the very poor condition of the forest. This being a strict reserve, the Hill Marias were at liberty to practise without restraint their own form of shifting cultivation. This entailed the felling in the early summer of all forest growth over a certain area. When it was dry, it was burned and a wide variety of minor grains was broadcast in the ashes as soon as there had been sufficient rain. This process was repeated in the same area for three years. Then they would move into fresh ground. The area pertaining to each village might be twenty-five square miles or so; and some thirty years would be the period of rotation.

The effect over the centuries was to prevent the growth of anything but scrub jungle. So long as the population remained small, this was the limit of the damage. There was none of the denudation and erosion of the earth which in some other parts of India accompanied this form of agriculture when pressure of population led to steadily lessening periods of rotation. At the same time it is necessary to take into account the fact that forests should produce something more than fine timber. In India profit accrued to the Government, to contractors and to local workers from certain minor products. For example, *lak* was a substance secreted by certain insects on the leaves of certain bushes. It appeared later in world markets as shellac. Another bush, the *tendu*, produced the leaves which ultimately composed the poor man's cigarette for hundreds of millions of addicts, the *bidi*. Such things, however, require care and attention at their source. A mountainous area closed to the world could not be that source.

Another result of this situation may possibly not have been anticipated. The tribal population of Bastar as a whole suffered grievously from the lack of protein in the diet. The craving so created is difficult to appreciate by those who have either not themselves experienced it or who have not seen its effects. One day I saw a youth sitting on a low branch of a tree in the jungle. A column of red ants was climbing the tree, as they often do for reasons of their own. The youth was catching them by the handful as they came level with him and swallowing them in a serious and purposeful way.

I have seen my two aboriginal companions, as I walked about a forest at dawn, share the eggs from a bird's nest, with well-advanced embryos, though not without first most politely offering me the whole lot. To most people this might seem simply an example of unfortunate habits. But the craving is the explanation. The Dandami (lowland) Marias would hold an annual ritual hunt, the *pharad*. At one time this produced meat in abundance. Shortly before I went to Bastar the ritual hunt, spread over a number of days, in one area produced a single hare. So it was in the Abujh Marh. All the game had been exterminated. Few birds were either visible or audible, much as was the case when in my childhood I visited southern

France. The inevitable result was serious malnutrition. They would occasionally emerge from their 'paradise' to buy cloth and salt.

Then there was the matter of disease. Captain Mitchell's work on yaws was widely known in India. It is a spirochaetal disease whose tertiary stage is crippling and debilitating to a high degree; and by 1940 the number of patients inoculated had passed the figure of 600,000. It was well known all over the state that sufferers from this disease could always go for treatment to certain centres. On this visit to the Abujh Marh I took a junior doctor with me with the intention of offering medical services in general.

The first response was a daily line-up of sufferers from yaws. It appeared that they had in many cases not had the resolution to go outside for treatment until they had reached the tertiary stage. Fortunately my medical colleague came south with me from Narayanpur, and had to return by himself the same way. This gave him the chance to inject the second dose of Salvarsan where necessary, and to spread the general impression that the Medical Department (known as Mitchell, from its head) was nothing of which to be afraid.

Yaws, however, was not surprising. To me at least hydrocele was, in its apparently endemic incidence. The doctor was quite equal to the minor surgery involved; but I was not so happy as I bribed the first patient with beads to submit to the operation; and kept his confidence firm as the operation advanced by supplying him with a small, gilt mirror with which to observe the results. His ultimate pleasure, which was not inhibited by western concepts of exposure, brought us many clients.

To bring such things as medical relief and health service to places where they are lacking is in my view so good as to justify occasional flippancy about the results. The places where they are so sorely needed are not appropriate for flippancy at all. I would end my description of this other Eden by leaving facts and adverting to what is purely subjective. As these simple people sat of an evening by my camp-fire and beat their drums and sang their songs, I thought that here too I had never heard anything so sad.

Grigson's successor, D R Ratnam, seems to have made no change of policy. Fortunately for the state he was a very active and efficient man and incidentally a first-class cricketer and Wimbledon tennis player. He did nothing but good for the reputation of Central Provinces administrators. Next came E S Hyde whose whole life during his years in the post was devoted to the welfare of the aboriginal population. Even thirty-five years afterwards it worries me to think that I could not wholly agree with, as I understood it, his complete support for Grigson's isolationist policy.

In one respect I largely agreed with him. The Foreign and Political Department was known in some quarters as the Forage and Plunder

Department. Hyde tended to endorse this view; and a certain puritan indignation brought him occasionally into conflict with officers of that service. Bastar was under direct administration; therefore there must be no foraging and plundering by disingenuous British officers who abused hospitality when visiting the state. Seen from this angle Hyde's view was right.

Later however, when I went to Orissa as Political Agent I met another aspect of this problem. Several of the twenty-two states were under direct administration. In certain cases this was simply owing to the minority of the ruler. In others, however, the rulers had been deprived of their powers either for incompetence or for misconduct. My predecessor, Cecil Griffin (later Sir Cecil, Political Secretary to the Government of India), had laid down for his staff that, when visits were made to states under management, everything must be paid for. He was a man for whom I had great respect, but quite soon I felt bound to disagree with him in this general order. Of course minority administrations must be treated very strictly as trusts. I could not, however, stomach the idea that this must apply *au pied de la lettre* to deposed Rajas and Maharajas living in their states in humiliation. They had to accept the decision of the Central Government that as rulers they had been found wanting. I was not prepared to inflict the ultimate humiliation of not permitting them to provide hospitality to the King's representative.

The fact was that a few officers had no scruples about sponging. In Bastar, not long after I left, the Political Agent in Raipur was guilty of a most regrettable example of this. He more or less announced to my successor, Mr Radakrishnan, ICS, that he would spend his Christmas vacation in Bastar. He would be accompanied by his friend Major Peter Fleming (a Guards officer) and a French lady, Mlle Maillart. He hoped that the customary big game beats and bird shooting would be available.

My wife and I learned of this when we arrived, by previous arrangement, in Jagdalpur late on the evening of December 23, 1942. We were to be the guests of Captain and Mrs Mitchell for the same Christmas vacation. The anger against the Political Agent and his outsiders was strong. As usual however, an element of farce recoiled on the invaders. The first day was the bird shoot. Between Jagdalpur and the border of the Koraput district of Orissa to the east there was a curiously flat area of many hundreds of acres which could not possibly be drained. It was, therefore, covered with tall grass and rushes and pock-marked with deep pools. Many species of duck came into this area in winter.

On that day I found myself a member of the bird-shooting party. More, I was to partner Mlle Maillart as we lurked on the margin of one of the pools. Unfortunately Major Fleming, who, in addition to his distinctions as an author and a traveller, had also become one of Orde Wingate's Chindits, had acquired on his way to Bastar some most unusual cartridges. They seemed in daylight somewhat similar in their effect to Very lights. When he fired his gun the sky was rent by a red flame. The duck soon decided that this was unsporting and disappeared eastwards to the Koraput District of Orissa. Any who came back met with the same eccentric reception and did not stay long. The number killed was in consequence small.

For me this was fortunate as I was able to converse under the winter sun with Mlle Maillart for several hours. It was she who accompanied Peter Fleming on the journey across Central Asia from which arose his book *News from Tartary*. At this time she was sympathetically interested in the philosophy and the actions of Mahatma Gandhi. It was not often that an administrative officer in remote places was able to meet an observer and critic of such calibre. Perhaps it is permissible to say that the reverse was also true.

A subsequent beat for big game, with the possibility of a tiger, also produced very little for the game book. On that occasion I was far away, but I was not jealous. I could imagine from previous experience the hunters, under guidance, moving noisily to their perches (known as *machans*) in the trees. The ladies would look very trim in their clean starched jodhpurs and bush shirts, quite unaware that the cosmetics so alluring to their men companions were being wafted as a sweetly-scented barrier to a considerable distance through the jungle. A beat of any sort might reasonably take two hours. Men have been known to smoke in such a situation. Ladies would turn the pages of a paper-backed novel. The best *shikari* in the world might fidget.

All this would militate against the chances of any animals obediently passing under the appropriate trees. What no one had anticipated in this instance was the element of public interest. As Administrator I had on occasion been embarrassed, when organizing a serious beat for a cattle-lifting tiger, to find four hundred men turning up when I had asked for a hundred to a hundred and fifty. Among other things it came very expensive. This occasion was, however, unique. The young Maharaja had decided quite rightly that as the host of these persons – he had not met them – he must accompany them to the hunt. The news spread in the area. The demigod ruler was in their midst. In the sparsely populated forest reserve every man, woman and child moved out from their little forest villages to see the Maharaja as his car ploughed through the dust of the forest road. All those capable of doing so joined the beat. The visitors went empty away.

It was, as I have said above, in cases of this sort that I would always agree with Hyde, but not in the strong isolationism of the Grigson doctrine. This may seem a matter of little importance *sub specie aeternitatis*. Even so long afterwards I cannot agree. I have mentioned elsewhere the degradation of the so-called Gonds which I saw in the railway yards of Nagpur. In Chhindwara and Seoni their condition was better, though the story of Lotan Singh illustrates how vulnerable they were to exploitation and oppression.

Here in Bastar, thanks to the firm maintenance of isolation, most of the 600,000 aboriginals lived secure and contented lives. Only occasionally some gross conduct by a contractor or merchant, or some cruel humiliation by a Hindu schoolmaster, would reveal the horrid possibilities of contact with 20th century India. In 1940 it was manifest that the unprepared aboriginal exposed to the contemporary world outside was doomed to oblivion first and extinction later.

Very few people, Indian or British, cared to know that there were at least 18 million of these primitive people. In southern India some were only at the neolithic stage of development. In much of the western Deccan the aboriginals had been integrated to some extent. The Savara bowmen received greater respect from the Marathas than did the untouchables, but this is not to say much. The Bhils of north-east Bombay seem to have been tough men who benefited by being written about by Rudyard Kipling. The Brahui of Baluchistan had the good fortune to be converted to Islam centuries ago. Islam offers a pure faith and true brotherhood to its devotees. There we have one strong surviving example of an original people of India still speaking a language intimately connected with that of the people of Bastar.

There was then to my knowledge only one other, the Mundas of Gangpur State and the Ranchi District of Bihar. Of these Lutheran Christians there will be more later. Yet less than forty miles south of the main Bengal Nagpur Railway as it extended east from Nagpur to Calcutta there were some thousands of aboriginal forest dwellers whose scanty clothes were made of leaves and bark.

No administrative officer could ignore this problem. My own decision as to what to do was in the first instance taken as the result of certain chances. Of these the first was that, after I had only been in Bastar a few weeks, I received secret instructions from the Government of India to hold myself ready to go at twenty-four hours' notice on military service overseas. I heard no more. A year later I stood myself down from this peak of eager patriotism. Several years later I heard that I was one of two officers lined up for service in Mesopotamia, the other being a contemporary and colleague, the late Cecil Savidge. He was selected. Major Savidge was undoubtedly as good an officer as Mr Savidge, which is saying a good deal. From my point of view the uncertainty of the future made administrative planning difficult.

The second matter of chance was the presence in the State of Dr Verrier Elwin. It was a long time before I felt that I could form a final judgement about this unusual man. He was then in his middle thirties. His father had been an Anglican bishop in West Africa, and he himself, after graduating at Oxford via Merton College, likewise took holy orders in the Anglican church. I first heard his name in the winter of 1933–34, when, as Under Secretary in the Central Provinces secretariat, I used to receive CID reports on his subversive activities in the Jabalpur District. He had aligned himself with the Indian Congress Party.

So far as I was concerned there was then a time gap of six years. During that time he abjured his holy orders and moved the short distance eastwards to the Mandla District of the Central Provinces. There he settled himself as a lay missionary and social worker among the aboriginal Baigas, who formed the majority of the population. He also established an efficient leper colony. He wrote a comprehensive book about the Baigas which, with other anthropological publications, led to the award of an Oxford Doctorate of Science. He has recorded that it was E S Hyde who 'got me there', that is to Bastar. Before that Elwin was attracted to the study of the aboriginal tribes of Bastar by Grigson's contribution to the 1931 census.

One of Hyde's moves towards drawing this distinguished anthropologist to Bastar was to have him recognized as Honorary Ethnologist, and in due course he was assigned Rs 100 per month to apply his special skills in research to the census of 1941. Fortunately he would by choice walk barefoot. Otherwise his honorarium would not have carried him very far. It was at this point that I replaced Hyde. Elwin visited me very soon, and it was clear that we had much in common on the subject of how any territory should be administered in the best interests of an aboriginal population. He had just been put in more or less complete charge of the 1941 census in the state, and he asked me to contribute to his report a linguistic survey.

Apart from the fact that the idea appealed to me, I was already favourably impressed with the anthropological research in Bastar on which he had embarked. As time went by I became convinced of two things: first, his research and his writings were extremely thorough and of a high order of scholarship; secondly, the results of that research could be of great value to anyone having responsibility for the administration of aboriginals.

I would cite as examples two tasks which he performed at my request: a detailed study (later published) of a hundred murder cases in Bastar, and a detailed social and economic survey of a very primitive tribe in Keonjhar State of the Orissa States Agency (1942–43). I accepted the invitation.

My qualifications were not in academic terms impressive. Utilitarian might describe them. In a short time I was able to assess the field of languages involved. The final result was a grammar of Maria Gondi. The question of what use to make of it naturally followed; and it was here that I decided that development of the education of the aboriginals must be undertaken. The state had a good number of well-conceived primary schools. David Plumley, the State Engineer, could run them up with their brick walls and thatched roofs in a few weeks and for an expenditure of one or two hundred pounds. I retain a picture of a shaded lane of red, impacted soil leading to a verandah far overhung by thatch. The single-storey building would be in luxuriant greenery even in the hot weather, bougainvillea flowers contributing the spectacular element.

As always, however, the idyllic exterior – and indeed the cool interior with the diminished light – contained much that was wrong. These primary schools, as of course was much more the case with the few middle schools and the single high school in Jagdalpur, were staffed by teachers whose mother tongue was Hindi or Marathi. Any aboriginal child who might find his (or very occasionally her) way to school found himself being instructed in a language which he did not understand. Moreover, more than a few of these teachers were abominable men. The meek aboriginal was fair game in the school of a teacher who, however unjustified his arrogance, enjoyed bullying and degrading the helpless. I prefer not to give examples. Many of them would be revolting. The general effect was that the aboriginals were receiving no education at all.

My next decision was that conventional schools at the primary level were of no use to aboriginals. There must be schools based on crafts in the first instance. Even this was not easy. A craft such as weaving might be approved by one tribe but abominated for religious reasons by others. This could at least, however, be borne in mind when an anthropologist was available to advise. Ultimately I established one school based on carpentry and one based on weaving.

It was stipulated that the headmaster must himself be a qualified aboriginal. His assistants, to a maximum of two, might be Hindus; but they must have a knowledge of Gondi based on my grammar. This was in due course printed at our State Press. The Devanagri script was used for the Gondi words, so that no Hindu could be handicapped in his studies. Fortunately we did not wait for the book. I spent much time on my tours trying to ascertain whether the people really wanted this sort of thing. A craft was clearly a good starting point. Dancing and familiar games were an acceptable idea for recreation. But I had to emphasize that the state required more than this from its children. Specifically there would be teaching in reading and writing. Arithmetic would follow.

I had with me on these journeys the relevant volume of Grierson's *Linguistic Survey of India*, produced in the early years of the century. From that, as we sat round a fire in the darkness, I would read to them, in something recognizable as their own speech, the parable of the prodigal son. There were also similar transcriptions of their own myths. As I was reading more and more of them would get up and stand behind me following my finger as I, in the uncertain light of the paraffin pressure lamp, pronounced the living words from the incomprehensible script. The eager answer always was that they wished their children to be introduced to this new kind of school.

We established the first two in 1941. Each was intended for seventy children. Each enrolled ninety in its first month or two, when admissions had to be closed. More were in process of establishment when I was transferred in February 1942, but I heard no more on the subject. It has to be feared that the experiment was abandoned, even as it has to be emphasized again that Hindus care nothing for aboriginals. What little is known of the origin of the caste system seems to suggest that it was rigidly applied to Aryan invaders mainly because their breed was being diluted and polluted by unrestricted interbreeding with the aboriginal people. Pollution is a concept which governs the caste system to this day.

Elwin was given a post in the Government of India after the achievement of independence in 1947. It bore an ill-defined title indicative of care and concern for the aboriginals. He did not hold it long. He could not make any headway. No one can do that if no one cares in what direction the ship is intended to travel. It is much to Elwin's credit that he reached as far as he did; but it seems possible that he only did so because of his friendship with Pandit Jawaharlal Nehru.

I had arrived in Bastar at the beginning of the hot weather. My wife soon joined the children in Pachmarhi; and, after a few short journeys undertaken to learn as much as possible of the state in a short time, I set myself to the first major task of my new post. This was to write the Administrative Report of the year which was drawing to its end (a fiscal year to the end of March). I decided to go to a very remote and peaceful place.

In the very middle of the state there was a range of mountains of an average height of 4,000 feet. This ran about twelve miles from north to south. The steepness of its slopes on all sides made access difficult, and this difficulty was compounded by the fact that the range was largely composed of rock bearing iron ore equal to the richest in the world. From the point of view of anyone wishing to walk, this richness took the form of small stones, large stones, and huge boulders, all of a rufous tinge, comprising the surface of the ground. No timber could grow, but the usual indomitable shrubs would thrive among the rocks. Where by chance alluvium had provided some depth of soil, cool copses would provide shade for the few bison which survived there.

One took the main road west from Jagdalpur some fifty miles to the *tahsil* headquarters of Dantewara. This for me was always an uncanny place. For one thing it was situated a thousand feet lower than the 2,000 foot plateau to the north and east. It was, therefore, always hot, and night and day seemed to breathe silently in a stupor. It was named after a goddess, Danteshwari Mai. Her temple looked evil. She herself was clearly a local form of the Hindu Kali, who lived by destruction and slaughter. Mai, by a horrid paradox means mother. The first name probably points to her as a goddess connected with the elephant (*dant* has the same root as the Latin *dentem* and means the elephant's tusk or tooth).

Even in this century human sacrifices occurred in Bastar. Earlier this temple had seen them frequently. At the appropriate feasts in this century however, the goddess was worshipped with sacrifices of buffalo. There were priests skilled in the use of the sword. One of these could decapitate a buffalo with a single blow. This feat would be repeated at such seasons night and day as worshippers presented themselves; and the blood which spouted and gushed from the severed neck would flow down the runnels below the altars to vanish into unseen soak-pits.

I never walked abroad at night in Dantewara without feeling what in Scotland is called a 'grue' as I passed the temple. One soon felt free of this miasma, however, as one turned south along an unmetalled road through the jungle. Very soon the Bailadila* range began to rise very steeply to the west, the road actually skirting the lower slopes. After about a dozen miles the car must stop. From that point a footpath led up the mountainside for three miles and ultimately emerged from the jungle into a shallow valley ascending gently from north to south. A stream of very clear water ran down the centre and disappeared a short distance away over the east side of the range and so down to the plains. Along the east side of this stream the path continued for another half mile, terminating at a brick-built bungalow with deep verandahs and three or four steps leading up to the

* The word means 'the bullock's hump'.

plinth level. It was here that I had arranged to spend three or four weeks of quietude. A few Marias were very happy to make up the body of camp-followers. One had brought several cow buffaloes for the milk supply.

At first he seemed to be unlucky. Two or three days after we arrived a tiger killed one of his buffaloes a hundred yards or so from the path. The rumpus woke everyone, and the poor beast was actually alive when the tiger was induced to go away. It soon died however, and on the following evening I sat over the already smelly corpse. I would have got the tiger too if the Maria headman sitting in the *machan* with me had not indulged in an apparently uncontrollable bout of scratching just as it approached. I had, with a combination of stoicism and discretion, managed to cope with and endure the mosquitoes for three hours in silence. The headman's trouble, it is only fair to say, had nothing to do with mosquitoes. It served all the same to scare off the tiger. The hitherto unlucky owner of the victim was in the end the only winner. I paid him the market price for his buffalo and, in what seemed to him and the others the height of liberality, I bestowed the now very ripe carcass on them for human consumption.

I enjoyed the silence for my three whole weeks. It was interrupted once a day when the mail runner arrived with papers from headquarters. One could hear the subdued chime of his bell from far down the valley. This bell, which was intended to frighten off dangerous animals, was slung from

On a 'machan', waiting for the tiger, 1941

the shaft of a formidable spear carried, head upwards, over his shoulder. How he carried the mail depended entirely on how much there might be; but it was never burdensome. Incidentally, this system was general throughout the state, except on the main road from Jagdalpur to the north.

The Indian Posts and Telegraph Service was always equal to its tasks. Here there were small thatched shelters by the roadside every four miles. Each mail runner (an elastic word) would daily cover four miles out from his home to one of these shelters, hand over his burden to his waiting colleague; receive the latter's burden, if any, and trot back home. Eight miles fairly gentle exercise each day in no way daunted these men. Indeed the employment was popular. The payment was Rs 8 per month, twelve shillings in those days; and the fortunate employees would often farm out the work to eager substitutes for Rs 4 per month and retain the balance for purely self-indulgent expenditure on themselves.

Q Horatius Flaccus said that those who flee across the sea might change their climate but not their conscience. So for me at this time there was still the news in the papers and on the wireless to remind me several times a day of the frequent disasters and the occasional triumphs of the British in many places in World War II. There was not much, until later, that could be done to assuage one's scruples. I was however, still on the twenty-four hour notice; and there was no reason why I should not be physically prepared. I would get up, therefore, at 4.00 am and walk those abominable iron-ore boulders, threading my way among the unsympathetic bushes and carrying my double-barrelled .450 rifle. Sometimes I would shoot something for all of us to eat; but the main point was to go as hard as possible for three hours or so, returning in reasonable time for ablutions and breakfast before starting the day's work.

Another similar but shorter walk in the evening, and early supper and an early bed would complete this rather silly regimen. At least however, it could do no harm. It also enabled me to see my first bison and to miss him at short range after trying too hard to run up through the natural obstacles to cut him off as he walked along the western rim of the valley. I cut him off all right. We confronted one another briefly. But I could hardly stand, let alone hold a rifle steady, and it was foolish to try. He and the cow who accompanied him disappeared smartly in the direction whence they came; and after a minute or two I was very glad. He had looked magnificent against the sunset sky with the mountain falling steeply away for three thousand feet below him.

So next day we left the Bailadila range to its normal uninhabited peace. In the political, economic and social changes of the past thirty-five years Bailadila has not escaped. It is not merely lachrymose sentimentality which makes me wonder about the condition of the Marias of that area today. It is certain that the silence no longer prevails, as is shown from a letter dated 16 May 1963 which reached me in St Andrews a month later. By that time Bastar was merged with the new Central Provinces, Madhya Pradesh. The writer was an admirable man who had been headmaster of the High School in Jagdalpur while I was there, Madhusudhan Narayan Deo MA, Dip Ed (Sheffield). His words were:

> Bastar now is entirely different. Once a backwater – quiet and peaceful – it is now in the main stream of civilization sharing all its advantages and disadvantages. Each Tahsil headquarters has a High School now and the number of Primary Schools is tenfold. There are Community Development Blocks. All the important places have now been connected by all weather bus services. Buildings have sprung up where there was forest. There is a tremendous influx of outsiders. The iron ore deposits on Bailadila are being vigorously exploited and there is talk of locating a steel plant in the vicinity of the Bailadila Range. A railway line connecting a village at the foot of the range with the East coast is well under way. Bastar has also been selected for the rehabilitation of refugees from East Pakistan. . . (The project) is particularly active in North Bastar.

The Maharaja of Bastar is dead. With all the other rulers of Indian States he had been dispossessed of his powers and his territory by Sardar Vallabhbhai Patel in particular and by the Government of India as a whole within a few years of the achievement of independence. Later he was even deprived of his status as maharaja. The aboriginals attributed to him semi-divine attributes and he was so ill-advised as to encourage them to rebel. One result was that the palace in Jagdalpur was surrounded by armed police, and he was killed in his own drawing-room during an exchange of fire.

I must hark back to 1940. Even the aboriginals acquired some dim concept of the war which was never out of our minds. One reason was their sight of the endless lines of bullock carts and lorries carrying north to Raipur the varying sizes of teak and sal (*shorea robusta*) for railway sleepers or for jetty piles in the Persian Gulf, and soon they would contribute quite astonishing sums in response to appeals for funds. These appeals might, for example, be for money to buy an ambulance or a Spitfire, things of which they could not be expected to have any concept; but one day the *Tahsildar* of Dantewara wrote to tell me that a man from the Abujh Marh had just come to see him, having travelled forty miles on foot with a very heavy bag of copper coins to help with the war. Another officer told me that he had asked a group of Murias what they would do if the Germans came to Bastar. The answer was that they would run away to Orissa. This meant crossing a boundary fifteen miles to the east.

I toured constantly during the two years 1940–41. In the rains one was restricted to the main roads, which implied that formal work was confined to visits of inspection to *tahsil* headquarters. With the return of dry weather in October it was once again possible to see the less accessible parts of the state, to inspect the work of minor officials such as *patwaris** and to see remote primary schools. Conditions varied. In the northern central plateau it was simple to travel in the conventional way with comfortable tents transported by bullock carts. Almost always however, I would take the elephants Motilal and Champakali. They enjoyed it. So did the *mahouts*. On easy tours they would carry my wife and perhaps the two older children. On the less easy they might be my only transport.

Unfortunately Motilal was afraid of tigers and Champakali was very small. There was thus none of that spectacular shooting of ravening beasts from the vantage point of a howdah with an ornate roof, which seems to have been (if one is to trust the illustrations of books) common form in days of yore. I once used both elephants to follow a wounded tiger. Naturally I sat on the taller one in accordance (I asserted to myself) with common prudence. When we drew close to the tiger, Motilal raised his trunk vertically in a defiant gesture. This obscured my forward view. He then backed under a tree, one of whose branches dislodged me to the ground before I had time to adopt a posture such as to suggest that I had dismounted intentionally. Motilal then took up position behind Champakali who was quietly browsing on spear grass. I decided to go from that point on foot. The lady might be placid, but as I sat sideways on her back my feet would be within snapping distance of any tiger.†

The southernmost *tahsil* of the state was Konta. Its area was 1,000 square miles and its population 13,000, which by Indian standards was very sparse. It was low-lying, adjacent to the basin of the Godavari river, and very hot. It was entirely covered by secondary forest growth and not very beautiful unless one liked the curious, almost pulsating silence of that type of wilderness. Here lived the Dorlas, the lowland family of the Marias. I would have liked to ask some of my predecessors how they would wish to preserve the ancient life pattern of these people. The isolation policy certainly gave them, at thirteen inhabitants to the square mile, plenty of room to live as centuries before their ancestors had learned to live.

---

* Literally an accountant. His work consisted in maintaining land records for a group of villages.

† We got the tiger ultimately.

One of their amenities might appeal to some western people. The forest grew countless palms known as *tari*. The word 'toddy' in English has here its birth. All through the dry months one might, if so inclined, repair to the forest with few if any possessions and, on the first morning early, make an incision in the bark of a tree. Below the incision one would lash an earthenware pot with a narrow neck and a fat belly. This would quickly fill with the sap running from the incision; and this, when fresh, was a very agreeable beverage. By noon however, it would have fermented to a remarkable degree. One could fall quite soon into an intoxicated sleep; and even if this lasted till next morning, it did not matter (apart from the mosquitoes) if the night minimum temperature seldom went below 80°F.

Apart from such adventitious aids however, the country had a certain dream-like quality. On my first visit I was met outside the little village of Konta itself by an unmistakeable Brahman priest. We clasped hands in an unexpectedly warm manner. His two hands enveloped my right hand and pressed into it a gift of a small orange. He then waved his hand towards the shrine over which he presided (the hand was not normal) and complained that ill-wishers had cast doubt on its sanctity. In consequence his income had been seriously reduced, and would I help him. I made no promises but moved on to the *tahsil* office where the *tahsildar* was waiting. I asked him about the priest and his troubles. He said that the poor man suffered from advanced leprosy and so people avoided him. Had I not noticed his hands? Yes, well a little carbolic soap would be advisable.

And so we would travel westwards from Konta along forest roads by car or lorry through the silent heat. Since villages were never less than thirty miles apart, any other way of travelling would have taken more time than I could spare or work could justify. In this way we travelled through the Bijapur *tahsil* to Bhopalpatnam and back by the west road to Jagdalpur. It was in the Bijapur area that I shot a tiger which had killed fifty-six head of cattle in a year.

My last tour was in the middle of December 1941. If I were to ask myself when anxiety for the future grew in my mind, displacing the pleasure inherent in the enthusiastic progress of a career, I think I would answer that it was in April 1937, the time of the Shahur Tangi ambush in South Waziristan. Colonel Claude Erskine, Inspecting Officer Frontier Corps, and I, discussing that tragedy in my office in Peshawar a few days later, each found the other thinking that it was a matter to be dealt with 'before the war came'. Increasingly during the next eighteen months this conviction seemed to influence thinking. The majority of people, like me, remembered the first war and inwardly feared the next; and it was this anxiety which made me cherish every day of my leave in 1938 in the certainty that none of these pleasures would ever recur.

For a brief time however, during this tour the world and its war retreated. I had driven north-west to the *tahsil* headquarters of Narayanpur. From there I rode first to Antagarh in the extreme north of the state, a journey under mile after mile of *sal* forest. These tall trees inhibit undergrowth so that one could see perhaps two hundred yards in all directions. The morning sun shone through the remote branches as it might through the 'Storied windows richly dight' of Milton's cloisters. The mare's feet, trotting steadily mile after mile made only the faintest thud in the earth. The effect was one of enchantment bordering on exaltation.

The map shows the distance as well over twenty miles, which would take three hours or so, depending on how considerate one was to the mare. Then quite unexpectedly the track emerged into a clearing of about four acres. The soil must have been very deep because the trees – mangoes, *nim* and banyan (*ficus religiosa*) mainly – were of exceptional height. Very little of the sunlight penetrated at all; and the shelter, made of branches for me, looked very small indeed.

My visit was a pleasant one. After some routine inspection of land records and the usual audience of grievances, I handed over to what in later life I would call an ad hoc committee of management a very large battery wireless set. Once it got going, I have to admit, any brief interest in my visit evaporated. This present however, was not in the least intended as a placebo designed to divert attention from fundamental hardships or injustices. It was one detail in my effort to provide, as it were, a window on the outer world for these completely isolated and primitive people. I never knew the end of it.

For the next three days I walked eastwards along the top of the escarpment that rose at its western end from the Drug District of the Central Provinces and further eastward from Kanker State. I had been joined again (and for the last time) by Motilal and Champakali, since we had to travel thirty miles of rough country to the *dak* bungalow at Keskal. Before we left Antagarh we had tried to earn our keep by shooting something for the local people, and, since the shooting of big game was at that time for me both an interest and a duty, I was glad to record two bears by Police Havildar Hira Singh, my orderly, and two tigers and a panther by myself. Against such beasts the local people had very little protection. I also got them a *sambhar* (a large deer) for the pot.

Each day's journey was restricted to ten miles since I had to consider the condition of my very small company. The elephants could bring the essential equipment. The local people were well content to build shelters

On horseback, 1940

of branches and be well paid. But a single servant, for example, – and it was still Chandu – could hardly be expected to feel the same exaltation as I might as I eagerly covered the miles of dusty, rutted track to the next halt. If he sat on one of the elephants, and if he was constructed as I was, he would feel all the time as if his spine were being forced through the back of his neck into his brain. If he walked . . . well, that was something outside the limits of possibility.

There were others to consider: the village watchman (*kotwal*) who would see me through the territory in which his duties lay; the *manjhi* (literally skipper) of the *pargana*, who would also wish to come, was usually stout and becoming inactive. Ten miles a day was plenty. Then, if I could get a little food some time between noon and 2.00 pm, with the help of the local people (if any – the first halt was in an uninhabited area) there could be some indulgence in our common interest, shooting.

There could be little work to do in such country: no land records to inspect, no police stations or dispensaries. No doubt plenty of work was piling up at the Keskal *dak* bungalow, only eighty miles north from Jagdalpur on the main road, visited daily by the Royal Mail bus. Here however, there were, as everywhere in Bastar, poor, simple people who were glad to greet and know the person to whom they could always refer their troubles. If those words sound as if they reflected a special type of self-conceit, I must instantly record that I ranked in their estimation second to the two elephants. Had the Maharaja been there, I would not have been noticed at all.

I was back in Jagdalpur in good time for Christmas. There was an active Methodist Mission in Bastar with some hundreds of converts. It was not only they, however, who celebrated the Feast of the Nativity. All the children of Jagdalpur knew about it. In Hindi it was Bara Din, the Great Day, and the little town was lit up almost as if it were the Hindu Diwali, the festival of the *dipa* or little oil lamps.

In the small club, of which anyone who wished could be a member, there would be on Christmas Eve a larger than usual turn-out for tennis or gossip. Then as darkness fell our short, stout, strong, round-faced Mr Mayberry, his brown rosy cheeks obscured by a white beard, clad in the raiment of Father Christmas, took his seat on Motilal, emerged from the club gates, and rode round the town. I never knew whether the children knew that this was really the Superintendent of Police. No doubt there, as in many other lands, some did and some did not. It was a strange thing to watch however. Motilal was very tall. Behind his great ears his *mahout* was clearly visible. Further back however, the light of the little lamps barely reached to where Mr Mayberry sat at ease on a very comfortable pad. An arm could be seen moving in the half light as he distributed packets of sweets in all directions; but to the unsophisticated mind and eyes of young children it must all have been a spectacle for awe.

Soon after the New Year orders came for my transfer, to take place early in February. We were all very sad; and to this day it is unhappy to recall the farewell parties and the illuminated addresses in English, Hindi and even Urdu. We left on a dull cold morning and it was a relief when we finally dropped down the *ghat* at Keskal and crossed the northern border into the other world.

A FAREWELL TO A. N. MITCHELL, Esq., I. C. S.

ADMINISTRATOR-BASTAR STATE.

ON THE EVE OF HIS DEPARTURE FROM BASTAR STATE.

Most revered Sir,

It is a joy for ever to have a view and a sweet recollection of your august self. But on this unique occasion, amid all pomp and grandeur my heart aches even sitting and talking in close touch with you. In all prosperity and with all hail a superior office you are going to adorn but still the very word 'Farewell' moves a chord of this lyre and, alas, it breaks.

FATHER AND SAVIOUR OF THE ABORIGINALS!

Thou with thy manifold activities in course of this short period of administration hast led the mute aboriginals every tomorrow to a glaring vale of life and light of civic test. Under thy enlightened patronage of education, protection of life and right, and above all a melting heart in famine, distress and disease, a new life has dawned upon them. To these neglected millions it was a bliss indeed to live in an elysium tasting of its ambrosia under thy protecting arms.

GREAT FRIEND OF HUMANITY!

Blessed though with higest rank of service, true you are still to the kindered points of heaven and home. I had the opportunity to feel the pulse of your inner-man on occasions more than once but yonr real man revealed and attracted me the most when once during summer in heavy shower near Farashgaon, the gloomy veil of the dawn was not still unfurled, my truck stood before a damaged diversion-bridge and you came down in mire and to make the bridge motorable started setting stones and bricks with your own hands while sufficient menials at your command stood by watching the scene. Ever remained your door open to the rich and the poor and alike you have extended your healing and helping hands to redress their grievances, pain and pangs. The appeal of the afflicted ever found an echo in your heart and it is for your humane heart that the local Maharani Hospital gets an extension with the opening of a 'Veterinary Vaccine Laboratory' in your hands. Thrice welcomed thee, the glorious son of the Almighty.

I cannot lose temptation of speaking here of the perennial affection of a mother we have enjoyed from Mrs. Mitchell and with heavy heart I convey my heart-felt gratitude to her.

PRIME EXPONENT OF JUSTICE AND EQUITY!

I congratulate you upon your elevation to the higher rank of service. May Heaven shower His choicest blessings upon thy head and a long, happy and bright life be bestowed upon thee.

Jagdalpur,
The 16th January, 1942.
Bastar State, C. P.

With best regards I remain,
Most revered Sir,
Your most law-abiding subject
R. L. Samajdar.
(Manager.)
Messrs. Himatsingka Timber Ltd.,
Jagdalpur.

Farewell speech on Norval's departure from Jagdalpur, Bastar State, 1942

Chapter 10

The lone and level sands stretch far away.
Shelley

MY NEW POST WAS that of Political Agent, Sabar Kantha, in the Kathiawar Peninsula. The whole area of the peninsula was comprised of Indian States, large and small – some indeed not true states but groups of a few villages. The proprietors of the latter held the title of *thakur*. At the other end of the scale were such extremely distinguished figures as the Maharajas of Jamnagar or Bhaunagar. The senior political officer for the whole area was the Resident for the Western States, equivalent in rank to a provincial governor. The so-called first class states communicated with the Viceroy through the Resident. The less distinguished were in political relations with three Political Agents, distributed territorially, of whom I was one.

Our depressed feelings on leaving Bastar were not improved by anything that happened for a long time thereafter. The journey to Raipur was its usual dusty misery, but that was only the first stage. From Raipur to Bombay by train involved approximately one full day. A brief pause in Bombay was succeeded by another journey of 500 miles north by the Bombay, Baroda and Central India Railway to Ahmedabad.

I had up to that time believed that Nagpur was the worst place in the world, but I had been learning better as the years went by. Now I was prepared to say that all large Indian cities were an insult to the teeming myriads of human beings who flocked into them from the rural areas. The processes and the effects of the industrial revolution in the British Isles were reproduced with striking similarity. People for various reasons gravitated to the cities. They were usually the untouchables and the dispossessed; that is the aboriginals, for example, of whom I have already written much; and the sweepers, the tanners and others who lived on sufferance on the fringes of prosperous agricultural communities. Islam and Sikhism indeed offered them brotherhood. Hinduism rejected them wholly. This was in spite of Mahatma Gandhi's efforts on their behalf. After all, he invented the name Harijan, that is, the lordly ones, as a generic term for all untouchables.

To some of us however, it seemed suspiciously similar to the half-contemptuous, half-kindly nicknames already applied to sweepers. Over much of India it was *maharaj*, great king; in areas where Urdu prevailed as the general language it was *mehtar*, prince. It was not a matter of surprise if such people moved into such places as Ahmedabad where work was available in the textile mills, with reasonably clean quarters and running water, at worst from a stand-pipe in the street. There were, of course, many other types of people, even Pathans, in and around the textile industry in Ahmedabad, as in Bombay, but this did not affect the fact that the former was a dirty, congested slum with constant heat varying from simply hot in winter to perhaps 120°F in summer.

We were eager to leave the railway station and drive the thirteen miles to our new headquarters, Sadra. My mother-in-law, anxious to know where her daughter was, failed to discover until she had enlisted an old friend of the family, Andrew McNally, head of the American map publishers of that name. Even his expert cartographers took several days to produce the answer. The place lies north of Ahmedabad. The car abruptly left the tarmac streets and plunged into a deeply rutted road consisting solely of grey dust or sand. Speed was out of the question. Wheel-spin and skidding were constant, involving the driver in much healthy exercise. There was no danger, only discomfort. The road was bounded by cactus hedges, which one soon noticed were also 'field' boundaries. Since the bushes were always a yard or two apart, they were of no use as barriers, but I assumed that they did delineate something. The thirteen miles took about forty minutes to cover. Then we found ourselves on a stretch of tarmac again. For two or three hundred yards we drove between rows of ordinary Indian shops. Then came the almost laughable climax of our fifteen hundred mile journey. It was the Political Agent's house and office.

It was a Moghul fort of the 16th or 17th century. In area it was about fifty yards square, its walls about forty feet high. The entrance was through an arched gateway on the south side, and on the right of that was our house, which formed the eastern half of the south wall. The windows opening to the outside of the fort were of dark green glass. My predecessor's wife told my wife that this was intended to mitigate the glare of the sun in summer, and this became clear as the weeks went by. In the Scottish baronial manner there were rounded turrets at each corner of the square, and these, with their accommodation built into the inside of the walls, contained my office and staff, my personal office in the south-east turret, stables at ground level and so on. In the courtyard were several large *nim* trees, so that little sun penetrated to the ground.

This improbable edifice dominated on its west side a cliff of forty feet dropping down to a small, clear, fast running stream some twelve feet wide and perhaps eighteen inches deep at that point, the Sabarmati river. All around was grey sand. The rainfall seldom exceeded four inches in a year, although when it did the sandy fields proved themselves very fertile. Fresh water must be drawn from wells. (For the children aged 9, 8, 5 and 3 the fort was straight out of 'Beau Geste' and other novels about the French Foreign Legion. It was 'Fort Zinderneuf', and for a few weeks its turrets and battlements in the middle of a desert provided a wonderful setting for imaginative play. Ed.)

I was only left in this post for six weeks. This brief pause in life's journey, therefore, did not suffice to give me any real knowledge of the area. I gained a liking for my Gujerati staff and an admiration for the Rajput population whom the terribly arduous climatic conditions did not overcome. Since I expected to be there for at least two years, I travelled over the agency as much as I could from the start. One journey may be taken as an example. I left my house at 5.00 am one day, drove to Ahmedabad and left there about 6.00 am on the narrow gauge railway to the north. We alighted at a simple platform where a car was waiting for me. We drove westwards to Palanpur, the capital of the state of that name. There was no road. The country consisted of the usual grey sand which supported a fairly heavy growth of *babul* trees.

The town of Palanpur itself, with an adequate water supply, was a most attractive oasis. We stopped at the guest house, since I had previously written to the Nawab for permission to have lunch there. What I had not expected was that he would have lunch with me, acting in a very easy way as a personal, as he was also the official, host. He was so perfectly familiar with the English language and everything else English that I actually felt awkward when addressing him as Nawab Sahib. Since he was my senior by about ten years, 'Sir' would have been much more appropriate.

One of the sad aspects of the coming transfer of government in India was that men such as I would never again converse with men such as he on matters of mutual concern in a way based on mutual liking and respect. There remains to me the recollection of how easily he accepted my excuses for continuing my journey, and of the vain hopes expressed by each of us that we would soon be meeting again. At 5.00 pm we went on our tortuous way through the *babul*.

Two hours later I was met by the customary reception committee at a *tahsil*, Rhadanpur, which was under my control. Strictly speaking I should have inspected it, but I was far too tired. Having been conventionally garlanded, met the staff, drunk tea and eaten iced cakes, I made eloquent

Ceremony at Sadra. The editor is seated on the far right, looking bored! 1942

excuses and once more went on my way. As the sun set we reached the *dak* bungalow near the eastern edge of the Great Rann of Kutch. The cold, dry air had to an exceptional degree the bracing quality of all desert air, but nothing could prevent me sleeping from 10.00 pm to 8.00 am.

I did nothing of importance here any more than I did elsewhere during my brief sojourn in Sadra. Everything was however, new and interesting. There was the so-called Salt Line. It ran north and south across the neck of the Kathiawar peninsular, and looked very much like Rotten Row in Hyde Park. Its object was to delineate the boundary between the Kathiawar States, which produced salt in great quantities, and British India, where salt was a government monopoly.

Imported salt was liable to customs duty. Smuggling had to be prevented. To this end the line was patrolled, in what Gibbon might have called a regular or capricious manner, by fierce horsemen. They were armed with large, curved swords. They were very hirsute and sun-burned. Their uniforms were mainly red. This point was important since the colour made them visible afar off. Any desperado trying to smuggle a few donkeys laden with salt across the line by daylight would be provided with a fair warning. He would, if he were prudent, turn back. Flight or other erratic action with loaded donkeys is not feasible. In future he would ply his nefarious occupation by night. The opposition would be at home then, possibly cogitating tactics for the morrow. What I have never been able to understand was how the expenditure on this formidable apparatus could be justified in respect of a commodity which was almost literally dirt cheap.

Mahatma Gandhi took advantage of this, as all his followers are happy to recall. He led his well-known march to the sea through Gujerat, a latter day Xenophon, in order to commit the technical offence, when he got there, of 'manufacturing' salt in contravention of the law. You could do this, if the driving force of your idealism was strong enough, by improvising a salt-pan and waiting for the sun to evaporate the water.

At one point adjacent to the Salt Line I came upon another instance of futility, an abortive well. In this case, however, it was not anyone's fault but rather an example of nature in her most contrary mood. Water was desperately needed. Money was provided by the Government of India in fairly generous quantity for boring wells. After several failures, on one conspicuous day water gushed from the pipe. It proved to be a strong solution of magnesium sulphate.

My last interesting experience in the neighbourhood of the Rann was in the field of wildlife. On my second morning I left the *dak* bungalow before dawn and, on a borrowed horse, rode seven miles westward to a shallow lake about a mile long in search of food for my camp. This lake would dry up in the hot weather. Meanwhile it was a staging post for many species of duck on their northward migration to their breeding grounds in northern Russia.

It was also a drinking place for both the common and the imperial sand-grouse. It was for these that I had started so early. It is their habit to drink in flocks both soon after sunrise and shortly before sunset. Even where water is plentiful they keep to this habit, though the flocks may be quite small – similar to coveys of partridges. Where water is scanty and its sources far apart, the flocks are literally uncountable. At first light I sat myself in a very small hide made of branches some twenty yards back from the eastern edge of the lake. The high water mark was about sixty yards further back.

From about 7.00 am the sand-grouse began to fly in from all the quarters of the sky and to alight at the high water mark, the common variety immediately behind me and the imperial about two hundred yards further south. By the very rough count which I made there were ultimately between eight and nine hundred of the former and about two hundred and fifty of the latter. At a precise moment about 8.10 the whole concourse took wing and hurled themselves into the water four and five deep to right and left of me. It reminded me of the quails in Exodus XVI, 13. Shooting was out of the question. In time it was possible to frighten them once more into flight, and I obtained what I wanted. In a few minutes all the quarters of the sky were once more bright and empty in the winter sunlight. Having eaten my portable breakfast, I turned to the duck.

Here again the numbers which rose from the reeds were countless. When I thought that I had enough for the needs of my camp, having been shooting fast for twenty minutes, I stopped and told my party of assistants that they could have everything over twenty. But, they protested, the day was young, much more could be shot. They believed me, however, when I explained that butchery was not in my line, and there were, as I could see, plenty of birds to supplement their cash wages.

Chapter 11

Bricks without straw.

DURING MARCH I RECEIVED orders of transfer again. This time it was to the post of Political Agent, Orissa States, and one thousand eight hundred miles by rail via Bombay.

Twenty-two states in the Uriya-speaking area of east-central India formed one of the components of the Eastern States Agency whose headquarters was in Calcutta. Other units were certain large states, such as Cooch Behar in Bengal, which were in direct relations with the Resident, and the so-called Central Provinces States (of which Bastar was the southernmost) whose Political Agent was stationed at Raipur. He lived 180 miles due west of my new headquarters, Sambalpur.

The Province of Orissa and the Orissa States bordered one another in a somewhat confused way. Since however, the latter no longer exist, it would be pointless here to do more than mention the general position. First, in the matter of size the states comprised approximately 7 million people and 17,000 square miles. Sambalpur was the headquarters of the district of that name (in Orissa Province), situated on the north bank of the Mahanadi river. The name means 'Great River' and is well deserved. It rises far off under the northern escarpment of Bastar State, flowing first north and then east to Sambalpur. At that point it is in the rains a stormy, muddy flood half a mile wide. With the cessation of the rains it shrinks to a point where it is only a clear channel through the sand and rocks of its bed. Its course continues south-east to Cuttack 170 miles away, drawing strength from great tributaries, and finally reaches the Bay of Bengal, about 50 miles further on, by way of a delta.

The basin of the Mahanadi contains most of the Orissa States. They were mainly populated by aboriginals and, almost as a corollary, were largely made up of thickly forested and rocky hills. That in the idiom of Orissa was the place for aboriginals. The area on the south bank was the more level and fertile. That lying back from the river to the north contained much commercially valuable timber. Further north again ran the main line of the Bengal-Nagpur Railway, which marked the end of the primitive people and the usual over-population of British India exemplified in this case by the Ranchi District of Bihar Province. The few remaining states included Gangpur, lying between Ranchi District and the railway on the north western end of the Agency; and others in the coastal plain north and south of Cuttack.

The domestic arrangements for this move were complex. Two sons returned to school in Simla; my wife and two younger children came to Sambalpur at first, preparatory to a later move to Mussoorie, there to stay until cooler weather returned. We reached Sambalpur by train late at night, the last thirty miles being by the branch line from Jharsuguda, the junction to the north. The full horrors of the place did not therefore assail us till next day. And yet perhaps I should not in retrospect think in such extreme terms.

My first day was 8 April and the maximum temperature was 107°F. This rose steadily till mid-June, when the maximum approached 120°F and the night minimum was 97°F. This was enough to put me off at any time, but especially in 1942 when I was increasingly suffering from a vitamin B deficiency which had started in 1935. It was on that morning of April 8 that I was able for the first time to see our house. It was built in two stories in a style very close to the Scots baronial. Inside the turrets at the corners were spiral stairways of stone which gave access to the bathrooms for the waterman and the sweeper. It stood on a hill of rock and shale, looking out on all sides over the countryside. The radiation of heat from the rock and from the stone of which the house was built passes my power of description. Even the verandahs on the ground and upper floors could not mitigate the heat and glare.

But there was one unexpected relief. All through the hot summer months the strong hot wind called the *lun* blew from the south west from dawn until after dark. On our hill it blew unimpeded. This was ideal for the operation of the one available form of air-conditioning, the *khas-khas tatti*. This was a mat woven of a certain very coarse grass. It would be made to fit on one or more open doors or windows on the windward side of the house. A coolie employed solely for the purpose would keep pouring water on it, keeping it in a soaked condition, and through it the wind would blow a scented draught some twenty or twenty-five degrees cooler than the temperature outside. One other amenity of the place was the superb view from south-east, over the Mahanadi, round to the west where the horizon was marked by forest-covered hills. During the rains in particular, when heavy cloud formations were so often towards sunset shot through with great shafts of light in all colours, I would repeat R L Stevenson's words, 'The incomparable pomp of eve.'

The year 1942 was for the people of the United Kingdom, whether in their own islands or on their other battlefields, a very grievous one. Those who were serving in any capacity in the east were naturally prone to see most clearly the tragedies by land and sea of the Japanese victories in Malaya, Singapore, Indonesia and Burma. My appointment to the Orissa States was almost entirely related to what happened in Burma; and in April it was not possible to foresee what would come next.

On the military side the question seemed to be whether the rearguard action in Burma could delay the Japanese advance long enough for the arrival of the rains to make an immediate invasion of India impossible. It is a matter of history that they were stopped at Imphal as the result of a prolonged demonstration of endurance, discipline, skill and courage which to those of us much further back was nothing less than inspiring. My brave and efficient assistant, Captain Dudley Biscoe and I had, as our first and most urgent duty, the preparation of action to be taken in the event of a Japanese landing on the coast of Orissa.

During the whole of 1942 the east coast of India was almost defenceless. I was informed that only one division of troops was in position to protect the coast line from western Bengal to Madras, a distance of close on 900 miles. The available troops were, therefore, disposed in such strength as was possible in a limited number of strategic positions well back from the coast. It was, for example, essential on the north to defend the railway junction of Kharagpur and the armaments factories to the north-west in the Jamshedpur area. From such prepared defences it was hoped (or so I understood) that counter-attacks could be mounted after Japanese landings. News of such landings would be communicated rapidly (personally I never knew how) by the humble *chaukidars** of the coastal villages.

There were also small advance units of troops whose task seemed to be much the same as that of the Balearic slingers in the Roman army's battles in the later years of the Republic. The last thing that I would wish to do would be to aim ignorant mockery at what the military authorities were doing at that time. Their resources were so small and the situation was so desperate. Indeed, although my commendation must be based on the same ignorance as my mockery would be, I thought that what was done was absolutely correct. Whether it could work seemed doubtful, but there was nothing else to be done.

My doubts may be illustrated by two examples: first, one of the advance units was a squadron of States troops, the Hyderabad Lancers, quartered just within the southern border of Keonjhar State where in those days it bordered with the Balasore district of Orissa. In effect, this was the coastal plain, where height above sea level was twelve to fifteen feet and about

* Watchmen.

fifty miles from the coast itself. The idea is clearly right. Indeed, when I paid a courtesy call on them, their enthusiasm for the defence of their country was unmistakeable. Yet it was obvious that, other than dying, there was nothing that they could do to resist a Japanese invasion. They could, however, pass information up to, say, Kharagpur, although accuracy would be difficult.

This point links my first example with my second: during that summer a Japanese fleet entered the Bay of Bengal and sank an entire fleet of merchant ships, sailing at that time without air cover. Word of this spread very quickly. Many faces fell wan and drawn when it was officially confirmed that in one of those ships whiskey to the value of £2 million had sunk without trace. The effect of the enemy being so near to our shores tended to become more obvious than heretofore.

One evening during the monsoon a *chaukidar* of a coastal village in the Balasore district had a vision against the eastern sky of an endless procession of funnels of enemy ships; he acted on his instructions by hastening to the nearest post office and ensuring that the alarm was given. Those to whom it was given were in no position to know whence it had come. The fact was that the *chaukidar*, possibly affected by his own equivalent of the lost whiskey, had seen toddy palms bending to the wind against a darkening sky. As regards action taken on his warning (which never reached me), all that I know was that the Deputy Commissioner of Balasore worked all through the night burning hundreds of thousands of currency notes, lest they fall into enemy hands, and depositing silver and copper coin in wells of unplumbed depth.

Biscoe and I had one clear task to perform. It was liable to be called the scorched earth policy, which sounded rather apocalyptic and was not very accurate. One has to appreciate however, that with so few troops available a Japanese landing would initially be unopposed. From events in Malaya one knew that the Japanese would not wait about on the beaches. They would instantly generate a momentum of advance which would carry them on indefinitely. Death to them was so little in their thoughts that they were content to be sacrificed to strategy with little regard for tactics. In our area this meant that they could reach Cuttack and then find the road to the west open to them to Sambalpur, Raipur and Nagpur – at this point having travelled from 450 to 500 miles as the crow flies – until even Bombay was within their reach. Alternatively, they might cut the vital Bengal Nagpur Railway at Raipur and turn north to Kharagpur and its industrial neighbours.

Fortunately it turned out that the Japanese, even in Burma, seemed to have to a considerable extent out-run their supply lines. As they entered

Assam they met very solid resistance. And so in due course the rains arrived in June, and even the Japanese would have found it very difficult to carry out a landing on the open beaches of the Orissa coast in the heavy monsoon seas.

It was however, essential in the hot weather to act as if a landing was imminent. To that end Biscoe and I toured widely. We dealt with the Diwans of all the states and organized refugee routes, emergency food arrangements, and such unromantic but necessary measures as a census of bicycles so that, when the alarm was given, the local police might call them in, remove the chains, dump the latter in the nearest deep water, and return the emasculated machines to their owners. There was an interesting mixture of farce and good sense in all this – a vision of frustrated enemy unable to pedal away to the west; and a much clearer vision of all local transport being denied. The Orissa Public Works Department and their equivalent in the states had (I sometimes wonder how far this was true on the spot) every bridge mined ready for demolition. Police and others were organized to sink all boats on the Mahanadi and its tributaries. Well, we could only try.

One thing worried Biscoe and me and, I imagine, all officers of our type. Orders had been issued by the Government of India that all Deputy Commissioners and their juniors of what in the army would be commissioned rank must stay at their posts if their districts were over-run by the Japanese. The same applied to Political Agents. There seemed to be no clear idea of what such officers could do in such circumstances. News from Malaya and Burma suggested that they could but go to their prison camp with a good grace, their services being lost to their employers. I was told that a friend of mine, a Deputy Commissioner in Orissa, spoke out strongly against this order in an official meeting in Cuttack. He said it could only have been issued by a fifth columnist. The statement was well received; it was relayed to the Government of India, and the order (whether *post hoc* or *propter hoc* I do not know) was rescinded.

Meanwhile Biscoe and I had acted differently. We had assumed that the orders would stand. Any of our duties in respect, for example, of refugee camps would in the event of a successful Japanese invasion fall away like a snake's skin in spring. We would simply remain in a sort of noble limbo. This did not appeal to us, and we decided upon another approach. We had both served on the frontier and we thus had experience of mountain warfare. This could hardly be said to resemble jungle warfare at all closely; but if it were tactfully introduced with becoming modesty in a letter to the Resident, it might support a proposal for something not wholly different in principle. This duly went to Lt Col Cyril Hancock (later Sir

Cyril), Resident for the Eastern States, in Calcutta. The letter suggested that to stay ornamentally at one's post was, as a concept, less attractive and less useful than to take to the jungle and wage guerrilla war against the enemy. We would recruit Pathan traders as being more martial than Uriya cultivators; but we would need some .303 rifles and a supply of ammunition and hand grenades.

Colonel Hancock was a fire-eater. He had won the MC in the 1914–18 war for (so I was told) an action involving machine guns. Shortly before this episode he had let all concerned know that his advanced headquarters would be at a station on the Bengal-Nagpur railway south west of Jamshedpur, this providing a point from which rail communications were good in general, and from which roads to the south-east, Balasore and Cuttack, were available. His receipt of my message was enthusiastic. His only criticism was that I had not proposed a scale of blood money graduated to the rank and importance of those we would be killing. This was not easy. If an aboriginal killed a Japanese major with an arrow (as might happen if our campaign caught on), he would be happy with five or ten rupees. A Pathan with a grenade, like some East Anglian wild fowler with a punt gun, would be likely to choose his moment carefully, lob it into a conference of battalion commanders, and expect to retire on the proceeds to the mountains of his homeland.

I did my best however, being careful, as a true civil servant, to emphasize the importance of elasticity in uncertain times. Meanwhile Biscoe was summoned to Calcutta. There the Resident sent him in his official car, the Union Jack fluttering on the bonnet, to the Fort. In this way he was able to indent in person for our weaponry and to arrange for its delivery in due course. He said he felt more important than either he or I thought was justified by our scheme. Yet in all seriousness something of the sort was essential. It had been observed in Malaya how much could be done behind the enemy lines by parties of troops with no support from outside.

About this time I came to know that my friend of Bastar days, Herbert Mooney, Indian Forest Service, Forest Adviser to the Eastern States Agency, was already committed to remaining behind the Japanese lines with a view to conducting an intelligence service to a military centre far away. All of us hoped to conduct our resistance efficiently. All of us had lost friends or relations in the preceding months. None of us felt any disinclination to undertake any eccentric task which might bring us back into line with them.

Our final task was one which carried little inspiration. The Japanese danger receded with the arrival of the rains. I then took three weeks' holiday with my wife and the two younger children in Mussoorie, a hill station in the United Provinces. On my return to Sambalpur my malady was no better, and I obtained entry to the School of Tropical Medicine in Calcutta at the end of July. Before I went in we had been warned by the Government of India that the Congress Party were planning a general revolt. This would be the logical development of their 'Quit India' agitation. The so-called Cripps mission on the subject of political reforms in India arrived in India in March 1942. The general terms of His Majesty's Government's offer, communicated through Sir Stafford Cripps, implied the grant of full Dominion status after the war and the concomitant right of secession from the Commonwealth.

The Mission failed in its object of conciliating Indian nationalists, largely because the Congress Party did not expect that Great Britain would win the war and so be in a position to implement the proposals.* Mr Gandhi referred to a post-dated cheque on an insolvent bank, or words to that effect. Those of us on the spot heard, for example, a 'more in sorrow than in anger' broadcast from Sir Stafford. We read Mr Gandhi's views on the benevolent intentions of the Japanese towards India's political aspirations. We waited for the explosion.

The Executive Committee of the Congress was to meet in Bombay on 7 August. The Government of India had given all officials with responsibility for the maintenance of law and order a code word which would be telegraphed to them as soon as that Committee's decision was reached. I understood that the Intelligence Directorate had also made their own arrangements for the decision to be reported from the conference room as soon as it was reached. Certainly the code word reached me in hospital, relayed from Sambalpur, before the news was published. The Congress would put into effect their plans for rebellion. The cry of 'Quit India' was to be reinforced by action.

In 1947 I had occasion to write to a Member of Parliament who had been a friend of mine and a rowing colleague at Oxford. In the course of my letter I mentioned the Congress rebellion of 1942, and in his answer he expressed surprise. He was in fact of the extreme left wing of the Parliamentary Labour Party, but even so I found strange his comment that he had always supposed that the so-called rebellion was invented by Winston Churchill. Since then it has become clear that in Great Britain there was very little news permitted of what went on in India in August

---

* Sir George Cunningham, Governor of the North West Frontier Province, learned on 5 July 1942, that the Viceroy had been forbidden by the British Government to consult Governors and others about the scheme. Cunningham, in his diary, refers to this as 'a revelation' of political folly 'which deserves to be more widely known than it is.'

and September of that year. Likewise in India only such news as would cast discredit on the rebels, and such as would not damage public morale, appeared in the papers. Of the former type there was plenty.

In India as a whole there were violent, often bestially cruel, uprisings in all provinces except the North West Frontier Province, the Punjab and Madras. Railways were one of the main targets. Stations were destroyed, signal boxes put out of action, rails torn up. For three weeks rail communication between Delhi and Calcutta was cut. There were some shocking murders of railway staff. At one station in Bihar two Canadian Air Force officers sitting in an immobilized train were induced to give up their revolvers. They were then hauled out of the train and beaten to death. Their bodies were thrown into a flooded stream nearby.

After railways came police stations, district treasuries, and sub-treasuries at *tahsil* headquarters. I never heard of any dereliction of duty by the police in the ranks from inspector downwards. Like the vast majority of Indians they seemed to be capable of a loyalty to their salt which, while not driving out fear, superseded fear as the dominant influence in their conduct. There were numbers of examples of mobs attacking police stations, or treasuries with police guards. So far as my information went there was never any surrender. The reward of such staunchness on the part of the defenders, if they were overwhelmed, as was often the case, was to be burnt alive.

With the whole structure of defence on the eastern boundaries of India in mortal danger; with the individual crimes of barbarism acting to feed the fires of vengeance, it was only natural, however regrettable, that there was a risk of violent retaliation. From my point of view violent reaction was the only and absolute answer, provided that suppression and not retaliation was the only objective. This pious observation is less easy to adopt on the spot and at the time if one is there.

I left the hospital in Calcutta as quickly as possible. There had been riots of a very unpleasant type from the moment that the August 7 decision became known. The nurses and sisters in the hospital, for example, had been terrified as they reported for duty at their various times. My time came at about 4.00 pm one afternoon. The Indian equivalent of a hospital porter whistled for a taxi to take me to Howrah station. The first two drivers refused to go. The driver of the third taxi was a Sikh, and rather disingenuously I suggested that he, like myself, coming from the north-west of India, should not be unduly daunted by Bengali mobs. All Sikhs are brave. He grunted and accepted my baggage. By the grace of God there then hit that area of Calcutta a violent thunderstorm. We drove through empty streets, but from the windows of the taxi I could see, all along the road, the rioters sheltering in their hundreds under the awnings of shops. Indeed, my Sikh friend and I seemed to be the only things then moving. We reached Howrah station unharmed and exchanged sighs of relief.

On arrival at Sambalpur the next morning I learned that on the previous day (Friday) the small state of Talcher had experienced our first subversive action. The town of Talcher stood on a branch railway line running from Cuttack north-west to the British India enclave of Angul. The whole state lay north of the Mahanadi, and the road from Cuttack to Sambalpur cut through its southern borders. A mob had derailed a locomotive, torn up the line and stolen a number of objects, such as fish-plates, which must have been of doubtful use in ordinary life.

The mob then moved on the palace. They had however, under-estimated Raja Harishchandra, a square figure of medium height and apparently ignorant of fear. He personally directed his twenty or thirty policemen to charge the mob and arrest the lot. This they tried to do, but were frustrated when the superintendent of the jail objected on humanitarian grounds to admitting more than two hundred prisoners to a jail possessing accommodation for only forty. One policeman was wounded by an arrow. The Raja was assisted by a Hudson aircraft from Cuttack. This *deus ex machina* did not use its so-called belly-gun, which was kept in reserve against a desperate situation. Instead, it made great play with low sweeps and a generous spraying of flares from a Very pistol. The affair reflected great credit on all concerned.

Although Talcher was by no means pacified – for example, a village headman, loyal to the Raja, had been murdered in the north of the state – I could not go there at once. The Resident had already received the news and had informed us that he was coming on Sunday for consultations. He did so. Most of what he said was in the highest degree encouraging, and in effect meant that this whole affair was an acute national emergency. No officer of his need look over his shoulder at remote authorities when coming to grips with local examples of the emergency. He stood by this throughout. Only once was he somewhat blood-curdling. That was when he said he expected such and such a number of dead miscreants (the accepted word for rebels) by such and such a date. I assumed that I need not look over my shoulder if I failed him in this.

The Resident went back to Calcutta that evening. On Monday Biscoe and I embarked on action against 'miscreants' which in the case of the Congress rebellion covered some four weeks. Rumblings of trouble had come from Nilgiri State whither Biscoe went to take a look. I went to

Talcher, where, by arrangement with the Inspector General of the Eastern States Agency Joint Armed Police, a platoon of that force had already arrived. I should mention at once however, that these men were armed only very simply. Their firearms were old .303 rifles bored out to make .410 smooth-bore muskets. These had a maximum range of 100 yards and were inaccurate at any range beyond 30 yards. They were strictly for close quarters. Apart from the muskets the men had bayonets, which, even when blunt, can also be, or at least appear, useful at close quarters.

On that Monday afternoon we made a show of force in the small town of Talcher and recovered much of the stolen railway property. Room was found in the jail for some obvious looters, even though it meant releasing some less obvious culprits. Next morning I moved out northwards along a dirt road with a force of a very mixed nature. The platoon of armed police numbered something over thirty men, Muslims from the Punjab. The *subhedar*, with medal ribbons on his breast, was over military age. The others were young and untried. Then there were another thirty or so Talcher citizens, enlisted as special constables. They were identified by arm-bands and armed with *lathis*, the six foot bamboos bound in three or four places with iron bands. A junior magistrate, a doctor and a handful of State police made up the party. As ever there was Chandu to see that I received proper food and dry clothes each morning.

This could not seem a formidable force without a good deal of bluff; and we must have seemed even less formidable that morning when we reached the south bank of the Brahmani river only three miles north of our starting point. In pouring rain which had been ceaseless for some days before, we looked across half a mile of silt-laden flood water with never a boat in sight. There was no option but to return to Talcher, but not before very strong orders had gone out for boats to be available next morning.

Next day, Wednesday, we transported our whole party to the north bank in three large oar-propelled boats, and resumed our march northwards. The objective was the village (near the northern boundary of the State) where the headman had been murdered. The hope was to arrest the culprits.

So far we had been unopposed; but towards noon the road narrowed to a defile with the river on the west side and a steep, thickly wooded hill about three or four hundred feet high rising abruptly on the east side. This seemed an obvious place for an ambush. I halted the party, therefore, and sent twenty of the special constables, with a police officer in charge, far out to the right in an encircling movement. Their instructions were to take the enemy, if any, in the rear and to bring in as many prisoners as possible.

Having given them half an hour's start, the rest of us moved into the defile. It reminded me of the pass of Brander as it was about 1930. When we were halfway through there came a noise of crashing from some distance above us. I thought that we had disturbed a herd of bison, and I stood uncertainly, waiting to see where they went. Then occurred something which has stayed clearly in my mind ever since. Among the special constables was a Pathan shop-keeper who traded in the town of Talcher. When he presented himself for enlistment I greeted him in Pakhtu, feeling a genuine friendliness for a man from the North West Frontier. I had also suggested that he should stay by me to help with interpreting if need should arise.

So as I stood uncertainly (incidentally holding a ridiculous little .22 revolver, borrowed from the Raja, and wondering what part of a bison would even feel such a bullet) this man pushed me roughly against the vertical bank on the inner side of the road. He stood over me, his arms extended over my shoulders and his hands against the bank, and told me to stoop. He then explained that the crashing came not from bison but from rocks rolled down upon us by men waiting in ambush. Two days before, we had never met. As a shop-keeper he was not really fighting fit. Yet he had conceived a loyalty which involved my protection in all circumstances.

The release of the rocks revealed to my flanking party where the enemy were. They moved in and caught six; and when we emerged from the northern end of the defile they joined us with their prisoners. I had given much thought to the question of what to do in such circumstances. No doubt my decision may disgust many people today, but in the circumstances I could conceive no other course. The war as a whole was at a point where the Germans and the Japanese were everywhere winning victories. Nearer home the Japanese were collecting themselves for the final assault which would destroy British rule in India. The Congress Party was committed to action which would help that consummation.

Here in the Orissa States (as in Orissa Province) the people were in revolt, ignorant of the greater issues no doubt, but persuaded that violent subversion was their duty. My forces in terms of numbers were negligible, though they were capable of fidelity and staunchness if correctly treated. None were to spare for escort duty, and even if there had been any, there were no jails for the prisoners whom they would be escorting. This led inevitably to some form of summary punishment on the spot. I acted within the Government of India's Defence Regulations and adopted two lines – collective fines on communities; and for people caught in the act of, for example, rolling rocks on Government forces, six of the best on the back-side. It was for this reason that I had with me a magistrate and a doctor. My own authority to act in Talcher State was legally dubious and certainly could only derive from the Raja. The magistrate however, had local criminal jurisdiction. He carried what seemed to be his register of summary cases.

So on this occasion, as on other subsequent occasions, the magistrate duly tried those brought before him charged by the police under the appropriate Regulation. If they were found guilty – and in the circumstances any other finding by the magistrate would be perverse – the doctor would be instructed to examine them and pronounce how many strokes of a bamboo cane their physical condition could tolerate. His approach with a stethoscope was one of the most formidable weapons in the suppression of rebellion. If, after examination of heart and lungs, he prescribed a maximum of four strokes, then that was the sentence. In fact, throughout these troubled times no man received more than four. The effect of these sentences, summarily inflicted, was immediate. Rebels would prefer being shot in hot blood to being painfully humiliated. The six men so punished on that Wednesday were released forthwith.

We moved on towards the village which was our objective. The dull skies and the rain persisted. One quite narrow tributary of the Brahmani could only be crossed by wading waist deep. Then the village came in sight. It was mid-afternoon. I halted the party and gave them a time when they should move in. Then I in my turn embarked on a flanking movement. This time it was over flat but very wet country, first east, then north, then west, so as to prevent the escape of, in particular, the individual murderer. It was necessary not to be seen. This meant a very wide circle.

In due course we – my Pathan friend, two special constables and I – reached the road out of the village on the north and started moving south again. Some men were moving up the road towards us, fleeing from the main party coming from the south. I told them to stop, flourishing the Raja's .22 pistol. There was a slight hesitation. One of my special constables said 'That's him'. I moved towards the man, who was clearly more impressed by the pistol than I was. He fainted. That was the end of that day.

I made my quarters for the night in the village primary school. I clamped a collective fine on the village of five or six hundred rupees from which was deducted at a valuation the cost of all supplies provided for my men – goats, rice and so on. Not a shot had been fired in the three days during which I had been in the State. Yet everyone was now obeying orders. Authority was restored. An example of this was the unexpected arrival in a car of the Diwan of Pal Lahara State, the border of which lay about three miles to the north. In the first place this had involved a journey through continuous jungle over an unmetalled road while heavy rain fell incessantly. The Diwan, a vigorous man in his early thirties called Hara Babu, thought nothing of this; nor did he have any fear of travelling with no escort and no modern communications to report to me that all was quiet in his area. He started back as darkness fell.

Next morning, Thursday, we again embarked in large boats, but this time it was only to drift quietly down the flooded Brahmani River back to Talcher. We disembarked there in the early afternoon. The latest news was that there had been some disturbance in Dhenkanal State. Its western border at this point was the left bank of the Brahmani River, across which I was looking. At its capital town of Dhenkanal, on the main Sambalpur–Cuttack road there was stationed a force of the Joint Armed Police. It was good to hear that one of their platoons (of Sikhs) had had a successful brush with some miscreants, and was now on its way to meet me. I sent the boats back across the river. An hour or so later the platoon arrived. They came ashore, where I was waiting, and reported for further duty in a manner which showed that their morale was high. In less lofty terms, they were very chatty.

My only regret was, assessing the situation, that I might indeed spend a quiet, dry night in the Raja's palace, but that I must cross the river next day and spend two days on foot on the journey to Dhenkanal town, where I had arranged a meeting with Biscoe. Pacification was essential. Odd skirmishes would achieve nothing. I sent cipher telegrams accordingly to Calcutta and to Biscoe in Nilgiri. I also petitioned the Raja for one further piece of help. So far all of us had been handicapped tactically by having to conduct all our operations on foot. This was slow enough on muddy roads. If, as had happened to me on the previous day, encircling movements were called for, running through flooded rice fields in *chaplies* was very slow indeed. Could he possibly find some horses for us? As ever the answer was yes. He had three beasts in his stables, which he would put at my disposal. After close enquiry there were found three men in the two platoons now available who said they could ride. So the next morning we had equine company in the boats which took us across to our next task.

We took two days over our trip through Dhenkanal State and were nowhere attacked. Our three horsemen were particularly impressive, sloshing through paddy fields with bayonets fixed on their muskets and going through the movements of being lancers. And so late on Saturday afternoon I kept my appointment with Biscoe at the Dhenkanal Guest House. I was surprised to find others there too. There was the Inspector

General of the Eastern States Agency Joint Armed Police, with whom, so far as my memory goes, I never saw eye to eye. And there was also Herbert Mooney, with whom I never saw reason to disagree.

Incidentally, he had been on duties other than advising on forests during previous (Congress) disturbances in 1939 in the Orissa States Agency. In that year the Political Agent, Major Bazalgette, was beaten to death in the small state of Ranpur, and his sole companion, a police sub-inspector, having been left for dead, recovered only to be a cripple. In that same year the Assistant Political Agent, Captain Magor, was actually beaten to the ground during an unpleasant confrontation in Gangpur State. So Mooney knew well enough what was going on now.

For my part I was puzzled to know what these two men were doing here. I asked them straight and they showed some embarrassment. Finally two things emerged. The Resident wished to provide me with support at a senior level. After all I was only 35. At the same time he felt uneasy at certain flippancies in such cipher telegrams as I had been able to send him during the past week. Two senior men might convince me that the situation was grave.

I immediately saw the Resident's point of view. Being a man of action, he detested the necessity (and it was indeed a necessity) of sitting most of the time in Calcutta while news trickled in from the very large area for which he was responsible. His subordinates were much younger men of whose reliability and similar qualities he knew nothing. His position was very different from that of the commanding officer of a battalion of a regiment of the Indian Army, where everyone from the top to the bottom, from battalion to battalion, was conscious of the integrated, mutual trust of men and officers. Naturally I did not say anything like this to Mooney or the Inspector General. I did however, move into another room with my elderly, staunch stenographer, Mr Mahanty, and dictated a dispatch running to eight pages of foolscap. I might well have started it, since that was its nature, with what Robert Burns wrote at the beginning of his 'Epistle to a Young Friend':

> Perhaps it may turn out a sang;
> Perhaps, turn out a sermon.

It was sent off by the hand of an armed policeman, who was given a car to Cuttack so that he might catch the Madras Mail for Calcutta. The Resident would get it before breakfast. When he did get it, he was satisfied that things were as good as could be expected, even if he might still disapprove of my interpretation of *dulce est desipere in loco* (to forget one's wisdom is sweet, in the right place).

Biscoe's news of Nilgiri* was not good. The spirit of rebellion was abroad and was encouraged by the many contacts with the Orissa Province which its geographical position made possible. No grave riots had taken place, probably because of Biscoe's demeanour during his five days alone there with no reliable armed force. He tactfully took over control of the untrained and not very imposing State police. Each day he gave them musketry training and so provided warlike noises to deter enemies. It was however, clearly necessary to take measures for the suppression of rebellion. This was in the first instance a matter of principle. It was also a matter of practical importance, since the main railway line from Calcutta to Madras ran through the Balasore district only a few miles beyond the State border to the east. I arranged accordingly for two platoons of the Joint Armed Police to be sent there and I joined them on the Monday following the events in Talcher and Dhenkanal described above.

The days which followed were for me much more unhappy than they were wearisome or alarming. After twelve years of training and experience in working for Indians I had acquired the habit of thinking that it was all very much worthwhile. Moreover the people seemed to appreciate one's services and to express their appreciation far beyond the normal calls of flattery. That on the frontier one might be killed at any time by yesterday's friends was a different matter altogether. After all, the trans-border Pathans in particular owed the British (certainly in their own view) very little. We and they equally had interests in the Frontier, its military and civil administration, and these interests usually conflicted.

India proper however, had not for generations been a theatre of war. *Pace* the Congress Party, there had been no oppression whatsoever since the administration had been taken over by the Crown in 1857; and successive constitutional developments, in my view most unjustifiably slow, had nonetheless shown that Queen Victoria's proclamation of 1 May 1876 was still a binding promise of ultimate self-government. Every district officer remembered the years of friendliness and the mutual trust.

It seemed that this had all gone. I myself should have been warned. I used at one time to read the well-known Hindi newspaper *Bharat*, which means India. Tucked away under the title of the paper on the front page was a quotation from Tulsi Das, the 17th century poet, which may be transliterated, '*Paradhin swapnehu sukh nahin*'. It is as difficult to translate as some of those phrases of Tacitus; but certainly what it means is that even

---

* Nilgiri means 'blue mountain'. This feature rose very steeply a thousand feet behind the town from the coastal plain whose average height above sea level was 14 feet. For several centuries it had been a land-mark for British seamen, to whom it was known as Nelly Gray.

in his sleeping hours a man cannot be content with subjection. This was clearly the feeling of some millions of educated Indians. It was likewise the mainspring of what happened in 1942. What to me was so shocking was the form that the upsurge of the idealists took. Fire and slaughter were abroad to the war-cry of '*Mahatma Gandhi ki Jay*' (Victory to Gandhi, the Great Soul.). The name of the prophet of non-violence was being blasphemed. I take leave to doubt whether the prophet minded much.

In relation to what happened in Nilgiri that week this is no more than an explanation of my unhappiness. On the Tuesday we showed the flag by marching for some hours in the south of the state and back. There was no reaction to our presence; but at one point along the road I recognized a prominent Congress leader walking in the opposite direction. The hatred in his face was shocking. Next day we marched north-west. My intention was to levy and receive collective fines from two villages which had in several ways, short of violence, broken the law. There can be little doubt that my police regarded this as a licence to loot.

For example, one of the villages sat as it were on an island among the flooded paddy fields. Houses and lanes were bordered by high green hedges; and a raised road provided a causeway to the so-called main road. The latter could not carry motor traffic after heavy rain. I sent parties to left and right over the fields so as to cut off any people who tried to leave the village, and then moved in myself along the causeway. As I reached the houses I heard a woman scream on my right. By standing on my toes I was able to see over the hedge one of my men bashing at a cash box with the butt of his musket. There were no means of breaking through the hedge, and even in those days I could only stand on my toes for very brief spells. I did however, utter some menacing shouts. I was able to see that the man dodged away behind the house. The woman, cowering on the verandah, seemed unharmed. The cash box would never be the same again, but it seemed, as I hopped up and down to obtain a view, to be basically intact.

I immediately terminated the exercise and moved the two platoons to a mango grove adjacent to the village. Suppression of rebellion was one matter; to let loose Punjabi and Sikh armed police on a small Oriya village to indulge in loot was quite another. Yet these men were not regular soldiers, nor had they been subjected to true military discipline. The Joint Armed Police had only been called into existence after the disturbances of 1939. For all their uniforms and their oaths of allegiance after the probation period following the initial recruitment, they owed direct loyalty to no one. Finally, these two platoons – factors of geography meant that I never operated with any others – had recently been through a very rough time.

These were the points which I had to look at in the mango grove while (as so often) I ate my sandwiches. To do nothing would be craven. To adopt a domineering approach would probably lead to some sort of mutiny which, even if I survived it, could do nothing but disaster to the cause which I must serve. After careful thought, I called up the two *subhedars* commanding the two companies. I told them straight that I knew that their men had been looting. The *subhedars* may perhaps have tried to restrain them. I did not know. But, if so, they had not succeeded, and here in this mango grove was enough loot to bring shame on the platoons concerned. It was part of my duty to avert this. Of course in these special circumstances there might indeed have been a misunderstanding. I had no doubt that a criminal court would have accepted such a defence. Some distance away yonder there was a clump of bushes; every man must move from right to left behind those bushes and shed his loot as he went. This would in due course be collected and inventoried by the civil authorities as property seized, quite legitimately, in lieu of the collective fine already due from the village.

The sixty odd men moved as ordered. When they had all passed behind the bushes and out on the other side, I went down with the two *subhedars* to see the results. There on the ground lay an astonishing miscellany of private possessions and jewellery. To this day I can see in the eye of memory an umbrella flanked by brass vessels and pieces of silk cloth. My inclination to weep was strong. The men had, however, been shamed into this surrender and I could now proceed to salvage their honour. I called the headman and the other elders and showed them what had been done on my orders, and I explained that all these articles might be claimed from the State treasury as soon as the fine was paid.

Next day, we moved against another village and were resisted with much show of violence. As we marched along a forest road the air was loud with the beat of drum and the blare of conches. When we reached the outskirts of the village I was met by a very brave man. He was the sub-inspector of police in charge of a little post which would normally have had a staff of six constables. On that day four of them were absent on routine duties in their area. The remaining two were present. He marched smartly up to me and saluted. His uniform was clean and starched. Behind him was the pandemonium of shouts, conches and drums. I was able to make him hear me when I spoke, but he was unable to speak. His determination to do his duty, to stay at his post and, if necessary, and as seemed very likely, die at it in good order had governed his conduct. But the poor chap could not control his jaws or his voice. He was later decorated on my recommendation.

Even the armed police seemed shaky. Accordingly I paraded them and went through the old exercise of 'For inspection port arms'. Sure enough one of the younger men had a bullet in his magazine, which duly went off when he 'eased springs' and pulled the trigger after I had finished peering down the barrel. Fortunately he had his musket pointing upwards at exactly the right angle so that he did not blow his neighbour's head off, he only deafened him. This familiar routine had a good effect at least in producing steady ranks. Then I suggested that, since we were really up against large numbers of miscreants (in Hindustani '*dushman*', in English enemy, and no nonsense about euphemisms), then each platoon, Muslim and Sikh, should shout their appropriate war-cry. This suggestion was well received. It was time to move; and when we did move I was glad I was not on the receiving end of '*Allah-o-Akbar*' and '*Sri Sat Akal*' as they gave full vent to their wrath.

I sent one platoon out to the east of the village, partly to keep it disengaged, partly to protect my flank and rear. This left me with thirty men with which to attack the village itself. It all sounds silly in retrospect, but there is a lot to be said for routine tactics. So we had an advance guard of four men, who enjoyed my company. Then a 'link' of one man. That left twenty five, of whom twenty were the main body, for the rearguard, and one the link from the latter to the former. I could only hope that I was not falling short of the standards of the Shrewsbury School OTC, or of the Nagpur Rifles, Auxiliary Force India, in which I learned what I was now putting into practice.

This type of frivolous thought soon had to be abandoned. Our advance guard was charged down a narrow lane by a substantial band of hostile men. I gave the order that each of the four should fire one round. From the point of view of my future remorse it was fortunate that only one shot registered, hitting a poor fellow in the shoulder. We picked him up and handed him over to the doctor while the enemy withdrew.

As we moved on it became clear that stronger aggression was coming. I consolidated a party in an open space and faced west where the mob was concentrated in a pattern of streets. Some shot arrows into the air, over the houses, designed to fall on our heads. The *subhedar* kept one which landed at my feet. Then some charged us. One rather drunk aboriginal came for me with an axe, and for the second time in my life it seemed that I literally saw red. At least the Talcher .22 pistol was in my hand and my finger on the trigger when the *subhedar* crashed his *lathi* on the man's head.

The *subhedar* raised the *lathi* again for the death blow when I suddenly came to my senses. If I gave way to rage there was no knowing what the police would do or what atrocious climax the day would reach. It was too late to stop the blow, but I thrust my walking stick with my left hand into the ground beyond the man's face. The *lathi* slithered down the stick and hit the ground. A word to the *subhedar* was quite enough. Another casualty went to the doctor. The charging enemy were discouraged. The arrows ceased to fall, and we moved cautiously out of the village into open ground to the west.

Here there was a mob of about a hundred or a hundred and fifty men in and about a temple, shouting their heads off, waving a variety of weapons, beating drums and blowing conches. It was clearly essential to retain the initiative; but shooting would have meant many enemy casualties at what had now become close quarters. I could only hope that my men in their heavy boots would be less speedy than the bare-foot enemy as I 'fell them in', went through the drill for fixing bayonets, and then gave the order to charge. '*Allah-o-Akbar*' and '*Sri Sat Akal*' were again a deep-throated roar. The enemy fled. We could not, by the grace of our gods, catch them.

The incident would have been bloodless but for one miserable accident. One of the police, young and fit, and I, not so young but lightly equipped, very nearly caught one of the fleeing men. The policeman at my right elbow inadvertently pulled the trigger, having inexcusably left the safety catch off, and at a range of three feet the fugitive was instantly killed. This was the only fatal casualty in all the operations which Biscoe and I had to undertake during the last five months of 1942. Moreover he was such a small man, one who could hardly have been a menace to anything,

Indeed our real opponents were few and always *embusqué*. They were the agents of the nationalist politicians, stirring up simple cultivators, seducing aboriginals from the mountains and forests to the north-west and supplying them liberally with intoxicating liquor. This was the explanation of the archery to which we had been exposed shortly before. Later this became quite obvious. For the moment this day's work was not over.

We moved back through the village to our starting point and began to eat whatever rations we had brought with us. I tried to pretend that I could not hear the tumultuous noises coming from the east side of the village where the reserve platoon had been posted. It was no use. A runner came with information that large numbers of the enemy had emerged from the forest to the north and were advancing across the half-mile belt of rice fields. So we put away our food and proceeded smartly to join our colleagues. Their message was fully justified. I estimated that not less than two thousand men were advancing, though slowly, across the young green rice growing from its flooded fields and along the little *bunds* which, in grid-iron pattern, demarcated the fields and retained the water. There was the usual orchestral accompaniment.

Here again the initiative had to be seized. The police knew enough about military training to act quickly on my next order, which was to extend at the double to five paces to left and right of the central position which I had taken up. This gave us a front of three hundred yards. I also authorized them to shoot whenever they felt that it was essential to do so, but that no man must exhaust his ammunition on pain of court martial.

I blew a whistle and off we went. The enemy were overawed and fled. A few shots were fired by some of our optimistic young men, something which I could condone so long as the enemy was manifestly out of range of our out-of-date weapons. Then I blew the whistle again and we went back to the village once more.

At this point I took a risky decision. It was based, first, on the success of what we had done that day. It seemed that we had quite simply routed the rebels. That this was true became obvious next day when I was informed of propaganda from the enemy telling the population of the area at large of our atrocities and of my own competence with regard to rape. This simply meant that local vindictiveness must be introduced in place of nationalist idealism.

That evening however, I was firmly determined, as I remained throughout these disturbances, not to evacuate and withdraw from the smallest nuclear point of law and order. The brave Sub-Inspector who had met us in the morning was told that his *thana** was to be maintained. The Musulman platoon was left to provide it with a garrison. This order was not well received by the *subhedar*. I met this difficulty by pretending I had not noticed. I collected the Sikh platoon and, as the afternoon drew on to darkness, moved very fast through the jungle to where, many hours before, we had left our motor transport. So in due course some of us were back in the town of Nilgiri.

I received two letters next day. The first came as a situation report from the platoon which I had left behind. Everything seemed to be quiet in that area, so I brought the platoon back to headquarters. The second was a challenge from a village called Ayodhya to try my offensive tactics on them. This could not be ignored, but I took it up in my own time. The foremost consideration in my mind was still to retain the initiative. It seemed to me however, that I could no longer do this with so few men with such obsolete equipment. The adjoining parts of the Orissa Province were in complete turmoil and the state boundary was after all only a line on a map.

---

* Police station.

I resorted, therefore, to two courses then open to me. At dusk that evening I drove to Balasore station, paid a call on the Station Master and obtained his permission to use the railway telephone in his office. He was also good enough to leave me alone. I then telephoned the man in charge of a particular signal box in Kharagpur. He was my link with the Brigadier, who had shortly before driven down to Nilgiri to see how we were getting on, and who had made this arrangement with me. Now I said that I would be grateful for the supply of a platoon of troops as soon as possible. To be brief, I met them at dusk the next day when they alighted from the Madras Mail. Trains were full of troops in those days. This arrival was in no way conspicuous, and the arrangements for their accommodation, which could not be concealed, did not reveal in the darkness that these reinforcements were drawn from a modern army. We moved off at dawn on Thursday, 1 October 1942, in our motor transport.

As soon as I knew that the troops had been allocated I sent a cipher telegram to the Air Officer Commanding at Cuttack. This requested air support at 9.00 am for an attack on Ayodhya. Such map references as I was able to give came from an atlas borrowed from a local school, but they sufficed. Finally I sent Chandu down to the bazaar to buy two cotton *dhotis* (loin cloths). I had them folded in my haversack when we started off early next morning, now quite a formidable force. The Indian troops under a young and intelligent *subhedar* were armed with real .303 rifles (Lee Enfield Mark 5) and a proportion of Browning automatics, similar to, if not identical with, those used by American gangsters and referred to in the associated literature as 'typewriters'. My original two platoons after several days' rest were in good fettle. I had also for the first time in Nilgiri enrolled some special constables, included among whom were a handful of rascally Gurkhas, long resident in the slums of Calcutta. They had been recently employed by the Raja as watchmen at the palace. They bore no resemblance to the Gurkha soldiers whose record in the Indian Army was so shining.

After ten or twelve miles in buses, we alighted at a forest road which after three miles would bring us to the back of the village. I hoped this would be unexpected, and to some extent it was. Soon however, the conches and drums began. We reached the end of the trees about 8.45 am and looked across an uncultivated clearing which extended northwards and north-eastwards to a large grove of ancient mango, *nim* and *pipal* trees which embowered the village. The distance was about 800 yards. Under the distant trees a large number of men, difficult to estimate, was dispersed. They shouted and flitted in the shadows which, since for once the sun was shining, were relatively dark. Now and again a few men would rush forward, perform what must have been partly ritual movements, and then retreat into the shadows.

I was waiting for the aircraft from Cuttack, but I thought the troops might be glad of some action, and that I could derive some benefit from it. I asked the *subhedar* for three marksmen. They stood forward. The leaf-sights on the Lee-Enfield only catered for distances up to 600 yards. These men were, therefore, highly unlikely to make contact with a moving man at 800 yards. The crack and whine of the bullets should nonetheless start some wild surmise in the minds of the enemy, expecting by now only our very different weapons. I ordered two rounds to be fired by each of the three men. I could see leaves and small branches falling in the distance and in fact there were no casualties.

On the stroke of 0900 hours a Hudson appeared overhead. I ran out in the open with my two *dhotis* and spread them on the ground in the form of an arrow-head pointing towards the enemy – the Popham panel in the twilight of its use. The pilot took the point and did several hair-raising runs from behind us towards the trees. There appeared to be two men in the plane. The pilot took it in at about thirty feet and at a speed (if I may venture a guess) in excess of 150 mph. Just short of the trees he did an almost vertical climb in order to clear them. His companion, using the hatch (if that be the word) from which the so-called belly-gun would normally fire, fired Very pistols very fast both on the run-in and on the precipitous ascent.

The enemy fled and we saw no more that day. We could hear the Hudson roaring around at a greater and greater distance, which showed that it was demonstrating against parties of men either coming up to support the villagers or dispersing from the village. It was completely successful. I had sent our motor transport back to Nilgiri when we first alighted with orders to meet us later in the day at a point about ten miles north of the village; and thither we marched without meeting with any opposition. The disturbances in Nilgiri had finished.

The same, with one exception, was the case throughout the Agency. The exception occurred in Nayagarh State, which was situated on the south bank of the Mahanadi and south-west of Cuttack. There a mob had attacked a police post manned by five or six men. The latter resisted stoutly, killing one man and wounding several others. The mob carried their wounded away. I had this news in Nilgiri, and, although the authorities in Nayagarh seemed confident that they had the situation in hand, I decided to pay a visit with some of my Joint Armed Police stalwarts. This I did in the following week after a short visit to Sambalpur to deal with my much neglected correspondence and administrative work.

Our march through Nayagarh was not opposed, but that did not imply that all was well. The local police had not been able to lay hands on more than one or two of those who attacked the police post; and this even extended to the wounded, whose wounds would provide mute testimony of their guilt in the absence of oral evidence. We collected a few, including a man who would undoubtedly have died if he had not been given up. I heard of him by roundabout ways, and his village was one of those which we visited. Everywhere such few people as we met wore the now familiar look of dumb hatred.

As a momentary digression I would point out that this, with more spectacular indications of hostility, occurred in small states with long common borders with Orissa Province. Those states isolated from Congress propaganda seemed to be contented with their lot. This meant that, for example, in Nayagarh *fortiter in re* (strong in action) simply had to precede *suaviter in modo* (gentle in manner). This is always the point where the administrator with humane scruples is confronted not only with rampant violence but also with the categorical imperative of restraint.

So far as Nayagarh was concerned I dealt with this daunting dilemma in two ways. Three aboriginals identified, and later self-confessed, as attackers of the police post, each received three strokes of a light rattan cane. I doubt whether clemency could go much further. Incidentally they made no fuss at all. This pleased me, as a champion of aboriginals, very much.

As regards the badly wounded man, it became obvious that he had been carried from his hut into the surrounding forest so that we should not arrest him. He must not be left to die. I rehearsed this threat and that in my mind and finally came out with an ultimatum based on North West Frontier procedure. If the man were not produced within such and such a number of minutes, I would arrest and carry off to jail six men of those now listening. There they would remain as hostages for his production until further notice. The poor man was brought in on a *charpoy* (a rope bed) very soon. He was in a very bad state with a septic wound in the left shoulder from a musket ball. I am glad to remember however, that he recovered to serve six months, less remission, for participating in a riot.

The cessation of the insurgence which had been instigated by the Indian Congress in the Orissa States Agency did not mean that for Biscoe and me there was to be freedom to return to routine work. There remained another nucleus of insurgence in Gangpur State. This state lay north of the Bengal Nagpur Railway line from Jharsuguda, immediately north of Sambalpur, and extended for about seventy miles eastwards. Here the vast majority of the population – several hundred thousand – were aboriginals of the Munda tribe, which also extended northwards into the Ranchi district of Bihar Province. For many years they had been converts to Christianity in the Lutheran church, the result of hard work by a German missionary organization. To journey through their country was to meet a unique feature in rural India, the church tower in every village.

Unfortunately the German provenance of their conversion was accompanied by steady pro-German propaganda. Shortly before the outbreak of war on 5 September 1939 the German missionaries, of whom the senior man was named Schultz, quite simply went back to Germany. They had instilled into their converts a strong corporate sense, both tribal and religious; and the Mundas of Gangpur State had been instigated in 1939 to mount a campaign for the non-payment of land revenue which had been increased by a recent settlement. It was in that connection that the affray took place to which I have referred already.* This was not creditable to either side. The Mundas actually felled Magor, whereupon the State police opened fire unordered and killed several Mundas. Magor got back on his feet and with difficulty stopped what was in fact panic action. The incident left the Mundas resentful and unsuppressed.

During the subsequent three years there took place an official review of the land review settlement which was alleged to be so oppressive as to have led directly to revolt. The verdict of the officer who performed the review was that the enhanced assessment of land revenue could in no way excuse the reaction of the Mundas. There followed a quiet period; and my predecessor as Political Agent had reason to think that this matter was closed.

In 1942 it re-appeared. To the best of my belief this was directly caused by one Jaipal Singh, though his motives were certainly not those of Herr Schultz. He was never an enemy of the British. To me however, in that year he was a perfect nuisance. I only wish I had met him and told him so.

Jaipal Singh was a Munda. He was initially educated by the Lutheran missionaries and, on the basis of their recommendations and others, was nominated (a process then possible) as a probationer for the Indian Civil Service. I think that he must have been a very pleasant man to know. He was also a brilliant hockey player and represented India in the Olympic Games of 1928. He was at Oxford during my undergraduate period. As an Indian probationer he was required to spend two years over his probationary studies; and he was naturally a very welcome recruit to the Oxford University Hockey Club. At the end of his two years he was unable to pass the necessary examinations and his connection with the Indian Civil Service was terminated.

---

* See p. 168.

He returned to India and for some years was a master at the Rajkumar College in Raipur. A large proportion of the boys at the school, although technically Rajputs, had in varying degrees, consanguinity with the aboriginal Rajas of the Eastern States Agency; and from Mr Smith Pearce, the Principal of the College at that time, I gathered that Jaipal Singh was a valuable member of his staff – up to a point. His mind seemed to be going towards a form of nationalist politics. This did not, however, mean Indian nationalism. It meant a return to his own people, the Mundas, to lead whom had become his aspiration.

When I arrived in Sambalpur in April 1942, Gangpur State was under the management of the Political Agent. This was because the Raja was a minor; and his mother, the Regent Rani, was not regarded as legally competent to exercise full powers on his behalf. One consequence of this was that I bore full responsibility for what went on there. The Rani Sahiba was a sensible lady whose excellent English reflected the standard of conventional education which she had achieved. The state was well administered. Such major problems as confronted it seemed to originate only from Christian missionaries. Of the Lutheran Mundas there will be much more to relate.

There were also however, some Belgian Roman Catholic missionaries who probably came under the general description of White Fathers. Where the Lutherans were truculent and subversive, the Roman Catholics were, as it seemed to me, insidiously penetrative. Simply from the point of view of the Christian faith, which I profess, I could see no reason why Christians of any sect should not be free to testify to that faith and (probably inevitably) proselytize by example and by service. The medical missionaries were outstanding examples.

The Belgians gave anxiety to the Regent Rani, however, by repeatedly asking for grants of land, fiscal reliefs and similar privileges, with no administrative or legal basis for the requests. Rather there was a subtle underlying suggestion of two things: refusal might lead to discontent, discontent to disloyalty. Consent would no doubt be followed by increased devotion to the *darbar*, ie the State government. The Belgian mission tried this approach on me. Very early one morning in August or September 1942 I was visited by a tall, bearded man in a white cassock. He appeared to be about fifty years old. He presented what was clearly intended to be a grave presence. I had been working in the office, but I ushered him into the drawing room where we sat down. 'Yes, what may I do for you?' said I, producing as polite a manner as was within my power at 7.50 am with an empty stomach.

'I came to ask you, Mr Mitchell, if you would wish me to use my influence with the Roman Catholic community in Gangpur State to persuade them not to join the Lutherans in their present agitation.' I have never been proud of the fact that I have a violent temper; and on this occasion I tried very hard to suppress the rage which this question, sanctimonious, sly, dishonest, aroused. By the grace of God I preserved my self-control. I asked him quite quietly, with what I hoped was a neutral expression, 'Are you not already doing so?'

This both disconcerted and annoyed him. He went away. For the rest of my time in that post I heard no more from the Regent Rani about the activities of those men.

When the Congress troubles were allayed I turned my whole attention to Gangpur. We were able to list by name and domicile some of the leaders, but of course Jaipal Singh was the chief of these. He was no longer a schoolmaster. He held a commission in the Indian Army and in the middle of 1942 was Captain (later Major, I believe) Jaipal Singh, Recruiting Officer, Ranchi. This was very convenient for him in respect of the Mundas both of Gangpur State and of Ranchi District. For the former he could provide a refuge from the state authorities when necessary. For all he could offer gainful employment either in the fighting formations of the Indian Army or in the numerous ancillary arms. All the time he could advise and control the no-rent campaign.

In September the Commissioner of the Ranchi Division, Mr Swanky, and his wife very kindly gave me hospitality while I paid a visit to the place. I discussed certain matters of mutual concern with him. More especially, however, I sought and obtained an interview with the Brigade Commander with a view to discussing what could or should be done to control Jaipal Singh. To me it seemed obvious that an officer of the Indian Army should not be allowed, as a sideline to his military duties, to conduct subversive activities of a basically political nature to the detriment of the government and the Crown. Even this presentation of the case omitted any attempt to assess the context – the Japanese on the door-step.

My words fell on deaf ears. The Brigadier seemed to know little about India. Oh, yes, he was quite prepared to believe that Jaipal Singh was a 'naughty boy' (his very words), but he was not prepared to take any action of any sort against one of his most valuable officers. No harsh words were spoken. We parted with smiles. It was however, borne in on me how relatively unimportant in 1942 were the problems, the excursions and alarms, the anxieties of the Orissa States Agency.

I had now to fall back on my own resources. I consulted the Resident before issuing notice to the Mundas that all arrears of land revenue must be paid before midnight of 30 November, otherwise they would be collected by force. The Resident was warned by one of his advisors that this might result in open rebellion, and he asked me to comment. I asked what the adviser imagined that we were facing at the moment other than open rebellion. So the notice went out. It was becoming clear in the later months of the year that the notice had not impressed the Mundas. In a way I was pleased with this. I certainly had not wished to move in on a certain area to be met by a hostile mob and to have to open fire on them. I hoped that the desired result could be achieved without bloodshed and that we could convince the opposition that we disposed of irresistible power. At the same time it seemed that the truculent defiance of the law by the Mundas could not be stopped except by strong counter measures. These I now took.

Several weeks before the appointed date I completed the plans for what had to be done. I obtained the services of six platoons of the Joint Armed Police. These had not been with me before. The two at the Dhenkanal depot had earned a rest, and the fresh ones came from other depots. They too proved to be very good. Three of them were allocated to Biscoe, who would operate from the town of Gangpur itself at the western end of the state. Three would be with me operating from a *tahsil* headquarters at the eastern end. Accommodation was arranged for them; and they would move in during the late afternoon of 30 November.

There were also recruited nearly two hundred special constables from the Hindu population of the state, serving for one rupee a day. In a situation where there was sufficient time to plan, I could see no reason why for once the forces of law and order should not be adequately mobilized. Earlier in the year we had been compelled to take risks with scanty force. In Gangpur we knew that our opponents were a cohesive population to be numbered well into six figures. Our forces, even in their increased form, only numbered a nominal three hundred armed police; and the word nominal is significant. In our experience so far, six platoons would not muster for action much more than two hundred men. The special constables, to put it gently, would not have done for Gideon. Nonetheless it was clearly seen on the part of our forces that resolution, discipline, surprise and above all speed, must prevail over any odds. This was proved in the event.

The collection of numbers was not, of course, the only element of our plans. The enemy, whether followers of Schultz or of Jaipal Singh, had been specifically warned that the only point in issue was the payment of land revenue. On our side likewise the collection of land revenue was the first objective. If this were achieved, the Mundas might reconcile themselves to the authority of the *darbar* or they might contrive some new subversion. If the latter were to occur, at least it would be manifest that they were embarked on subversion for its own sake. Anything that we were about to do was designed to foreshadow what that might mean for them.

One other measure was, therefore, taken unobtrusively. At both ends of the state we prepared a train of several scores of bullock carts. They were to receive their orders after dark on 30 November. That day everything was ready. I left Biscoe soon after lunch and moved off in our motor transport eastwards, arriving at our destination as darkness was setting in. I had privately arranged for myself to be the guest of an elderly Scotsman named Alexander who was the owner and managing director of a limestone business. He was supplying very large quantities of limestone as a flux for the iron foundries in Jamshedpur and its neighbourhood. As a man he deserved more than the passing mention which I can give him here.

That evening, after I had seen the three platoons to their quarters and told the *subhedars* to report for instructions at 7.00 pm, he met me on the verandah of his house. He was short and plump, straight out of a bath and wearing cotton trousers and shirt of a dazzling whiteness; the shirt was topped at the collar by a black bow tie. The verandah was heavily festooned with scented flowering creepers. To the south a walled garden of about half an acre, part lawn, part herbaceous borders, was being generously watered from *mashaks** by four coolies and giving off the humid scents of earth and flowers. His welcome was kindly, and his first enquiry was 'would ye like an egg tae yer tea?'

The tea was taken about 5.50 pm with two other Scotsmen and the wife of one of them. The briefing of the *subhedars* followed, at which Mr Alexander asked to be present. Then for the first time I explained that the whole force would parade at 2.50 am, this to include motor transport. The objective was a village eight or ten miles to the east – a village of some size which was the home of several rebels and a staging post for many, since it lay very close to the Ranchi border. We would use transport up to a point two miles from the village, using only sidelights. We would have to go slowly in any case because we would be driving only on cross-country cart tracks. The last two miles would be covered on foot with no lights and no talking.

My map was a good one. From it I was able to show where one platoon would halt at the western outskirts of the village. This would be my headquarters where my staff as usual would include a magistrate and a doctor. One platoon would circle right, the other left, and they would join

* Goat-skins.

up on the east of the village. As soon as I judged the light to be sufficient I would blow a whistle long and loud. All three platoons would extend right or left until each one had made contact with its neighbours. This primarily involved contact with my platoon on the west. The village would thus be surrounded. Bayonets would be fixed, but muskets would not be loaded. Another whistle from me would be the order for the circle to be closed.

The *subhedars* were very intelligent and the exercise went off as if one and all had done it often before. At my end we enjoyed a bonus. When the moonless darkness had absorbed us all, I walked forward very quietly to a small clump of mango trees, more for something to do than with any clear idea in mind. Most unexpectedly I saw dimly in the starlight a number of *charpoys* under trees with humps on them which could only be men sleeping under blankets. I retraced my steps even more quietly; instructed a few men in whispers what to do; and a few minutes later found that we had taken prisoner in complete silence six of the leaders of the rebellion. Even they were not eager to protest noisily in face of bayonets.

By the time the force had moved into the village it was broad daylight and the bullock carts were beginning to roll in from the west. We seized every scrap of moveable rice which we could find. This meant not small quantities ready for husking and so for immediate use, but huge balls of rice confined by thick ropes, the diametre of each ball being about four feet. The magistrate, who was also the local *tahsildar*, stuck on each ball a label with the name of the owner written on it, and gave to the owner a receipt. It was explained that the rice would be instantly returned to those who paid their land revenue in full at the *tahsil*.

There was no need to fix a time limit. The rice was vital to them. Payments were being made very soon after the loaded bullock carts had returned to the *tahsil*. With Biscoe meeting with similar success at his end, the whole subversion collapsed. I did another march on the 2 December towards the west. This time I took no bullock carts. It was a calculated show of force; or perhaps a matter of trailing one's coat. At no time was there any opposition. No shot was fired. No blow was struck.

Once only, on this second day, there came the beat of a drum from a village nearly a mile away across the fields. We ran at the village across the fields which were now dry and provided good going. When we reached it there was no man, woman or child in sight. I peered into some of the houses, not wishing to be attacked from the shadows. All I found that was of any significance was, in every house, a photograph with the subscription 'Captain Jaipal Singh MA, OUHC' (Oxford University Hockey Club).

His hockey 'blue' at Oxford was easily adaptable to an impressive acronym!

On the afternoon of 2 December I said good bye to Mr Alexander and drove back to Gangpur town. Biscoe reported on his successes and warned me that the Resident might possibly be annoyed. He had received no report from me on the previous day. Ever anxious to support his officers, he had (by what means I never knew) obtained the services of a platoon of the Leicester Regiment and had them sent at once to Gangpur. This explained the unexpected presence of British sentries before I could get into the State Guest House.

The trouble was that I had no clerical staff with me during the previous two days; there was no telegraph office where I had been; and in any case I had not burdened myself with the necessary cipher books without which it was only possible to send messages in clear – which was out of the question. Having returned within reach of all these essentials of efficient practice, I sent that evening to Calcutta a report which, by sheer dullness, was calculated to allay all anxiety. It is only right to record however, that the presence of British troops represented a very wise precaution. Moreover, as the news of their presence went about the countryside, it was brought home to the Mundas that the Government really did mean business.

So this year of troubles drew to its end. The Orissa States were quiet. The Japanese were held on the northern frontiers of Burma. In the war as a whole there began to be light in the darkness. In India as a whole the turmoil was subsiding, and some of us were able to concentrate more on administrative work. The year 1943 was, however, to be a very difficult one. My staff in Sambalpur numbered nineteen. Owing to the great amount of time which I spent away from headquarters – inevitable with twenty-three states to deal with – all the burden of office supervision fell on the Superintendent. In 1943 he asked for leave of absence one day and died on the following day. He was riddled with tuberculosis. The life of a brilliant man in his mid-thirties had been surrendered for reasons which only he could explain. Three more of the older members of the staff were invalided out of service, They included my elderly stenographer and friend Mr Mahanty. He was succeeded by a good-looking but also frail-looking Bengali young man named Chatterjee, who in no way fell short of his predecessor. Of the remaining seventeen all except three had to be granted lengthy sick leave. A man would need to have a heart of stone not to remember these devoted men.

So far as the Orissa States were concerned it can be recorded that in 1943 it was possible to administer and to plan without the irrelevance of violent insurgence. The atmosphere had cleared. In Ranpur State, a very small area east of Nayagarh and forming a promontory into the province of Orissa south of Cuttack, I was a visitor on 25 February of that year. Only a short time had passed since the rebellion had been at its height; and I went there with no escort but solely in my capacity of Political Agent, responsible for the administration during the minority of the Raja.

At that time Mr Gandhi, in detention in Poona, was (in his own words) fasting unto death. His motive was not wholly clear but could be inferred. The rebellion had failed. Most of the leaders of the Congress Party were in custody. The Party had thus lost the initiative in its attack on the British in India. Mr Gandhi was seeking to regain that initiative. I had to expect, therefore, that in Ranpur, and in other places, there would be a recrudescence of rebellion in his support. It was not surprising, therefore, that there, and in most other places which I visited on tour at that time, I was always asked in public what I thought of the stand which he had taken. I always answered with another question. The word for suicide in all the Sanscritic languages of India was *atmahatya*. This meant 'the murder of the soul'. It was a fundamental tenet of Hinduism that this was a sin involving posthumous damnation. Was it not for them, as Hindus, to answer their own question? It applied, after all, to the Mahatma, 'the great soul'.

There was always complete agreement; and there nowhere seemed to be any resentment remaining from the action taken against rebels. In Ranpur the conciliatory attitude of those whom I met was indeed embarrassing. In a single day I formally opened, by invitation, a Social Club, a cattle-breeding centre, and an orphanage. I still have the illuminated addresses in which the history of each project was set out and I was (to quote one of them) asked 'to impart your blessings in a formal way'. In the case of the cattle-breeding centre the Viceroy, Lord Linlithgow, was especially praised for his unceasing concern with Indian agriculture. My contribution was to be my 'Kind blessings as its God-father'. In the subscription of two of these addresses occur the words 'Your most loyal subjects'.

Later I paid a visit to Nilgiri. The state had been brought under management after the disturbances. I had felt bound to recommend this measure to the Resident since it was clear that bad administration had contributed very largely to the discontent of the people, which in turn made them emotionally susceptible to subversive propaganda. I was at the same time sorry to do so. The Raja was a good man with cultured tastes and a special interest in Indian ballet. The interview at which I communicated to him the decision of the Government of India was distasteful to me. It was made less so by his quiet and dignified, even friendly, acceptance of the orders.

He also welcomed the new *diwan* whom I intended to appoint. This was T C R Menon, an outstandingly able young man whom the Bastar *darbar* had agreed to put at my disposal on deputation for two or three years. It was Menon who greeted my wife and me with our two younger children, and who told me that the people of Ayodhya, of all places, hoped that I would find time to do some duck-shooting there. One could hardly refuse; but when we were close to the village I turned the car so that it was facing the way from which we had come and told my wife to drive fast away (for the children's sake – she would never be concerned about her own safety) if sounds of tumult should come from the village. There were none. There was only a friendly reception. The only unfortunate thing was that the duck had to be shot from a dug-out canoe. Such things have no keel, preclude standing and make the actual hitting of the birds almost impossible.

Visits to states now became a pleasure. Most of the Rajas were at heart good men. Even those who had been deprived of their powers were mainly the victims of their own incompetence or self-indulgence rather than monsters of iniquity. Every state under administration was now visited and inspected twice a year. Since the *diwans* (the chief executive officers) were appointed by the Political Agent, inspections and administrative planning became purely professional exercises with no breath of politics or corrupt self-interest affecting decisions. In one such state only was there a somewhat different relationship between the *diwan* and the Political Agent, and for the amusement which it gave me I would not have had it otherwise. This was Bonai, a small state which lay north-east of Sambalpur at a distance of forty miles. The Raja was elderly, pleasant and hopelessly incompetent. His people liked him and his *diwan*; and the latter was retained in the post when the state was taken under management a few years before I arrived. He was middle-aged, of medium height, somewhat portly and possessed of the type of benevolence which characterizes some of the less dynamic bishops of the Christian Church somnolent here on earth. Verily he, like they, would in due course have his reward.

He had a genuine interest in primary education, which he linked closely with a concern for the proper nutrition of young children. The latter can be passed off quickly, since it mainly showed itself in his demonstration to inspecting officers of children consuming with obvious reluctance saucers full of cold raw germinated *gram* (*cicer arietinum* or chick pea). The spectacle reminded me of the maize puddings at St Ninian's School during the

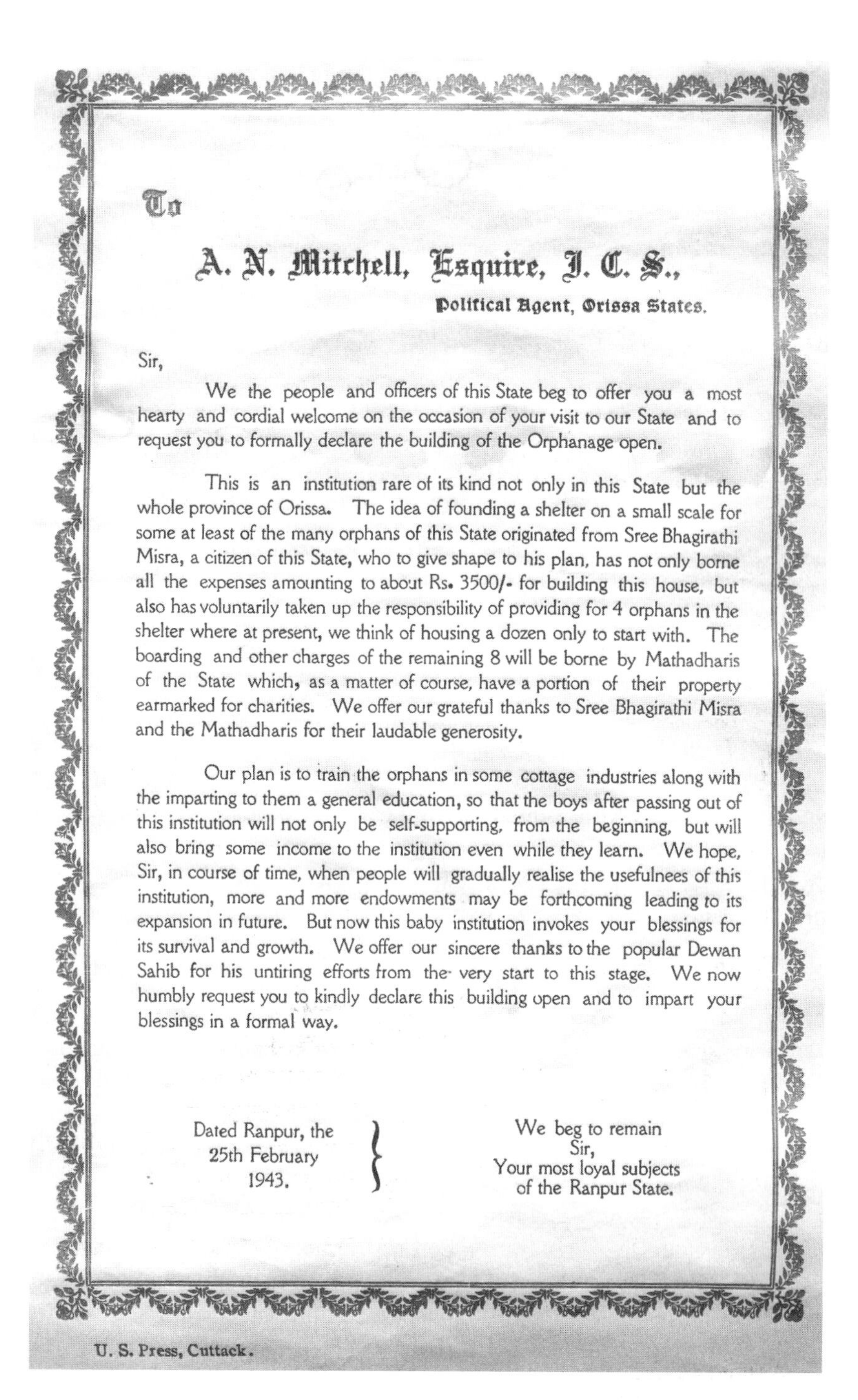
To

A. N. Mitchell, Esquire, I. C. S.,

Political Agent, Orissa States.

Sir,

We the people and officers of this State beg to offer you a most hearty and cordial welcome on the occasion of your visit to our State and to request you to formally declare the building of the Orphanage open.

This is an institution rare of its kind not only in this State but the whole province of Orissa. The idea of founding a shelter on a small scale for some at least of the many orphans of this State originated from Sree Bhagirathi Misra, a citizen of this State, who to give shape to his plan, has not only borne all the expenses amounting to about Rs. 3500/- for building this house, but also has voluntarily taken up the responsibility of providing for 4 orphans in the shelter where at present, we think of housing a dozen only to start with. The boarding and other charges of the remaining 8 will be borne by Mathadharis of the State which, as a matter of course, have a portion of their property earmarked for charities. We offer our grateful thanks to Sree Bhagirathi Misra and the Mathadharis for their laudable generosity.

Our plan is to train the orphans in some cottage industries along with the imparting to them a general education, so that the boys after passing out of this institution will not only be self-supporting, from the beginning, but will also bring some income to the institution even while they learn. We hope, Sir, in course of time, when people will gradually realise the usefulnees of this institution, more and more endowments may be forthcoming leading to its expansion in future. But now this baby institution invokes your blessings for its survival and growth. We offer our sincere thanks to the popular Dewan Sahib for his untiring efforts from the very start to this stage. We now humbly request you to kindly declare this building open and to impart your blessings in a formal way.

Dated Ranpur, the
25th February
1943.

We beg to remain
Sir,
Your most loyal subjects
of the Ranpur State.

U. S. Press, Cuttack.

Speech during visit to Ranpur, 1943. Note 'Your most loyal subjects'

1914–18 war, and induced a mood of self-pity which most culpably ousted my feeling of sympathy for the contemporary infants. The matter of primary education was different. So also was the *diwan*'s approach. He saw with unerring eye two things: first, there must be school buildings; secondly, such buildings must get off to a good start.

The question arose as to how both objectives could be achieved rapidly. He found a method whereby they could be achieved both simultaneously and in the twinkling of an eye. First, it was necessary to wait for a visit by some distinguished person. The ideal visitor was the Political Agent. These officers never stayed long in their posts, especially in war time. Moreover it was the Political Agent who controlled the state finances and might be (dare one say unsuspectingly?) influenced to allocate any amount of money to primary education if suitably handled. So when his routine visit was intimated, the *diwan* got to work.

The acknowledgement of the receipt of the intimation would include suggestions for actions of an extra-curricular type. He would write, for example, that there was a strong public demand for a primary school on the outskirts of Bonai town. The Political Agent's paternal interest in this field of administration was well-known, although everyone appreciated that he had been hampered by the scanty revenues of Bonai State from proceeding as far as he wished along this path. In this instance however, a partial solution to the problem had been reached after exhaustive discussion. The building would be constructed of timber with a thatched roof. These materials would be provided by the *darbar*. Strict costing procedures might put a price on them, but in effect the structure would cost nothing and only the labour would have to be paid for. If this relatively trivial expenditure were approved, the only remaining request from the public was that the Political Agent would lay the foundation stone.

I was partly taken in by this when my turn came. After all, I myself had been the *diwan* of a state under management and had been through the experience of visits by officers of my own service. My method of dealing with them was to ensure that they were offered big game shooting, bird shooting and fishing of a quality and in a degree of comfort which ensured acceptance. The addition of one or two banquets ensured that there would be no time for inquisitorial action in respect of the administration. I did once however, have a visit from a Political Officer junior to myself. Him I would not dream of hoodwinking, so we arranged his visit for the occasion of our annual, genuine and very satisfactory agricultural show. To the *diwan* such options were not open. I accepted, therefore, in a spirit of sympathy his proposals for expenditure and the invitation (I suppose literally) to found the school.

The ceremony took place one evening. Variegated bunting adorned a small pavilion constructed of newly-culled branches of mango trees. Tea, iced cakes and betel nuts were enjoyed as much by the teeming spectators as by the privileged participators. At the precise moment prescribed by the resident astrologer – the *kshubh muhurth* – I laid the foundation stone. Of course, it was not a stone. How could it be so for a building destined to be constructed of timber and thatch?

The *diwan*'s ingenuity had however, been equal to this challenge. A deep hole had been dug approximately 2′ × 2′. At an acute angle a tree-trunk had been placed with the bottom end in the hole and the top end, some ten feet away, supported by two muscular men stripped to the waist. The astrologer negligently cast a silver rupee in the hole. In my turn I gave a token upward push to the tree-trunk. The muscular men wrestled it into a perpendicular position when it slid into the hole. The applause could at best be described as polite. Later that evening I strolled out from the guest house for a breath of cool air after dinner. As I approached the scene of the ceremony I could not help noticing that the foundation 'stone' was no longer in the hole. It was too much to expect that the silver rupee would still be where I had last seen it. Indeed some enthusiastic singing from an adjacent liquor shop suggested that the muscular men had been the ultimate beneficiaries.

It is only fair to record that the *diwan* conceived his own agricultural show later on. This was organized to impress the Resident. No one so distinguished had ever visited Bonai. Apart from the space and the stalls allocated to animals and vegetables, there was a central space of beaten earth about half an acre in area. At the northern end a stage, or dais, suitably over-arched with canvas, had been set up, on which sat the Resident, the *diwan* at his elbow, and other honoured guests.

By this time the citizens of Bonai, unless they were very ungrateful, must have felt themselves well entertained in return for their taxes. We more or less processed from the south end of the concourse area to the stage. The Political Officers were in uniform, which really meant that they were wearing bush shirts with medal ribbons and white-cum-gold gorget tabs. The *diwan* was more than ever episcopal in cream-coloured silk vestments. Even the British ladies looked, and probably felt, upstaged.

I had done my best not to interfere with any of the *diwan*'s arrangements, not least because I was confident that he was in close touch with the charming little old Raja. Unfortunately I had not wholly assessed the extent of his showmanship. We saw as we drew near the dais that a hole had been dug in the ground immediately below it. It measured about 3′ × 3′ and may have been six or seven feet deep at the deepest part. About four feet down the soil had been left untouched on one side to form a shelf.

The *diwan*, as if announcing a cabaret show, explained from the dais that for our delectation and admiration a certain holy man would be voluntarily buried alive. Later the miracle of his survival would be revealed. Amidst appropriate applause a small man, stripped down to his loin cloth, embellished with ashes and varied pigments, and looking rather glum, was led forwards. In a trice he was sitting in the hole on the shelf. A board was placed over the hole; over the board was heaped the excavated earth to the depth of a foot; and all was made tidy by enthusiastic bashing of the soil with spades.

I looked at the Resident. He seemed to approve – as if, while this was no novelty to him, he saw nothing wrong and indeed some interest in this bizarre form of gambling with death. His facial expression was a combination of academic interest and a wish for someone to offer him attractive odds.

My feelings were different. As the speeches went on and on, I could only think of the progressive fouling of the air in those fifty or sixty hermetically sealed cubic feet. It was well over an hour and a half later, when the speeches were over and the *diwan* was escorting the Resident round the exhibits and urging him to restore the tissues with some germinated *cicer arietinum*, that I returned to what I had now come to think of as the arena. There were no spectators. The disciples of the holy man were chewing pan as they squatted round the tomb and quietly awaited orders. I gave them a very sharp order to get the poor chap out. He was duly exhumed and I saw something really interesting. He was beyond question in a coma. Not for several minutes was he aroused, and even then he looked very much as does a boxer recovering after a knock-out. One may wonder how much longer he could have lived.

There were matters of greater and wider importance in the wind in 1943. From my point of view as a product of the Central Provinces' system of training, and as an adverse critic of its purblind administrative outlook, the first action must be the development of this primitive country. I had in time toured, visited and inspected all the states comprising the seventeen thousand square miles of the Agency. I had persuaded the higher authorities to commission Verrier Elwin to write a report on the aboriginals of the south-west of Keonjharh State. Here was a state, whose main road north from the capital town provided an hour or two's driving to a station on the main Bengal Nagpur Railway line, and many of whose people in the opposite direction were clothed only in bark shirts.

Garlands at an official visit, 1943

The report was exceedingly useful. It more or less completed my conspectus of the people of the Agency; while my numerous travels, including those not of my own choosing, had given me a good knowledge of the country and its economy. I proceeded, therefore, to write a paper on methods of development for the whole area. It covered all the obvious subjects – agriculture, forestry, which was already in the safe hands of Herbert Mooney, roads, education, medical services and public health in particular.

The states in all these aspects were shamefully under-administered. They typified what I have criticized several times already, namely the unimaginative approach by the Government in large areas of India (but not everywhere) to the whole essence of administration. Financial ideas were too often those of bank managers administering trust funds on behalf of minors. Vision, enterprise, and especially the proper appreciation of credit, were too often absent.

The fate of my paper might have been foreseen. However sound I might be in my grasp of the mechanics of administration, my views on finance were clearly unsound. Having set out what was wanted for millions of people and many thousands of square miles, I recommended that the Government of India should make available a loan of the equivalent of £1 million secured on the revenues of the states themselves, so that true development should go ahead.

There was much else, and especially proposals for the joint administration of many subjects by groups of states. How, for example, could tiny individual units of government offer medical services above the level, say, of cottage hospitals in the United Kingdom; and even those services not in the smallest degree supported by the necessary system of general practitioners, central hospitals with consultants in all the fields of clinical and para-clinical medicine and of surgery? There was no need to emphasize the fact that anyway four out of five rulers spent the greater part of their small revenues on themselves.

The paper did not get beyond Calcutta. Moreover it came back smartly with numerous criticisms by Authority marked in the margins in red pencil. Most of these could no doubt have been contested and discussed, but one was incontestable. The Government of India did not favour the incurring by Indian States of public debt, and in the case of states under management, would not permit it. I could do nothing without capital; so the paper was consigned to the record room. I continued to do what was possible with the resources of states under management, and to nudge the rulers in the direction of material progress.

A few months after this set-back a very large and heavy envelope arrived in my mail one day. It contained twenty-eight copies, one for each state plus a few spares, of a letter running to seven or eight foolscap pages of single space typewriting. The subject was 'Post-War Development'. The concept and the context both seemed to me to be commendable. I distributed the copies and invited proposals from all the states for schemes of administrative development to be embarked upon when peace returned. One point in the letter I especially drew to their attention. It reminded me of certain lines by Ralph Hodgson:

> 'Twould ring the bells of Heaven
> The wildest peal for years,
> If Parson lost his senses
> And people came to theirs,
> And he and they together
> Knelt down with angry prayers. . .
>
> (*Bells of Heaven*)

The poet went on to wave a banner against mindless cruelty to animals. My own thoughts then and later were often occupied with the similarly mindless neglect of the nutrition, health and happiness of hundreds of millions of subjects of the Crown in India. Yet in this letter there was a dim glow of light. Every recipient was urged to plan without restraint and without regard for the financial implications. Someone in Delhi certainly lost his senses when such a letter was permitted to say 'the sky is the limit'.

My original paper had asked for £1 million. When all the replies had been coordinated the demand was for £60 million.

This year and 1944 saw the attempt to implement a policy of the Government of India which might have been of great importance if it had been formulated earlier. This aimed at persuading all the rulers of all the agencies to federate and, in the interest of their subjects, to provide joint services with some form of central control. The word 'agency' in this context meant a group of states whose relations with the Central Government and the Crown were conducted through a Resident of the First or Second Class. Smaller groups in communication through a Political Agent with a Resident, such as the Orissa States Agency, would for the purpose of this policy not be considered separately. They would be subsumed in the vast areas such as the Eastern States, the Punjab States, the Western India States, and so on. Incidentally the policy could not apply to Hyderabad. There the Nawab was in a literal sense the feudal ruler of an area (as mentioned earlier) comparable with that of modern France, and his administration could stand on its own feet.

Such federation would not only have been in the interests of the common people. It could also have ensured the survival of the states themselves. For example, the Eastern States could have produced a unit similar in size and resources to a province of what was then still called British India. There was however, a curious similarity between this concept in 1943 and that of the European Economic Community in the seventh and eighth decades of the 20th century. In the latter case the opinions of both voters and their representatives alike on the matter of joining the EEC cut across the boundaries of normal political tenets and objectives.

In the United Kingdom the three major political parties were all, in respect of their individual members of Parliament, divided. The basis of opposition to joining has been an emotional rather than a rational, a selfish rather than an enlightened determination not to cede any individual sovereignty, however partial, to a composite organization where a form of democracy is elevated beyond their own sphere. In the case of the rulers of the Eastern States the attitude was the same, but at least they did not

Standing left to right. The Raja of Nayagarh. The Yuvaraj, Kharsawan. Captain R.D. Metcalfe, I.P.S., A.P.A. The Raja Bahadur of Talcher. The Maharaja of Kalahandi. The Maharaja of Sonepur. Captain A.C.K. Maunsell, Secretary, East States. The Raja Bahadur of Hindol

Sitting left to right. Mr L.G. Coke-Wallis, I.C.S., P.A. Chhattisgarh. The Raja of Korea. Mr A.C. Carter, O.B.E., I.P., I.G. Police East States.The Raja of Dhenkanal. Lieut. Colonel C.P. Hancock, C.I.E., O.B.E., M.C., Resident, The Host. The Raja of Seraikella. The Raja of Raigarh. Mr A.N. Mitchell, O.B.E., I.C.S., P.A. Orrissa. The Raja Bahadur of Sakti. The Raja of Bamra.

Eastern States Rulers' Conference, 10 August 1943. Norval is seated, 3rd from the right. Lt Col C P Hancock, Resident, is seated 5th from the left. Some of the Rajas are mentioned in the story.

pretend that they spoke for anyone other than themselves and their families. They clung to their inheritance: autocracy, reverence and wealth, and in many cases self-indulgence, made possible by wealth. Responsibility for the welfare of their subjects was a sense which many of them did possess; but it was a feeling which came second in influence to that fundamental determination to retain power.

Two conferences of rulers were held, one in Gangpur in the Orissa States Agency, and one in Bolangir in the Central Provinces States Agency. Very little came of them apart from the nominal establishment of a joint High Court. The Resident, presiding, tried in vain to convince the rulers that their survival depended on joint action and pooling of authority. Their ears heard but their minds rejected the idea. At Bolangir the Raja of Seraikela said, 'Gandhi is friendly towards the Princes'. After the transition of India to independence three and a half years later it was only a matter of months till Sardar Vallabhbhai Patel, in charge of Home Affairs in the Central Government, abolished the Indian States altogether and evicted the rulers on pensions. Less than thirty years on, Mrs Gandhi's government has abolished the pensions. As Froude said of the Middle Ages, echoing Shakespeare, the Maharajas, the Nawabs, the Nizam, and all the lesser nobility have like an insubstantial pageant faded after a history of three thousand years.

Chapter 12

Hopes are dupes.

IN APRIL 1944 I was transferred to Kolhapur State in the Deccan; and I remained there for nearly two years with an interval of six months' leave in England in 1945.

Kolhapur was the premier Maratha State. The Chhatrapati* Maharaja was the successor of the 17th century hero Shivaji, who rebelled against the Moghul Emperor Aurangzeb, and set the Marathas on their astonishing course to empire. They stabled their horses in Cuttack. They were only checked by substantial defence works a few miles west of Calcutta. Their first major defeat was by the Afghans at Panipat, west of Delhi in 1761, when they were said to have suffered (including camp followers) 200,000 killed. Sir Arthur Wellesley finally broke their power but not their spirit. In modern times their regular units of the Indian Army accumulated battle honours in, for example, Abyssinia and Italy. When I reached my post there were in existence two battalions of the state's own troops, one fully trained, one training for action in Malaya, with the designation of the Rajaram Rifles after the late Maharaja.

There were in India in the middle years of this century over sixty million speakers of the Marathi language. In approximate terms their country extended from Kolhapur State (two hundred miles south of Bombay) in an arc running north-east to Nagpur (450 miles east of Bombay), then north-west to Indore and finally west to the sea in Baroda State two hundred miles north of Bombay.

The imposing designation of my post was Prime Minister and Vice-President of the Council of Regency. The President was the Regent Maharani, senior widow of the Maharaja who had died about three years before. She took virtually no part in government. Her husband had left no issue, and her main responsibility was to act as stepmother to the four-year-old boy whom she had adopted as the successor. The little boy died three years later. On the occurrence of this second vacancy the runner-up in the previous adoption was instantly nominated, and went through the process of adoption and recognition in no time at all.

---

* Lord of the umbrella.

If one were to look at the new situation critically, one's first thought must be what the kindly, middle-aged Maharani thought of her new son. He was the Maharaja of Dewas Senior, a very likeable man of medium height and strong build. He kept himself very fit and among other things was an excellent shot with both rifle and shotgun. He had been on active service with the Maratha Light Infantry in North Africa, reaching the rank of Lieutenant. Unfortunately his men tended to cluster round him in battle in order to protect him, which made him something of an embarrassment. At the time of his adoption he was a mature, vigorous man in his thirties, who might have done well had not Sardar Vallabhbhai Patel expropriated his territories after about two years.

My own work in Kolhapur, on which I embarked with the enthusiasm which its importance (in my view) commanded, was also to prove in vain. Its objectives were long-term. None of those objectives was achieved, being overtaken and submerged by events. The work was, therefore, at best of only ephemeral importance, and some of it purely nugatory. A detailed account of it would thus be inappropriate. An outline may be of some interest.

As Prime Minister I gave myself responsibility for Law and Order, Finance, and Public Health and Medical Services. For a population of one and a quarter million in an area of about five thousand square miles, and with revenues falling short of £1.5 million, these subjects gave plenty to think about. I had three other ministers as my colleagues, two of them Marathas, one a Brahman. This detail is mentioned because it is illustrative of a radical division in Maharashtra (the great nation).

Throughout their history the Marathas had strongly disliked the Brahmans who lived in their country. They were often spoken of by English speaking people as Maratha Brahmans, but this was a contradiction in terms. It would be more accurate to call them Deccani Brahmans. That is, they were residents of the Deccan, which is an English corruption of the word *dakshin* meaning south. There were many sub-castes of them. They were all described by the writer of *The Lost Dominion*, Al Carthill, as the most outstanding people bred for intelligence that the world has known.

They were certainly in the main very clever and often brilliant. Their colouring varied from dark to very fair, many of them having blue eyes. One of them of my acquaintance told me that in Europe he was always taken for an Italian. This leads me to mention a legend which I have heard but not read anywhere. One of these Brahman castes is called Chitpawan. I was told that the word means 'born of fire', but my very slight knowledge of Sanskrit does not extend to confirming or denying this. The name was adopted (I once again tell the tale as I was told) by the crew of a vessel which in the dim past ran ashore on the west coast of India. They were large white men with golden hair. They conferred among themselves and decided to burn their ship and settle in the land whither fate had brought them.

Unfortunately the Marathas, who seem to have Dravidian links, although their language is highly Sanskritic and founded on as complete an analytical grammar as Attic Greek or Classical Latin, never took to their Brahman neighbours. This probably began when the descendants of Shivaji, like the Merovingian kings of the Franks, left the real control of government to their chief officials and receded into a strongly reverenced but physically obscure background.

In each case the tendency was for the position of *de facto* head of state to become hereditary; and in the case of Maharashtra these persons were Brahmans with the title of Peshwa. The word is adopted from the Persian *pesh*. It has many uses, all of them connected with the concept of being to the fore. It is odd that in many similar cases the vocabulary of the Moghul enemy was preferred to good sound Sanskrit. In recent times the Deccani Brahmans tended to fill a large majority of posts in all departments of the government. The Marathas were the farmers and the soldiers, in so far as any generalization can be accurate.

In Kolhapur the late Maharaja had done his best to elevate Marathas to high place. In some measure he was successful, though it is doubtful whether arbitrary appointments with a caste bias could be the best method of ensuring efficiency. In this situation my entry on the scene was for me a *damnosa hereditas* (accursed inheritance). My predecessor, appointed two years before on the death of the Maharaja, was a British officer of the ICS from the Bombay Presidency. His strong feeling for justice led him, with the concurrence of his colleagues on the Regency Council, to concede a number of appeals from a variety of people who claimed to have been unjustly dispossessed of their land. The allegation in each case was that it was the Maharaja who had appropriated the land so that he might confer it on his trusted Marathas, for example ADCs.

I arrived in time to inherit the onus of the further appeals, either to the Resident or to even higher authority, from the newly dispossessed Marathas. In retrospect I can only hope that when, in response to a demand from above for a report on any such appeal, I gave the right advice. The caste of the litigants was of no concern to me. What would happen would be that, on receipt of a demand for a report, I myself would call for the records and read them. Every such case involved many hours of work and sometimes the tracing of previous records and disputes covering many generations. In one case the records turned up a document in a script so old that only one or two scholars in the land of the living were able to read it. It is in no mood of vanity that I recall the results. Every draft report which I submitted for approval to the Regency Council was accepted without discussion. Every recommendation contained in such reports was accepted by the higher authority concerned. The only possible conclusion was that no one except myself could be bothered to tackle each case in detail. Many of them resulted in the restoration of the Maharaja's original grant which did much posthumous good to his reputation.

Another matter requiring immediate attention was the application of a new constitution.

Many of the rural areas of the state lacked good roads and were as backward in many ways as was rural India in general. The state was however, in many respects a modern (in the then contemporary sense of the word) organization and society. The capital city's population was 125,000. It contained three university colleges affiliated to the University of Bombay. On a point of detail, I was once invited to chair a meeting which was to be addressed by the well-known Parsee member of the Indian National Congress, M A Masani. The occasion was the one hundredth anniversary of the founding of a certain library, which by then was comprised in one of the colleges. A thousand students attended to hear Masani, who spoke in standard English and was brilliant. Their reception of my introductory remarks was surprisingly similar to what I observed on occasion, during my service in later years in a Scottish University; rather noisy, but good humoured and quick to take a point.

Also in the field of culture there were such things as an archaeological museum and several companies engaged in the production of moving pictures; there would be recitals of Indian music; there would be ceremonial parades of the States Forces. The position in fact was several centuries in advance of what obtained in the Eastern States Agency. It followed that autocratic government was wholly inappropriate. After the death of the last Maharaja, therefore, a constitution had been drawn up and approved by the Government of India which was designed to be the first step on the road to democratic government and to constitutional monarchy.

The constitution bore some resemblance to the Government of India Act 1919. For example, nominated members of the so-called Legislative Council, combined with the *ex officio* members such as the Ministers of the Regency Council, out-numbered the elected members. In other words, there was an official bloc which controlled the Council. One could well understand that anything so patronizing, so obviously jejune by way of concession to political appetite, must be received by a well-educated public with mingled mockery and anger. For my part I was restricted by the terms of my service to the Crown in the matter of criticism of, or resistance to, this product of the Government of India.

Moreover indignant gestures such as resignation are the one infallible method of ensuring that such reforms or progress as one may have in mind will never be achieved. I decided, therefore, that this housemaid's baby should be well nourished as long as I was there to feed it with thoroughly sterilized bottles. It is good to remember how sympathetic were the first two Residents under whom I worked: Lt Col Cosmo Edwards CIE and Herbert Thompson CIE, ICS, (later Resident for the Punjab States and promoted KCIE).

First, therefore, we provided a fitting inauguration ceremony. I administered an oath of allegiance to all the members. Then the Regent Maharani read a short speech which (I wrote it) was not in any way striking, but which she read very well. My speech was longer, containing historical retrospects and concluding with a most earnest quotation of Isaiah 54, xi–xiii.* Incidentally it held a reference to the possibility of further constitutional developments, which to my surprise was approved by the Government of India. At that moment I had one particular point in mind.

Kolhapur State possessed a well-established High Court. In my predecessor's time however, its competence and its administrative efficiency were widely criticized; and the Regency Council decided that it must be inspected in much the same manner as applied to subordinate courts. A retired Puisne Judge of the Bombay High Court, Sir Govindrao Madgaonkar ICS, accepted the invitation to conduct the inspection, and nothing could have been more satisfactory but for three things: first, Sir Govindrao was a Brahman; secondly, his report contained much strong adverse criticism; thirdly, the individual most strongly criticized was a Puisne Judge who was a Maratha. I stepped onto the stage at this point. We, the Regency Council, agreed that the report must be acted upon, but that to publish it *in toto* would be unfair to individuals. The Maratha judge in particular must be relieved of his post without delay; and this delicate job was left to me.

In a letter as firm but as gentle as I could compose I told him that his services would be dispensed with, and suggested that he might like to

---

* 'O thou afflicted, tossed with tempest and not comforted, behold I will lay thy stones with fair colours, and lay thy foundations with sapphires . . . And all thy children shall be taught of the Lord; and great shall be the peace of thy children.'

resign. He asked for an appointment and came to see me in my office, where we had something of a set-to. He was angry and rude. I said that I had not given him an appointment only to be insulted in my own office, and I indicated the door. Now, he was (as I knew) a very honest and decent man. I felt guilty, therefore, when he collapsed in his chair, apologized and asked me what on earth was the reason for his dismissal. I thanked him for his apology, and asked his leave to speak frankly. He agreed. I then told him of my regard for him as a man, but that as a High Court judge he was wholly miscast. Of course he knew the basis of my statement. I went on to say, however, that I would seek every opportunity to use his services in other fields. We parted friends and remained so. It is now necessary to collect the threads of the warp.

Under the new constitution I, as Prime Minister, was President of the Legislative Council. This was a provision so conservative as to be virtually primitive. In 1944 there emerged here a situation which had not been known in India since the Government of India Act 1919 came into force. It emphasised to the people the quiet, slightly contemptuous, paternalistic approach of the Government of India.

The same type of council survived in territories under the Colonial Office for many years after the 1939-45 war; but for many years after 1945 it was difficult to see an inclination towards constitutional progress in anything which the Colonial Office did. But we were in the India of the 20th century. The civilization of India in, for example, 1935, comprised of Hinduism and Islam with a Buddhist minority, was recovering from its earlier decline. The British rule had, of course, established the peace and the law and order which made this possible; but this fact constituted no excuse for retarding the return of self-government which Queen Victoria had proclaimed in 1876 as the ultimate goal for the country of which, under Disraeli's advice, she had recently become Empress.*

I took this point up with the Resident, and through him the matter went to the Government of India. I wished to achieve an object, not to alienate sympathy. I did not, therefore, write anything like what I have written in the preceding paragraph. Rather was I, in the good Scots word, 'sleekit' (cunning). I suppose I was learning from the Deccani Brahman the wide field of activity in which *suaviter in modo* (gentle in manner) was a vital principle.

My argument concentrated on the anomaly of the head of the administration presiding over the legislature. As President of the latter he was morally bound to be neutral. In the former capacity it was his duty to lead a party (however amorphous) against local elected opposition.

---

*Empress of India Act, 1876.

Moral obligation surely must take precedence. It followed that the Prime Minister, the nominee of the Government of India, was not able to fulfil all his duties in the Council without, quite immorally, becoming a biased President. My suggestion was that the constitution should be so amended that the Prime Minister should vacate the Chair and become Leader of the House. The way would then be open to the appointment of a distinguished man in local public life, one who enjoyed the confidence of . . . preferably with legal qualifications . . . and so on, to the Chair. Such a man had become available in the person of the recently retired Puisne Judge, whose appointment I recommended.

All this came to pass. The Secretary (in Westminster it would be the Clerk) of the Council was a pensioner whose main career had been spent as Secretary of the Bombay Legislative Assembly. He was a first-class officer, and although he was a Brahman he and the new President proceeded to run an efficient and decorous institution.

Unfortunately the Government of India on several occasions issued general orders, affecting all states, apparently without regard to their timing or their appropriateness in respect of individual states. One could only do one's best by remonstrating to have such orders either modified or withdrawn. One example may illustrate this point. Early in the autumn of 1945 I was instructed to pass through the Legislative Council an instrument known as the Faridkot Act, so called because it was first applied in Faridkot State. It was intended as a measure to suppress political subversion, and its main provision was to make it compulsory for all clubs, societies, associations etc to apply for registration.

The machinery for registration was similar to that applying to the registration of companies; the Registrar was empowered to refuse registration, though the reasons for such refusal were not well defined. What was definite was that any body to which registration was refused immediately became an illegal organization and liable to prosecution. With such an act in force, any government could pounce on any opposers or critics, provided they were in some manner incorporated, disperse the organization and fine or imprison its members.

I had been instructed to apply the same act in Bastar State in 1941. Then it was laughable because there was only the social club in Jagdalpur which came within the mischief of the act, and most of its members were in some degree involved in the administration. In Kolhapur circumstances were fundamentally different. Clubs, political, social, cultural – indeed of any type of which one can think – were everywhere. Registration was, therefore, by no means an easy administrative task, and in the event of general refusal to register the enforcement of the act would be impossible.

More serious than anything else, however, was this further insulting example of the Government of India's myopia and lack of sympathy in respect of its hundreds of millions of subjects. Delhi was indeed far away.* If this went any further there would be trouble.†

I immediately sought an interview with the Resident, therefore, to discuss what could be done. This, the third occupant of the post since my appointment, was a man of no ability or understanding. He clearly failed in this instance to appreciate any of the points which I was trying to make. Ultimately I obtained his agreement to one course of action. The Bill would be gazetted (ie officially published). Then I would make a statement in the Council, which would shortly be in session, to the effect that there would be a free vote on the Second Reading. Since no one would vote for it except my unfortunate self, that would be the end of it.

Two or three days before the session started I happened to be with the Resident at an opening ceremony one evening in the city. More by way of making conversation than anything else, as we were leaving I mentioned that I would be making the statement on such and such a day. He turned to me and said, 'But I never agreed to anything of the sort. The Bill must go through'. I at once asked for and was given a formal interview. My last argument, based on the Atlantic Charter principle of freedom of association, was rejected.

I then said very well. I would not make the statement. Being in duty bound to obey orders, I would force the Bill through with the aid of the *ex officio* and nominated members, I would put the whole police force on stand-by alert; and I indicated that I expected him to have troops in Belgaum or elsewhere ready to support the civil power. When the inevitable riots took place, all my officers and I would perform our full duty however repugnant; but I would not accept any responsibility for the miserable consequences of action taken against my advice. He would receive all this in writing next morning. That next morning, as I was finishing the dictation of my letter, a messenger brought a letter from the Secretary to the Resident. The Government of India had instructed that the Bill should be withdrawn.

There were many incidents of this sort, though only one other with such potentially disastrous consequences. This one involved a very highly

---

* This Persian proverb was a cliché in India.

† It is relevant to mention, among other signs of national unrest, the reaction in November-December 1945 to the Red Fort trials outside Delhi of three Indian Army officers accused of treason in Burma; the Royal Indian Navy mutiny in Bombay and Karachi in February 1946; and trouble in the Royal Indian Air Force at the same time. Law and Order were precariously balanced. See Wavell, *The Viceroy's Diary*, edited by Penderel Moon, Chapters 8 and 9, Oxford University Press, 1973.

secret communication from the Government of India to the Resident, which was passed to me for information under double sealed covers. It was a detailed appreciation of the undoubtedly very dangerous political situation then prevailing, followed by further details of how British subjects were to be rescued and protected in the event of a general rebellion, which was regarded as quite possible. I regarded the document as so important that I personally addressed and sealed the two envelopes in which it was to be returned, and took it myself in the early evening to deliver it into the Resident's own hands.

I met him as he was getting into his car to go to the cinema. He greeted me jovially, stuffed the envelope into his pocket and drove off. When I reached my office next morning at 8.00 am, I found two men waiting for me on the steps. One of them was the manager of the cinema. He passed to me the said envelope, apologizing for troubling me so early in the morning, but excusing himself on the grounds that he felt that the thing must be important. Moreover the (outer) envelope indicated that it came from my office. He had found it on a seat in the cinema after the end of the programme the previous night; but by then it was pretty late and he thought it wrong to disturb me. I thanked him cordially but (I hope) without undue emotion. Then, as now, a temporization was called for.

A large tiger. L–R a headman, Bill, Norval, David, the driver Sher Prasad, 1943

Early in 1946 Sir Conrad Corfield, Political Adviser to the Government of India, visited Kolhapur and stayed at the Residency. I was called for an interview. In due course I was seated across the table facing Sir Conrad and waiting for what at least must be a reprimand over the affair of the Faridkot Act. Not at all. He raised this matter at once, smiled and said how sorry he was that I had been put to so much trouble. Those in Delhi had not appreciated how inappropriate the whole project had been. Naturally I was deeply grateful. At the same time I could easily infer that, until the resistance was brought to his notice, he had not known that the matter had arisen at all. This makes one wonder how often, when the Government of India was blamed for this or that, the real culprit was a civil servant behind the scenes.

This was my first meeting with this very good man. Had I known him before, I would have had no anxiety about his attitude to this unhappy business. Later, when I met him in Delhi I began to appreciate his sympathetic approach both to the rulers and to the people of the Indian states. Thirteen years later he dined with us in Lusaka (in what is now Zambia) and it was possible in a social meeting to appreciate further his fundamental kindness and sense of justice.

Recently he has produced a book of memoirs *The Princely India I Knew* (Madras: Indo-British Historical Society). I was very happy to read, in the *Times Literary Supplement* of 16 July 1976 the words of the reviewer of the book, Mr Paul Scott. In July 1947 Corfield had been ordered by the Viceroy to call a meeting of rulers. There they were to be told, in effect, that His Majesty's Government was about to ditch them. The constitutional position might seem to some to be in doubt. Not so to Corfield, who, in Mr Scott's words 'set the date for July 25. On July 25, determined to have nothing to do with it, he packed his bags and flew home – unregretted in Viceregal House but not, I should like to think, by history, in which men of firm opinion and adherence to principle are not all that thick on the ground'.

On my arrival in Kolhapur I had taken as one part of my portfolio the departments of Medical Services and Public Health. The state suffered, as did British India, from gross neglect in these respects. Both politicians and government servants knew well that the subject of education would bring them far greater public acclaim. At the risk of parading myself as an Athanasius against the world, I must record that I was seldom able to convince my superiors in the service or my politician friends that no one can educate an undernourished child or adolescent, or one who may be suffering from chronic disease or a parasitic infestation.

Now however, I was in a position to do something. The Chief Medical Officer, Rege, a highly-qualified surgeon, was already embarked on a project for the building of a new hospital. There was a strong committee to draw up plans. I was chairman, and the members included Rege himself, my colleague Bagwe, Minister for Public Works and the Chief Engineer of the State, and Albert Simeons, MD Heidelberg, Director of Public Health. We also had the services of a distinguished firm of architects in Bombay. The stage was soon reached where funds could be provided in the budget, and the Government of India approved. This was achieved in spite of the opposition of the Resident. He wanted a substantial part of the available money to be diverted to the reconditioning of a rest-house in a small hill station called Panhala, in order that he might spend the summer there in greater comfort than was at the time offered.

Progress was steady for a time, and the walls were some four feet high when His Highness the Maharaja of Dewas Senior was selected as Maharaja of Kolhapur. He indicated that the project must forthwith be abandoned for lack of funds. The people of the State must continue to sleep on the floors and verandahs of the existing hospital, provided mainly with facilities dating from the turn of the century.

Another project was more successful and caused great interest beyond the boundaries of the state. This was called the Village Sub-Dispensary Scheme. Its object was to supplement on as large a scale as possible the medical services supplied by the government dispensaries. These were always few and very far between. They were in the charge of doctors (if one may so call them) with very low qualifications, usually that of Licensed Medical Practitioner, and with the designation of Sub-Assistant Surgeon. I have inspected scores of them and was always impressed by the same things.

For example, the doctors always seemed to be devoted. The number of out-patients seen in a day often averaged over a hundred. I use the word 'seen' advisedly, since the provision of medicines and drugs was always hopelessly inadequate, and effective treatment of illness was impossible. Moreover the population served by such a dispensary might well be anything from one to two hundred thousand. There was always however, a standard and praiseworthy provision of surgical instruments. They were always in immaculate condition, apparently because few of them were ever used. I remember particularly the Lane's forceps. Indian rural society's conventions would never permit their use; and in areas where use of such instruments might have been permitted, the distances to be travelled on foot by patients and their helpers would normally make recourse to surgery almost impossible.

It was however, a fairly simple task to increase the availability of medicines and drugs. The information was widely spread abroad by officers on tour that villages which wished to have a Sub-Dispensary installed should apply to the Public Health Department. They must themselves make available a room with a chair, a table and a cupboard with lock and key. They must nominate someone to be the Sub-Dispenser. He was usually, but not necessarily, the primary school master. He must be literate. He would attend a three-week course at Kolhapur, and then go home with an honorarium of Rs 5 per month, the key of the cupboard, and a stock of twenty things. Only the last of the twenty would be normally comprehensible to the villagers, viz surgical dressings. Indeed the Sub-Dispenser himself would not be qualified to understand (any more than I would) the full significance of the other nineteen. He would however, know that number six (say) was for the treatment of malaria. At that time it might have been paludrine or mepacrine. Another number might be aspirin, which at worst might be prescribed as a palliative. For dysentery another number would no doubt be enterovioform. And so on down the list. Only one condition attached to all this. Every patient must pay one anna for every one day's issue of any particular remedy. This coin bore no relation to the value of the goods supplied; but it had been decided between Simeons and me that if one did not charge something, human nature being what it is, no one would have had any faith in, or respect for, what was being supplied.

The success of the scheme was immediate and the demand too great for the Department to meet it quickly. In my capacity of Finance Minister however, I saw to it that money was made available. Not more than twenty men at a time could be accepted for the three-week courses, nor was it possible to organize them continuously. Yet by the time I left Kolhapur in March 1946 there were more than two hundred and twenty of these dispensaries in operation. This meant that about half a million people were, on this admittedly simple scale, being offered relief from suffering.

There were other similar advances. For example, Simeons detected endemic sclerosis of the liver among infants and, having traced the cause, as usual produced a solution. An outbreak of pneumonic plague, normally at that time a disease with a death rate of over 80% accompanied by extreme risk to the medical and nursing staff, he attacked with all his medical and administrative skill. Of course by the years 1944–46 the availability of antibiotic drugs was fairly general, and it was these that he was using. At the same time I believe that it was he who, in his makeshift isolation hospital, all under canvas and attracting patients (sometimes moribund) from hundreds of miles away, was the first to show with statistically significant figures a recovery rate of well over 80%.

The greatest achievement however, resulted from a petition which came to me one day from a party of lepers. The poor fellows did not even come into the gardens of the secretariat, but waited on the road outside and were very surprised when I went out and spoke to them there. Lepers led a miserable life in India and very little was done for them. I have forgotten what the petition was about; but it did remind me that in Bastar State we had established a small village as a leper colony under the provisions of the Leprosy Act of about 1863. The grant of a home and some land was equivalent to restoring humanity to the subhuman and hope to the hopeless.

I discussed with Simeons the possibility of doing something of the same sort and in due course it was done. A vast stone-built stable, then empty, but which had housed the late Maharaja's racehorses and stud, was handed over to the Public Health Department together with two or three hundred acres of agricultural land. All this was well outside the city, which precluded social objection. One hundred lepers with their families (often of course infected) could be accommodated and there was soon a waiting list for admission. Above all the inmates could be cured in the sense that by 1945 leprosy could be arrested by a drug called promin although there could be no restoration of damage already done, for example to hands or face. They always seemed very happy. I hope that funds were available for the colony's continuance in later years.

It is sad to remember that my differences with the Resident finally led me to confront him and ask him to forward to the Government of India my request for a transfer. It is only fair to record that he was unable to conceal his delight; which drew my attention, I hope not for the first time in my life, to the possibility that all the faults were not necessarily on his side. The request was forwarded and quite soon granted.

I did not want to leave Kolhapur. There was so much to like about it and its people and so much to be done which actually could be done. For example, when I made my decision I was visiting an area called Raibagh forty miles east of the city and an enclave of the Bombay Presidency. Much of it was enclosed as a shooting reserve for the Palace, and for the very specialized sport of hunting the blackbuck with cheetahs. Imagine a shooting brake with two horses and half a dozen passengers clinging to handrails at the back, the cheetahs being towards the front. One cheetah would be unhooded and released as the brake reached the right position in relation to the herd. They were trained to kill the buck, which was black. The brown females were never touched. It was thoroughly distasteful.*

---

* Dr Simeons, in 1965 wrote a children's book *Ramlal* (Atheneum, 1965) about hunting with cheetahs.

There had been a complete crop failure in 1945 owing to lack of rain. Indeed four to eight inches of rain was the normal annual rainfall in a belt of country running south from the latitude of Bombay to the extreme south of India. The spectacle of withered crops was terrible. Men and cattle were starving. I spent several days riding over the area from 7.00 am till 2.00 pm acquiring a detailed knowledge of the disaster together with a disinclination to sit down when I finished each day's journey. A letter from me to the Regent Maharani produced an immediate permission for the enclosed parks, which were her property, to be opened for communal grazing. One evening the fodder, which I had been calling up from other areas, started to arrive in a train of lorries over a road from the west with the sun setting behind them. My colleagues on the Regency Council had been organizing the food grains for the people. I thought that I might now go back to Kolhapur where my wife had been nursing our youngest son through diphtheria. Simeons and his wife did all that was possible and the child survived.

Then there was the hydroelectric project based on the Radhanagri River. Near its headwaters in the south-west of the state there had been an unsuccessful attempt to build a dam some years before. My predecessor revived the project, and a lake 14 miles long was being dammed back into a valley of the Western Ghats. As the water rose slowly behind the dam it was siphoned down the river bed; and in the hot weather what had previously been a dry river bed became a quietly running river. For many miles it provided water for hoist irrigation of the flat fields on either bank. Sugar cane and cotton brought profit to cultivators whose livelihood without irrigation was always at risk. The turbines were ready for the generation of electricity when the Government of India as usual came in with its dead hand. The moment coincided with one of my tours.

I had left my motor transport in a valley some thirty miles to the east of the lake with instructions to meet me two days later at the Radhanagri dam. My journey south from Kolhapur had been a very moving experience. Within living memory no *diwan* or *pant pradhan** or any such person had toured that area in the sense of the word tour as understood by the ICS. I had performed two or three such tours already. So far as possible I would mount my horse at my house and ride off in any direction towards which no road ran. Since I was not at first confident in my knowledge of Marathi, I would take with me a *sowar* (a trooper) of the state cavalry.

* Literally 'Principal pandit', an illustration of the transfer of power from the Maratha rulers to the Brahmans as *de facto* rulers.

When this first started no one among the country people had the slightest idea what was going on. For example, I heard a long grievance in one village from an obese gentleman who was quite unimpressed by my neat khaki bush shirt, jodhpurs etc. He had been an expert wrestler in the days of the late Maharaja, who paid all the expenses of the gymnasium and its trainees. Now all that had gone. He was reduced to looking after his small piece of land. Who was I anyway? No doubt part of the new administration. He did, however, manage a smile when I had drunk his tea and my *sowar* spoke to him quietly.

Naturally however, as time went on more and more people came out and came forward. It was beyond description sad. On one journey, it took me eight hours to travel sixty miles by car. I halted whenever I could or whenever the road was blocked. Several tens of thousands of people saw me that day. About one thousand of them presented petitions against ancient wrongs – a quantity which, however I might show myself approachable and sympathetic, could not possibly be considered in a lifetime. I felt an imposter and I could have wept. The only consolation was that my wife was with me and had brought our youngest son, aged seven; his very fair complexion and vivid red hair seemed to delight the women and children wherever we were. Nonetheless one fact was clear. However much there might be an aura of divinity about their Maharaja, they had never before experienced close and personal attention from administrators.

So I started westward on foot one morning, aiming at a camp on the further side of the range of mountains which I was to cross. My companions were eager to provide me with big game to shoot; and towards evening I shot the fine bison whose destruction turned me against big game shooting for ever. There was another long walk next day; and when I was at the highest point of the crossing of the Western Ghats I reached a village set in a shallow valley. The fields and grazing grounds were bordered by forest, and the picture recalled to me something imperfectly remembered from Switzerland. As I stood and looked I saw a church, which enhanced the illusion of Europe.

The village was empty, so I sent one of my followers to call some of those who were working in the fields while the other follower and I went to look at the church. To anyone of Christian sympathy and belief it would have been moving. A thatched roof crowned walls of mud and timber. The simple altar at the east end held a small brass crucifix; and on the wall to the right, shining and new in a glass case, was a tableau of the Virgin and the Child in the manger. The tinsel and gilt were for the pleasure of simple and childlike people. Then, as I turned to go, on the wall to the right of the door as I then faced it I saw the predecessor of the other tableau. The gold and the tinsel had become dull; but it was clear that this visual centre of devotion could not be cast out simply because it had been superseded.

There were soon plenty of people to talk to. They had few grievances. They also floored me on a point of agriculture. Everywhere they were burning brushwood on their fields and spreading the ashes, in somewhat the same way as the aboriginals of eastern India would do. I suggested that more effect could be achieved if the material were mixed with refuse, cattle dung and so on and left to rot before being applied to the fields. No, they said, that would only encourage the growth of weeds.

As regards the church, they said that they had been Christians time without mind. Yes, they had guidance. Every sixth week a priest would climb the *ghat* from Portuguese Goa on the coastal plain below, and conduct the services of the Roman church. They may have been forgetting the world but they were not wholly forgotten by the world.

We went on our way to Rhadanagri, where a rest-house at the east end of the dam gave a view of the artificial lake winding southwards into what had been the valley of the river. Problems in the construction of the dam, especially at the shoulders, had compelled a stop. The trouble lay in geological faults. This involved, in respect of the shoulders, the process known as grouting, that is the injection under pressure of some form of concrete into the gaps in the mass as a whole. In charge of the grouting was the man whom I had met doing the same work on the pillars of St Paul's Cathedral one day in April 1928.

I have digressed in order to provide a background to my mention of the dead hand of the Government of India. Even from my obviously partisan description of this scheme it should be clear that its conception was enlightened and its prospects favourable. Moreover the state was not seeking financial help. Our revenues were adequate to provide the capital cost, although I would have expected the Finance Department in Delhi to have had enough understanding to permit capital for large-scale development to be provided from loan funds. Even their general approval however, to the launching of the project in a state under a minority administration was to be withheld until they were satisfied of one main condition. This was that we must prove that the return on the capital outlay must not be less than 3%.

My letter, which was intended to be the final one in a long correspondence, did not convince them. They did not however, immediately disapprove. Instead they sent down to examine the matter the Irrigation Adviser to the Government of India. After the lapse of so many years, I cannot recall his name. I can clearly remember however, that he had been Chief Engineer, Irrigation, in the Madras Presidency, and on retirement had been employed by the Government of India in his present capacity. I had invited him to stay with me, and he had accepted.

He must have been twenty years my senior, a pleasant-looking man of large physique with white hair. I naturally greeted him and treated him with marked deference. Since however, his visit was to be short, I asked if he would agree that I should put my case over our whisky and soda before dinner. This would provide him with all that he need know from our point of view, and the whole of the next day would be at his disposal for the study of technical data, visiting the dam and so on. He agreed.

I then went to town. I said that I did not give a row of beans if the project produced its 3% or not. Within the bounds of normal prudence, the application of this norm was utterly misconceived. I could, for example, collect much more than the equivalent of 3% on the capital outlay from increased land revenue, income tax, octroi and a whole list of things. It boiled down to increased productivity. The Government of India seemed to be unable (apart altogether from an unimaginative approach to finance) to envisage the contribution to health and happiness that irrigation and electricity for industrial and agricultural purposes meant in simple human terms. I then sat back and waited.

My guest very slowly put down his glass on the flat surface of the arm of the long chair where he was lying back. He stood up and so did I. He came to me and embraced me in quite a cheerful way, but with obviously deep sincerity, and said that he had been waiting forty years and more for an administrator in India to talk in these terms.

At that moment, and in respect of one venture, the glass seemed to be set fair. So it was, as long as he and I had the reins in our hands. I have little doubt (in the absence of news) that the Radhanagri dam did not get any further.

Early in March 1946 my orders came to return to the North West Frontier Province. I was given to understand that I would succeed my friend and contemporary A P Low as Financial Secretary. I kept the information to myself until the day before I left, since I could not face a round of farewell parties whose speeches would all contain as an undercurrent the knowledge of my disputes with the Resident. This could have done much harm and could have served no purpose. My last service to Kolhapur was to discuss in Delhi with Sir Conrad Corfield the state's complete Development Plan. This was a printed document containing the narrative, with schedules and statistical tables, which often comprise parliamentary white papers. I can only hope, as was my position in many other matters to which I applied myself at that time, that something came of it. Almost certainly the hope is vain.

VE or VJ day, Kolhapur, 1945

Chapter 13

A time to pluck up that which is planted.
Ecclesiastes III, I i

On my journey to Peshawar I stayed briefly in Delhi. I visited the Deputy Secretary (among others) of the Political Department and, to my great relief, was informed that the circumstances of my departure from Kolhapur were appreciated and were not held against me. To those British officers, and to others of British nationality who did not see the secretariat in Delhi in March 1946, it may be of interest to read how it seemed to an outsider. I had heard in my remote office that there was marked demoralisation among the British members of the various branches of the Imperial Secretariat. I thought that the word 'demoralisation' was not applicable. Yet to analyse the situation and to provide another word was difficult.

What had happened to change the situation since I had last been in those magnificent buildings in 1934 was that Hindu politicians had moved in to control *de facto* the central administration. Field Marshall Lord Wavell, the Viceroy, did all in his power to introduce a form of cabinet government; and this meant proportional representation of Muslims. He never accepted that partition of India was the correct solution of the problem of those times. My friends in Delhi however, made it very clear that the Hindu leaders were constantly rude to British officers and at pains to snub them. People who have self-respect are not likely to be, or to feel, humiliated by mere rudeness. Yet if all action, all constructive thought, is simply puffed out of the window; if contumely is the only response to what government servants of the greatest experience and the greatest ability offer to their new masters as they did to their old, then there must be a change of attitude to their duty.

When constitutional changes were introduced in the North West Frontier Province in 1937 at the level of provincial government, there was nothing of this sort. Pathans and British officers always got along together except, for obvious reasons, when they were shooting at one another. With the attainment of power by the Kashmiri pandits and Brahmans of all degrees in India, the miasma of Brahman hatred quickly drifted up and down the corridors of power. This was so palpable that persons like myself (and there were many) who loved India, who respected and admired the people and their civilization, so much older than our own, tended to laugh in a bitter way. They went on working however, to the coming down of the curtain.

One evening I caught the Frontier Mail. It still ran to the same timetable as it had done twelve years before. The six hundred miles from Delhi to Peshawar took twenty-four hours; and the crossing of the Attock bridge over the Indus followed by the steady rallentando through Nowshera to the end of the long journey were unchanged. My arrival in the dusk of a March evening was so similar to my arrival more than eleven years before that the intervening years for a moment faded from memory.

The Frontier had been very stable all through the war. This was largely due to the solid and imperturbable conduct of the administration by Sir George Cunningham from 2 March 1937 to 2 March 1946. He was regarded with deep affection and respect by everyone, including the most perfervid politicians; and the value of his service at this time was by some authorities estimated as the equivalent of two or more divisions of troops. I have written in considerable detail of this in my memoir of him published by Blackwoods in 1968. Here it must be enough to summarize the development of political affairs since the outbreak of war on 5 September 1939.

The Congress Party government which took office on 7 September 1937, having defeated the coalition government of Sir Abdul Qaiyyum on a vote of confidence on 3 September, remained in power until the outbreak of war two years later. They then resigned in accordance with instructions from the central command of the All India Congress Party. There followed a period of administration by the Governor under the powers given by Section 93 of the Government of India Act 1935. In May 1943 moves began for the formation of a Muslim League government, and on 25 May such a government was sworn in under the leadership of a prominent Peshawar Advocate, Mohammed Auranzeb Khan.

He was tall and very stout. He and I had been on friendly terms in the past, when he practised in my court in Nowshera in 1934-35 and later in Peshawar in 1939-40. His simple geniality and friendliness is illustrated from an entry in Cunningham's diary in July 1943, 'Aurangzeb extremely amenable and anxious to do just as I want'. As time went by however, the political pendulum swung back towards the Congress Party. His own party acquired a bad name for corrupt practices especially (to quote Cunningham again) 'owing to the scandalous way in which they buy votes'. They were defeated in the Legislative Assembly on a vote of confidence on 12 March 1945. This fact was very remarkable and requires explanation.

In 1942, shortly before the Congress resolution of 7 August, it was the policy of the Government of India that all leading Congress politicians should be arrested and that the All India Congress Committee, its Working Committee and its Provincial Committees should be 'notified', ie proclaimed as unlawful associations. Cunningham, in direct communication with the Viceroy, refused to arrest anyone 'before Congress have shown their hand'. He saw no harm and no good in proclaiming the All India Congress Committee and the Working Committee; but he simply refused to proclaim the Provincial Committee. After the 7 August resolution he received on 12 August a telegram from the Viceroy saying that he 'ought to arrest all Congress leaders forthwith'. 'Put him off with a soothing telegram' was Cunningham's diary record.

The whole crisis in Indian affairs was treated by Cunningham with amused detachment so far as the Frontier Province was concerned. His absolutely dominant personal prestige in the eyes and minds of the six million Pathans, cis-border and trans-border, often meant that when he told important men not to do something they simply did not do that thing. As I look back, having had plenty of time to consider this phenomenon, I am convinced that this was the result of certain elements in his character and his appearance. The latter was not so irrelevant as people might suppose who never knew him. A man of medium height with very broad shoulders, appropriate to one who played rugby football eight times for Scotland, he could face any man with such complete determination as to give the impression of invincible rightness. He could smile charmingly. Within the limits of justice he could be ruthless. These were qualities which Pathans appreciated and deferred to, no matter what their political views.

As a result of all these factors, the Congress Party in the province was still at liberty in the literal sense, and also free to form a government if they could enlist sufficient support. After the defeat of the Aurangzeb government on 12 March, 1945, the Ministry resigned at 10.00 am on the 16 March and Dr Khan Sahib and two of his Ministers were sworn in an hour later. In January 1946 a general election was held, and Dr Khan Sahib and the Congress Party were returned with a comfortable majority.

Cunningham had retired only a few days before I returned to the Frontier Province. I was very sorry not to have been able to serve under him again as I had done for six years previously; but the wheel of fate brought me back into his field of administration fifteen years later for a period of two years. This was in the University of St Andrews, to whose service in high place he devoted much of the last seventeen years of his life.

He was succeeded as Governor by Sir Olaf Caroe, KCSI, KCIE. He was returning to the Frontier Province after six years as Foreign Secretary to the Government of India, but with many years experience of Frontier problems and administration before that time. In my memoir of Sir George Cunningham I wrote of Caroe the following, which was and remains my personal view of his achievement: 'His period of office was marked by an extraordinary degree of fortitude and distinction during a period of political and civil convulsion such that many might think that earth's foundations had fled.'

On the frontier the general scene was outwardly peaceful. My post as Financial Secretary was not yet vacant since, owing to the difficulties of postwar transport, it had not yet been possible to provide A P Low, my predecessor, with a passage to England for two or three months. I occupied, therefore, the posts of Home Secretary and Development Secretary in turn. In these posts, as in that of Finance Secretary in due course, I could for the first time since 1938 savour the pleasures of the *embusqué* bureaucrat. I could play golf, tennis or squash. I could go for cross-country runs in the winter, though pulled muscles occasionally reminded me that middle age was drawing on. Moreover, most of the work was both interesting and important; and some, as always, was funny.

The most improbable responsibility of all my time in India fell on me in the course of my work as Development Secretary. I held administrative control of a factory in Nowshera producing dehydrated goat's flesh. This was a product of the war. Tens of thousands of Muslim troops were serving overseas in Africa, the near and middle east, and in Italy. It was essential to supply them with this wholesome but uninviting food, tinned, in much the same way as bully beef was a staple for British troops.

In one respect however, the product was unique. Muslims may only eat meat which is *halal*, which is to say that it has been bled from the throat before life is extinct. How could troops so far away be assured that the contents of the tins conformed to this requirement? The solution was to enclose in each tin a small slip of paper on which was written a certificate to that effect. The stroke of genius (I do not know to whom it was attributable) inherent in this measure was that each certificate was signed by a Mullah. Two of these Muslim divines were engaged on salary for the purpose, not only to sign tens of thousands of certificates but also to witness the ritual demise of the goats and so be able to sign in truth.

I have said that the scene was peaceful, though political troubles were already brewing. Indeed the contrast with eastern and western India was difficult to assimilate. So far as the British were concerned the Pathans were as friendly as they had always been when not actually at war. The

Congress Government was administering an orderly and apparently contented province. All the members of the government were men of integrity whether Muslim, Hindu or Sikh. It was during the closing months of 1946, when I was Finance Secretary, that I came to know the Chief Minister, Dr Khan Sahib, better than I had ever done when I worked under him as Home Secretary in 1937. My immediate Minister was Rai Bahadur Mehr Chand Khanna, whom also I came to respect.

A few days after my return I went to pay an official call on the Deputy Commissioner of Peshawar, then Major A J Dring* with whom I had been friendly long before. The orderly who met me at his house (the same house from which John Nicholson started his march on Delhi in the days of the mutiny of 1857) was another old friend. When our greetings were completed and I asked for the DC, my friend said, '*spo tah tale dai*', which means in Pakhtu 'he has gone to the dogs'. I had not spoken Pakhtu for six years and failed to catch the significance of the words. They seemed to comprise a good deal of prejudice and disrespect. Slowly however, with the orderly's help, I understood. At this late date in the history of India the Peshawar Vale Hunt was still going strong. John Dring, DC Peshawar, was Master. And at that evening hour he was down at the kennels.

The Muslim League commanded overwhelming support from Muslims throughout India. Yet, as I have mentioned above, the Congress Party in the Frontier Province had secured a comfortable majority in the general election of January 1946. The flood of events however, was soon to show that their hold on the people of the frontier was not based on fundamental political loyalties. While the Deputy Commissioner of Peshawar was in his spare time directing hounds and hunt members in perfect safety over the countryside, the horrific virus of communal riots in Eastern Bengal spread quickly north-west. The province of Bihar saw massacres of Muslims. Meerut in the United Provinces saw massacres of Hindus. So the mischief advanced north-west like an infection,

In October 1946 I went to Delhi, in my capacity as Financial Secretary to attend two conferences as the representative of my Minister, Mehr Chand Khanna. I stayed as the guest of a friend in a house which was being shared by four or five senior officers of the imperial secretariat. One of these was Lt Col G C L Crichton, Deputy Secretary in the Foreign Department. He came in early on my first evening and announced that he was off on his 'death ride'. He referred to the decision of Pandit Jawaharlal Nehru to visit the Frontier Province with his Deputy Foreign Secretary in attendance.

---

* Lt Col Sir John Dring KBE CIE.

Crichton, as an experienced frontier officer, knew how futile such a gesture was on the part of so prominent a member of the Indian Congress Party at that time. In fact it turned out much more than futile. The Muslim League staged a very aggressive demonstration at the airport when Nehru's plane arrived; and Dr Khan Sahib's car, with Nehru as a passenger, was stoned as it went away. It was on this occasion that my wife, with our youngest child on the carrier of her bicycle, met the rioters as she was on her way to the Peshawar Club swimming pool. Those in control of them vigorously cleared a way for her and nothing but respect was shown by what was at that stage an orderly procession.

In the course of the next few days Nehru paid an official visit to Jamrud, at the east end of the Khyber pass. A *jirga* of Afridi Maliks treated him fairly politely but made it very clear that they disliked him and all that he represented.

His next excursion was to the Malakand, the trans-border agency north of Peshawar District. He was entertained there by the Political Agent, Sheikh Mahbub Ali Khan. When he left, and his car was winding its way down the road from the agency headquarters, it came under fire. No one was injured, but the Sheikh, following behind in his own car, was naturally extremely embarrassed. Apologies, unfortunately, were not enough. Nehru and the Congress Ministry in particular, publicly expressed the conviction that the Sheikh had laid on an ambush. An official enquiry was started, presided over by a senior judge, who ultimately acquitted the Sheikh of all complicity in the incident. The events of these few days however, were a clear warning of the determination of the Pathans not to be yoked to the Hindu governors of India.

I was given a peculiar insight into the intensity of communal hatred in the course of one of my duties. A lecture on the history of the Frontier and the policies of the government towards the Frontier Province and the trans-border tribes formed part of each course at the School of Frontier Warfare at Kakul near Abbotabad. There was a lecture in English to officers in the morning; and in Urdu to the Viceroy's Commissioned Officers and NCOs after lunch. My predecessor as Finance Secretary, A P Low, had been the lecturer for some time; and I was detailed to take on the job. It made a pleasant break from office work. I would leave Peshawar by the Frontier Mail at 9.00 am and get off at Taxila in the Punjab (with memories of its Graeco-Bactrian civilization and Alexander the Great). A military car would be waiting to take me north to Kakul in time to lecture at 12.00 noon. After the second lecture the same car took me back to Taxila to catch the Frontier Mail back to Peshawar at 7.00 pm.

This would occur every month. In the autumn of 1946, on one of these trips I was met at Kakul as usual by the Commandant of the school. He was a certain Brigadier Campbell whom I had known in Nowshera in 1934-35 when he was a major. He was short, slim and lacking one arm; he was a first-class soldier. When, therefore, his first remark on meeting me that day was to warn me to watch my words very carefully in my lectures, I took him very seriously. One of the officers on the course, who had been on duty in the recent communal riots down-country, had drawn a knife at dinner the previous evening on an officer who belonged to the other community. His witnessing of the disgusting atrocities committed on human beings in such riots had deprived him of all self-control in the course of some simple discussion.

I was appointed Chief Secretary on 1 April 1947. It was only many years later that I learned from Sir Olaf Caroe that my promotion was especially requested by Dr Khan Sahib although it involved the supersession of at least two of my seniors. This fact even today rouses an unhappy memory. The sequence of matters was this.

On the day on which I took over as Chief Secretary Sir Olaf asked me to write for him an appreciation of the political situation in the North West Frontier Province. I later learned that he thought that such an appreciation by an officer who had considerable experience of the Frontier, but who had recently not been involved in political affairs, could be valuable support for the arguments which he was preparing for the Viceroy in respect of the policy to be adopted for the political future of the province. The main point in the policy was to hold an election on the issue of whether the province should, in a divided India, be assigned to Pakistan or not.

I prepared my note in complete secrecy. I dictated it to my wife who typed it in my house, retaining a single carbon copy myself. I delivered it to Government House myself, addressed to the Governor personally, in two envelopes sealed with my own seal. It was mainly to the effect that the Congress ministry had strong support in two areas of the province. The first was the Charsadda subdivision of the Peshawar district, lying north of Peshawar itself. It was the home country of the Chief Minister, Dr Khan Sahib and of his brother Abdul Ghaffar Khan, the leader of the Redshirt uprising in 1931. The second was the Bannu district, where there was a considerable concentration of Hindu merchants in Bannu itself. Muslim Bannuchis were in many ways different from other Pathans, lacking the strong clan feeling and the conservative individualism of, for example, their Khattak neighbours to the north in Kohat district. Apart from these two areas, in my view the people were solidly behind the Muslim League.

A few days later I began to hear from various sources that my note was more or less public property in Delhi and had given great offence in

Congress circles. Nehru had made contemptuous comments about it and its obscure author. Dr Khan Sahib was noticeably less friendly and his colleague in the Ministry, Qazi Attaullah Khan, would glare at me with burning hatred when we met. It was twenty-one years afterwards that I learned from Sir Olaf the manner in which it had been transmitted to the Viceroy, that is (without going into full detail) in a highly confidential manner. Thirty years later I still feel that somewhere there was a breach of confidence. It was then, as now, no consolation to know that my assessment, as shown by the result of the plebiscite, was correct. I had a deep affection for Dr Khan Sahib. Then, as now, I found it very hard to bear the thought that he might regard me as treacherous.

The Viceroy's visit to Peshawar followed in the same month. I have no word to describe the degree of anxiety and suspense which preceded it. It was as if clouds covered the sky from horizon to horizon waiting for the simultaneous flash of lightning and the crash of thunder. If Dr Khan Sahib really thought that he enjoyed public support, he must have had an exceptional faculty of self-deception. I am sure this was not so. He was, rather, a very brave man, prepared to resist to the last any opposition to his own conception of what was best for the NWFP.

In the days preceding the Viceroy's visit, however, reports of what was brewing were coming in from politicians and men prominent in other fields. Nearly all were Muslim League followers, but a few were Congress Members of the Legislative Assembly. The information was always the same. The Pathans were determined not to be assigned to India when partition arrived. To this end they were also determined that the Viceroy should see the strength and weight of their determination on his arrival. If he did not do so, if he drove from the airfield in a cavalcade of cars straight to Government House, then a hundred thousand Pathans would storm the gates and barbed wire fences of the cantonment and march on from there. One of them said to me that even the machine guns of the very substantial garrison could not kill all of the hundred thousand.

The threat was not empty. The word fanaticism could be applied to the mood of the people, but it would not be wholly fair. There were anger and communal hatred as ingredients in that mood. But above all there truly was an adamant, quite balanced, resolve not to be delivered into the power of the Hindus by their own unrepresentative leaders. Early one morning I met Mehr Chand Khanna out for a walk (when he joined the Congress Party he had rejected his title of Rai Bahadur). He looked haggard and ill, and he was flanked by three armed guards. This was a typical example of the Party's predicament.

On the morning of the Viceroy's arrival I reached the aerodrome very early. There I met the District Commander, an imperturbable Australian Major General whose intention was to suggest to the Governor that the only course was for the Viceroy to see the people and to be seen by them. This was in fact unnecessary. The Governor had reached the same decision. A few nights before, the General's residence, Flagstaff House, which was adjacent to the barbed wire perimeter of the cantonment, had been raked with bullets from a very nasty hazard on the golf course outside the wire. Golf architects never think of such contingencies; but at least he had evidence of what might happen.

More potentially disastrous was the fact that on this morning some 8,000 men had approached the airfield from a point north of west with the idea of standing more or less where the Viceroy's plane would land. In this way they could not fail to be seen by him. The police had very tactfully diverted them in such a way that they veered further north, skirted the northern and north-eastern limits of the airfield, and joined the vast assembly which was waiting, fairly quietly, between Peshawar City to the east, Peshawar cantonment to the west, and astride the Great North Road and the railway line to the Punjab and India. That assembly numbered well over one hundred thousand armed men. They were under no command or organization, under no control except the declared intent to demonstrate their feelings to the Viceroy.

His plane came down punctually. I noticed as I joined the reception line to have my hand shaken by Lord Mountbatten of Burma, that the *Daily Mail* correspondent, Ralph Izzard, had emerged from a verandah some distance away. He was a remarkable man in many ways. Later he was to pursue a Mount Everest expedition to their base camp at some extreme height without any equipment and with only one Sherpa as a guide. That day in Peshawar his equipment for a temperature of well over 100°F was a trilby hat and a smart lounge suit.

The Viceroy inspected the guard of honour and I could not help noticing his most impressive appearance as he took the salute. He has always been a fine figure of a man. Rightly, in my view, he tended to make the most of this on public occasions; and on this of all occasions a strong impression was vitally necessary. As a contribution to this he had rolled up the sleeves of his bush shirt rather higher than the normal, thereby revealing, as his hand came up to the peak of his cap, the hypertrophied biceps of a first-class polo player.

Freedom at Midnight by Larry Collins and Dominique Lapierre, (Simon and Schuster 1975), is a dramatic narrative of those times in India. In its account of this day the authors refer to the Viceroy's bush shirt as green 'the colour of Islam'. I cannot recall this; but it was certainly not the bright Islamic green, though it may have been what was called jungle green. The pages covering this narrative (128–151) owe something to dramatic imagination. The authors write 'the worried governor suggested* that there was only one way out, an idea condemned by his police and army commander as sheer madness. Mountbatten might present himself to the crowds, hoping that somehow a glimpse of him would mollify them.'

The Governor appeared unruffled but he might be excused if he was 'worried'. The possibility of his own death he would face calmly. His responsibility, in the circumstances of that morning, for scores of thousands of lives and the preservation of an entire provincial administration from collapse, chaos and slaughter, might excusably bring a furrow to Sir Olaf's brow. When the reception party had been shaken by the hand, the official procession of cars departed, and I drove, a little later, to my office. I had no information as to what the Viceroy had decided to do.

The whole morning was unusually quiet. For my part I grew increasingly uneasy and found it difficult to resist ringing up the Military District Headquarters on the radio telephone with which I had been specially supplied. I was, however, determined not to bother other people with enquiries when they had plenty of their own anxieties. So I sat on at my desk, convinced that bad news, if any, would reach me soon enough; and that this was in any case my post.

Several hours went by. No sounds of shooting were audible. Indeed the silence became deeper, which puzzled me until I realized that it was lunch time and the building, where it was not empty, housed only somnolent clerks. Still I did not feel justified in going home. I recalled some of the words of an 18th century hymn with which I was familiar as a choir boy in happier times:

> Ye servants of the Lord†
> Each in his office wait . . . .
> O happy servant he,
> In such a posture found!

The hymn goes on to assure the servant that he will 'Be with honour crowned'. I would not presume to aspire to promotion in the Order of which I was already an obscure officer (in common with most of my contemporaries). But it would be bad not to be found waiting if and when one was wanted.

---

*ie to the Viceroy.

†In the India of those days the Governor was the Lāt Sahib, ie the Lord Sahib.

As so often in my life it was hunger which dictated my next move. The time was 2.00 pm. Audible movements in the building conveyed the same impression of well-fed placidity as the clucking of hens in a farmyard. Surely I might now (after all it was the Chief Secretary speaking) lift the telephone and enquire the worst or the best. I did so. I rang up my friend Kim McCrae, Deputy Director of Intelligence, and asked him as casually as I could how things had gone off this morning. He was surprised to learn that I did not know, and told me of the Viceroy's and Lady Mountbatten's brave and brilliant conduct on the railway embankment outside the north-east gate. Incidentally, it has never been clearly put on record that they were accompanied by the Governor.

The immediate crisis was over. I had enough strength left to mount my bicycle and go home to lunch.

Unlike my odd situation that morning, it is now a matter of record that the Viceroy, on arrival at Government House, took into consideration the Governor's suggestion and agreed with it provided that Dr Khan Sahib also agreed. The latter was called and spoke to the Viceroy privately. The Viceroy shortly afterwards informed the Governor that Khan Sahib's response was that the Viceroy should indeed go to be seen by the people if he must; but he should know that the Governor had organized the demonstration. To anyone who knew how much the Governor had done from the start of his term of office to handle political and constitutional developments in the interests of the Frontier Province, present and future, this evidence of Khan Sahib's attitude at that time is shocking.

And so the party set off again and stood on the railway bridge at the east end of Peshawar cantonment where he could see and be seen by the vast congregation of armed men. Pathans seldom shoot sitting ducks just for fun. In this instance the vast inchoate mass received him and Lady Mountbatten rapturously and a great victory had been won.

There was still more to be done however. That afternoon the Viceroy attended a meeting, staged by the Governor, with the Ministers – the Governor insisting, as he had consistently done for many months, that the voice of the people should be taken on the main issue of the time. The Viceroy seemed to have dominated the meeting by the remarkable force of his personality. Papers began to reach me from Latimer (now Sir Robert), Secretary to the Governor and of the Cabinet, which surprised me by what seemed the statesmanlike decisions of the meeting. The vital one was the decision, not announced for several days, that there should be a plebiscite* to decide whether the province should be included in India or in Pakistan.

* The plebiscite, rather than an election, was decided upon in Delhi.

Then papers began to reach me from the Chief Minister's house. A meeting of Ministers was taking place there. In the idiom of later years, it was clear that they wished to set the record straight. On the vital issue, the plebiscite, the official attitude was that the Congress Party would take no part in it. Instead a new political, or national, concept was born. The reason why the Congress would abstain from voting in the plebiscite was that the issue as framed was irrelevant. What the Party in the province now stood for was the concept of an independent state of Pakhtunistan.

This came to mean a political unit embracing all Pakhtu speakers. The area involved is, with the exception of the North West Frontier Province, very mountainous and very poorly endowed with natural resources. The NWFP could then claim a population of three million. The tribal agencies were also estimated to provide three million. Afghanistan might provide twelve million. And then there were those areas to the north in the Kara Koram mountains in so far as they were inhabited by Pathans. I never heard or read a clear definition of Pakhtunistan; but one point was quite clear, namely that its eastern boundary was to be the Indus.

It is possible that the idea originated in the minds of the Afghan government. There might be great benefit to them as they fished in the troubled waters of Frontier politics. No doubt Russia would encourage this. One minister in Kabul, Abdul Hamid, concerned mainly with commerce, was said to be a particularly warm partisan of Russia. A few days after the idea was first announced, the Afghan Ambassador in Rome arrived in Bombay on leave, and as he motored from Peshawar to the border he stopped at Jamrud (the border post at the foot of the Khyber Pass), alighted and delivered 'to such as cared to attend' a harangue in favour of Pakhtunistan and hostile to the British in India.

In the turmoil of the time this incident did not attract much attention; but it did draw from the Government of India (at Caroe's instance) a very sharp protest to the Afghan government. In the subsequent thirty years the theme has been taken up by prominent politicians in the NWFP. To a distant observer this has appeared to be sometimes one of the causes, sometimes one of the effects, of the fissile tendency in Pakistan of which so far the most calamitous result has been the secession of East Bengal.

There is, however, no certainty as to where the concept originated. It may well be, and the possibility is one favoured by Sir Olaf Caroe himself, that Dr Khan Sahib and his brother, Abdul Ghaffar Khan, felt that they had been betrayed by Nehru's agreement that a vote should be taken at all; and fell back on a fanciful idea of some sort of Pathan independence as a reason for refusing to take part in a vote. However that may be, it was probably not in the minds of the Khan brothers that Pakhtunistan should include any portion of Afghanistan. Nonetheless the concept was adopted by the Congress Government of the Province.

I had the task of signing the passport of one of the junior ministers to enable him to visit Kabul at very short notice; and there could not be a shred of doubt that the visit, combined with all else that was going on, was concerned with Pakhtunistan. Yet only a matter of days earlier the Congress Government had been indissolubly wedded to the idea of union with India when partition was brought about. The Viceroy made it clear to them within hours of his arrival that there must be a reference to the electorate to determine this. They knew what the result of that would be, however angry they might be over my confidential assessment which was 'blown' in Delhi.

One might expect a reluctant acquiescence. Instead, this time in a matter of hours, not days, they voluntarily adopted an objective which in effect repudiated everything for which they had stood for nearly twenty years. The turning of the coats seemed contemptible. But these were by no means contemptible men. Dr Khan Sahib in particular was in my view a noble man. My own conclusion is that there were two motive forces. One was a feeling that they had been democratically and constitutionally elected and must therefore hold on to office as trustees of their constituents. The second was an absolute hatred for the Muslim League leader, Mohammad Ali Jinnah.

Dr Khan Sahib once said to me in private conversation that Jinnah was 'a horribly vindictive man'. There were admirable Muslim leaders in the Punjab who would hold the same view, as Jinnah declared war on them for not supporting his pure Islamic doctrine for the theocratic state of Pakistan. One of them retired to England because he quite simply feared some form of impeachment followed by execution. The tide was running against the Congress in the NWFP, however, and in 1947 Pakhtunistan was a meaningless word.

Pakistan was the vibrant word. One generalization which can never be shown to be invalid is the statement that Pathans are very strong individualists. Their revolt against union with India, which meant subjection to an overwhelming Hindu majority, was balanced by their revolt against anything which might involve subjection to Afghanistan. And so the plebiscite went overwhelmingly in favour of Pakistan. Of those who voted about 98% were in favour.

This was not, unfortunately, by any means a cure for the ills of the time. All through the winter of 1946-47 communal hatred had been growing in intensity, leading ultimately, both in the Punjab and the NWFP, to disturbances severe enough to cause a partial breakdown of the administration. As the year 1947 wore on, every day more and more villages were burning. The personal steadfastness of the Congress ministers was to no avail, though they quite correctly insisted that the Government's parliamentary majority gave it the right and the duty to continue to govern. It did not give it the power. The result of the plebiscite brought a form of political peace. Muslim League agitation, which had filled the provincial jails with respectable and respected Muslims who committed purely technical offences in order to embarrass the Government, ceased as soon as the holding of the plebiscite had been announced.

There was, however, still serious lawlessness on the part of the trans-border tribes. Tank underwent a siege by the Mahsuds for three days, and the Hindu bazaar outside the perimeter barbed wire was largely destroyed by fire. This affair was one of several which gave me an uneasy conscience at that time as I sat in Peshawar. One evening about 6.00 pm a telephone call came through from Tank two hundred miles away. Captain Raw, the Political Agent, wanted some precise orders in the light of a disagreement with an officer of the South Waziristan Scouts who was commanding a platoon of Scouts which formed part of the garrison. Each of them spoke in turn. Behind their voices I could hear the continuous rattle of rifle and machine gun fire.

Today I cannot remember what the disagreement was; but my orders were to hold on while I got something going . . . orders larded with appreciative remarks. Then I rang up the Commandant of the Frontier Constabulary, J F Scroggie, and asked him to come and see me. He was another of those steadfast men who were then holding things together. For three hours we assessed the availability of Frontier Constabulary platoons all along the border, telephoning from time to time to this post or that, ordering the immediate move of platoons through the night to Tank. At dawn fourteen such platoons, numbering between four hundred and four hundred and fifty riflemen in all rumbled into Tank and the besiegers were driven off.

This was one of many critical situations. It may be salutary to mention, for the benefit of the many who today sneer at the British Raj as if it were some self-indulgent tyranny, that Captain Raw was, in that desperate situation, accompanied by his wife, who had given birth to a son two weeks before.

In Dera Ismail Khan communal rioting and burning went on for several days. Dr Khan Sahib flew down to lend his personal support to the Deputy Commissioner, who, being a Hindu, was in an impossible position. For the first time in his life that I know of, Dr Khan Sahib fell short of his own standards of justice. The Superintendent of Police was a young man called Hallowes. He had virtually no sleep for forty-eight hours while he fought the rioters and flames in the intolerable heat of a frontier summer. At one point he suffered a burn of one arm.

The best that Dr Khan Sahib could offer was a rebuke, followed by a second rebuke when Hallowes partially broke down. When the day of Independence arrived, which was after I had left the scene, there was little enough law and order in the northern half of West Pakistan. It is only right however, to record that Lady Mountbatten flew to Dera Ismail Khan immediately after Dr Khan Sahib, and in the same intolerable heat walked everywhere offering comfort.

In Peshawar a matter of extreme constitutional importance had not been resolved before the Viceroy left. He was under pressure from all sides to dismiss the Congress Government (or instruct the Governor to do so) under Section 93 of the Government of India Act 1935. This would entail the Government being conducted by the Governor with advisors until the date of independence, when Mr Jinnah would take over. At dinner at Government House Lord Mountbatten consulted a number of people on this issue, of whom I was one. It seemed to me that mere dismissal of the Ministry could do nothing to restore order.

On one occasion when the Governor was in Delhi I was very sharply criticized (not by him) when I telegraphed a suggestion that Field Marshall Auchinleck might be approached with a request for more troops. I had carefully stated that the situation in the south of the province was at that moment deteriorating to the point where it differed in no way from that of the Punjab. Only the Indus, a geographical accident, separated two vast areas of burning villages, looting, massacre and rape.

It reached my ears that the Commander-in-Chief (goodness knows his burden must have been very grievous) only enquired who was the alarmist who had composed the telegram. I appreciated that in fact no troops were available. The authority for the moment was not available to restore peace.

On the matter of Section 93, therefore, the view which I offered the Viceroy was that it should not be invoked. My reasons looked beyond the immediate emergency. The British Government in India was on the way out. In April we did not know that there were only about three months to go. We were only to know this on 3 June. Nonetheless it was accepted that British rule was ended. I considered, therefore, that, with the Indian Empire's day far spent, any action against the Congress Party in the Frontier Province could only be interpreted in time to come as a vindictive move by the British against those who had deprived them of their empire.

The fact that this was nonsense would be of no assistance to the Muslims. It could always be alleged by members of the Congress Party and their historians that the Muslim League did not succeed to power on their own merits or even by their own efforts. It was obvious that Jinnah would dismiss this Ministry as soon as he succeeded to power – as indeed he did. There could, therefore, be no reason why this should be done now. It could only provide ammunition later for enemies of the Muslim League.

In the event it was not done. What was seen to be done thereafter was that Sir Olaf Caroe went on leave while the plebiscite was held. The suggestion that he should do so came from the Viceroy, who presumably felt that it would be better for a new Governor, or an acting governor, to preside over the plebiscite. Caroe himself expected to return if the issue of the plebiscite went against the Congress Party. The fact that he did not do so inescapably suggests that he was *persona non grata* with the leaders of the Congress Party then in high place.

He was replaced by Lieutenant General Sir Rob M M Lockhart. He presided with firmness and tact over the chaotic situation which prevailed in the province until the return of Sir George Cunningham on the 15 August 1947. By that time I was no longer in India, but the story of the invocation or otherwise of Section 93 may be completed.

It was Mr Jinnah who had stated in the proper quarters that he would like to have British Governors for all the provinces of Pakistan, of which he announced that he wished to be Governor-General. In particular, he was anxious to get Cunningham for the North West Frontier Province. Cunningham, actuated by an austere sense of duty, accepted the appointment; and was confronted with the problem on 8 August in the India office. He was 'horrified' at the suggestion that the Frontier Ministry should be dismissed. Such a word from someone so confident and strong is startling, but it is in his own diary.

Dismissal of the Ministry while they still had a majority in the Assembly, without even offering them the choice of dissolution, would simply be unconstitutional. On the practical side, dismissal would embitter local feelings to the extent of provoking violence. The India office shared his views. It was intimated to the Viceroy that the matter should be left for action to the Pakistan Government after 15 August, the date fixed for the actual achievement of independence. Of course Jinnah did what everyone knew he would do.*

---

* Caroe was very casually treated in all this. The first that he knew came in a letter from the Viceroy dated 15 July. He might have received it in Kashmir two or three days later. Cunningham received the offer of the post on 4 July. He wrote in his diary on 12 August: 'I was surprised to learn (in Delhi) that it was only last week or so that Olaf Caroe had been told that he would not be coming back to Peshawar. He surely ought to have been told as soon as they had decided to ask me, which is now five weeks ago'.

I was in Nathiagali on 3 June when I received information that a most important message was awaiting me in Peshawar. All India Radio had already announced that the Viceroy would make a statement at 6.00 pm. I reached Peshawar just before 6.00 pm after a drive in great heat which provided me with my last contact with the rural, friendly India whereon Indo-British mutual regard was based. As we drove south from Abbottabad through Haripur to the junction with the Grand Trunk road, the heat became so intense that we could not tolerate the wind on our faces and had to shut the windows of the car.

Soon afterwards we saw by the roadside, in the shade of a mango tree, a tea stall. The local name was *thela*, but sometimes they were assigned the name *hotel*, pronounced with the stress on the first syllable. We stopped – a servant, an orderly and I – and shared a pot of tea *à la maison*, that is a strong mixture of tea, milk and sugar boiled in a kettle together and served scalding hot. We sat with sweat pouring off us, gasping and joking with the owners and the other customers, and feeling increasingly refreshed until time ran out and we must go on.

The news in Peshawar was to some extent unexpected. A date in June 1948 had hitherto been the target for the advent of independence. Now it was to be 15 August of this very year, 1947. This decision has been variously assessed. Mountbatten and his advisers clearly thought that immediate surgery, and the handing over of power to the governments of a partitioned India, were the only courses open if a cataclysmic disaster were to be prevented. The whole truth of what followed may be read in H V Hodson's *The Great Divide*. The inability of any government to prevent one of the worst disasters in history was revealed. Another view, held by Cunningham among others, was that the original date in 1948 should have been adhered to. There would then have been time to organize the transfer without the irritant of urgency. It is all over now and the unnumbered myriads of dead have been forgotten.

Soon after the announcement of the date for independence I was informed that Lt Col Dudley de la Fargue, whom I had succeeded as Chief Secretary, would be returning from leave early in August and would be again posted as Chief Secretary. I wrote officially to the Provincial Government that, if my services were needed, I would be ready to serve on beyond 15 August in any post to which I might have to revert. Otherwise I would ask to be released, when relieved by de la Fargue, in accordance with the terms announced by the Viceroy on 6 June. The latter offer was accepted.

I thought that this was clearly enough the end for me. This need not have been so. One day in July I received a letter from Mr Jinnah's personal

Norval Mitchell's formal picture on his retirement from the position of Secretary and Registrar at St Andrews University, 1972

secretariat inviting me to join the service of Pakistan from 15 August. No post was mentioned, but the salary would not be less than that which I drew as Chief Secretary; and in addition I might enjoy my compensation for loss of office and such pension as I might have earned after seventeen years' service in India.

The offer, in terms of the contemporary purchasing power of money, was glittering. Yet I was not for one moment tempted. The reasons were various. I was now aged forty. For the past five years my responsibilities had largely consisted in suppressing social unrest or outright rebellion. Such work was both distasteful and exhausting. I was not either an Indian or a Pakistani patriot. I was a mercenary, though not in a military sense, and the opportunity for service which had been so inspiring in 1929 was no longer available. There was also the welfare of my family to consider. Both my wife and I believed that our immediate duty now was to serve the interests of our four children. This could not be done by accepting a post in Peshawar or Karachi. The same consideration applied later when openings in the British Foreign Service were made available.

On 1 August we for the last time took the Frontier Mail for Delhi and Bombay. The brief formality of handing over to my successor on the previous day differed from previous relinquishments of posts in that it was also the relinquishment of a life's vocation. It would be hypocritical to suggest that I was utterly cast down and grief-stricken. Rather I was numb, subconsciously suppressing emotion and trying to look forward cheerfully to the ill-defined future. I think (and I certainly hope) after the lapse of years that I could see the insignificance of an individual coming to the end of a road when world-shaking changes and human suffering on a stupefying scale were going on all around.

We were delayed for a few days in Bombay. Then we were ordered onto a troop-ship which was, like many others, two years after the war, still conveying men of all the services from the east to the United Kingdom. We met some of our own colleagues. When the ship moved away from the land I did what many of us rather foolishly used to do when going on leave, that is I threw my topi over the stern. It would not be needed for several months, and it would not cost much to buy a new one. In this case I would never need a new one. This struck me forcibly as it sank in the ship's wake.

Editor's Postscript

AFTER THE SYMBOLIC JETTISONING of the topi into the sea, Norval Mitchell's life took several interesting directions. He himself described his next duty as being to provide a settled home for the remaining years of the childhood of his four children. Sir Fraser Noble, in the Postscript to his memoir *Something in India* (Pentland Press, 1997), described him on the SS *Franconia* as being 'immersed in his reading for a new venture into hill-farming'. This took him to a remote sheep-farm in the Scottish Borders, where he spent the next ten years putting his children through school and into universities.

That done, he returned to public service. In 1957 he took the position of Clerk to the Legislative Council of Northern Rhodesia (which became Zambia in 1964). Then in 1961 his old friend and boss Sir George Cunningham sought him out and suggested that he should apply for the post of Secretary and Registrar of St Andrews University.

When he arrived at St Andrews the administration was quite outdated and unable to cope with the impending expansion of universities. His first task was to design and implement a blueprint for the administrative function which led to him being called 'a one-man O & M operation' and was a model for other Scottish universities at that time. It enabled him and his staff to handle smoothly and efficiently the vast expansion of St Andrews and the creation of the newly-independent Dundee University.

Perhaps more characteristically, under his influence the Senate co-opted two undergraduates from the Students' Union onto the Senate, a step which was ahead of its time but which contributed to the fact that St Andrews avoided almost all the student unrest which prevailed elsewhere. His Principal attributed to him the major credit for 'the good order and rational argument which have been maintained at St Andrews' and wrote that 'He likes young people without condescending to them. . . . As a result they have treated him as something between a father confessor and a family lawyer'. The same could be said of his relationship with alien cultures in India.

When Sir George Cunningham died suddenly in 1963 Norval Mitchell was asked by Lady Cunningham to write a memoir about him, which was published in 1968 by William Blackwood. The theme running through the book was the ideal of service, as shared and exemplified by both of them.

In 1972 Norval Mitchell retired to Galloway in Scotland's south-west corner, where he wrote these memoirs. On his retirement it was said that he had been a Political Agent, a Prime Minister, a Judge, a Finance Secretary in a Provincial Government, a Sheep Farmer, the Parliamentary Clerk to a National Legislature, a Chief Electoral Officer, an author, and Secretary and Registrar of the University of St Andrews. Truly a remarkable range of achievements. And yet we hope that readers will recognise in these pages qualities which say at least as much about him as those achievements.

David Mitchell

Index